THE
Luftwaffe
DATA BOOK

THE Luftwaffe

DATA BOOK

DR ALFRED PRICE

GREENHILL BOOKS, LONDON
STACKPOLE BOOKS, PENNSYLVANIA

The Luftwaffe Data Book
first published 1997 by Greenhill Books,
Lionel Leventhal Limited, Park House, 1 Russell Gardens, London
NW11 9NN
and
Stackpole Books, 5067 Ritter Road, Mechanicsburg, PA 17055, USA

ISBN 1-85367-293-9
Publishing History
The Luftwaffe Data Book is based on *Luftwaffe Handbook, 1939–1945*
by Alfred Price (Ian Allan, Shepperton, 1977) and has been
completely revised and expanded, with new material by Alfred Price.

Designed and typeset by Roger Chesneau
Printed and bound in U.S.A.

Contents

Preface

This is the sort of book I should like to have had when I first began my serious research into the *Luftwaffe*, some thirty years ago. Had it been available then, my task would have been a great deal easier.

The book is intended as a basic reference manual on the *Luftwaffe* during World War II. It is not intended to be a substitute for other works on the subject, but rather a supplement to them, giving much useful background information and increasing the level of understanding.

Chapter 1 outlines the working of the *Luftwaffe* High Command, from the Commander-in-Chief to *Luftflotte* and *Fliegerkorps* level. Chapter 2 does the same thing for the operational units, from *Geschwader* down to *Staffel* level. Chapters 3 to 9 list the strengths, serviceability states and equipment of *Luftwaffe* front-line flying units, at seven important dates between September 1939 and April 1945. Units are listed under their respective *Luftflotten*, allowing the reader to observe the changing strengths and force compositions in each major theatre of operations.

Other chapters give details of the tactics employed by fighter, night fighter, bomber, dive-bomber, reconnaissance and other operational flying units. Chapter 19 provides a detailed description of the composition and working of the *Flak* units, a major fighting arm of the *Luftwaffe* that has received relatively little coverage. Chapter 20 deals with the V.1 flying bomb and the ground organisation that supported it. To round off there is an analysis of the *Luftwaffe* fighter aces' victory scores, biographies of some of the senior commanders, and a critical bibliography of the available literature on the *Luftwaffe*.

In collecting the material for this work, several good friends allowed me to use documents and photographs from their collections. In particular, I offer my grateful thanks to Götz Bergander, Eddie Creek, Hanfried Schliephake, J. Richard Smith and Fritz Trenkle.

The first edition of *Luftwaffe Handbook 1939–1945* appeared in 1977. In 1986 an expanded second edition was published. This new work contains almost all the material from the second edition, and has been extensively revised and lengthened to include more than twice the material in the original first edition. Because this is virtually a new book, it has deserved to have a new title.

Alfred Price

Author's Note

Although this account concentrates mainly on the activities of *Luftwaffe* flying and anti-aircraft units, it should be borne in mind that the *Luftwaffe* sent large numbers of personnel to take part in ground fighting. Throughout the entire war the paratroop units, the *Fallschirmjäger*, remained an integral part of the *Luftwaffe*. Ten divisions of paratroops were raised, and these high-grade units were employed as shock troops in several critical areas.

Following the heavy losses suffered on the Eastern Front in 1941 and 1942, the German Army began to run short of fighting personnel. On Hitler's orders, *Luftwaffe* flying and other units were combed of men judged surplus to their units' combat requirements. Several tens of thousands of *Luftwaffe* personnel were collected in this way and, rather than pass them to the Army, Göring formed them into *Luftwaffe* ground fighting units. The highest-quality unit raised and equipped by the *Luftwaffe* was the *Hermann Göring Panzer Korps*, comprising one *Panzer* and one *Panzer Grenadier* division.

At the other end of the scale of effectiveness were the twenty-two Field Divisions raised with the rest of the redundant personnel. Hastily formed, these divisions were poorly trained and badly equipped. Although they were intended as low-grade infantry units for use in the static defence role, when desperate situations arose on the Eastern Front *Luftwaffe* Field Divisions were often pressed into action to help stabilise battle fronts. When they got caught up in fierce ground fighting they usually suffered severe losses. One by one the depleted *Luftwaffe* divisions were forced to disband, the survivors being incorporated into the Army.

When they went into action, the *Luftwaffe* ground fighting units almost invariably operated under the control of the local Army commander, and fought in the same way as normal German Army units. For this reason the *Luftwaffe* ground units will not be considered further in this book.

A.P.

The High Command

The Air Ministry

The *Luftwaffe* was directed from the *Reichsluftfahrt Ministerium* (Air Ministry), which had a dual function. First there was the *Oberkommando der Luftwaffe* (Luftwaffe High Command), concerned with the military direction of the Air Force, and secondly there was the office of the *Reichsminister der Luftfahrt* (State Minister for Air), which dealt with ministerial problems, long-term administration, financial control, civilian aviation and, until 1944, aircraft production. Almost until the end of the war Hermann Göring headed both sections with the titles of *Oberbefehlshaber der Luftwaffe* (Commander-in-Chief of the Air Force) and State Minister for Air.

The *Oberkommando der Luftwaffe* was divided into several numbered *Abteilungen* (Directorates), of which the more important were:

1 Operations	4 Movements	8 Historical
2 Organisation	5 Intelligence	9 Personnel
3 Training	6 Equipment	

Of these Directorates Nos 1, 3 and 5 came under the control of the Chief of the Operations Staff. He was responsible not only for operations but also for basic decisions relating to the implementation of the air strategy as laid down by the Chief of the General Staff. The 8th Directorate (Historical) came under the direction of the Chief of the General Staff. The remainder of the major Directorates, Nos 2, 4, 6 and 9, came under the *Generalquartiermeister* (Quartermaster General). In addition to the Directorates there were several Inspectorates, which came under the Chief of the General Staff. These dealt with specific flying matters such as the fighter arm, the bomber arm, the reconnaissance arm and flight safety.

'Robinson' and *'Kurfürst'*

For the greater part of the war the *Oberkommando der Luftwaffe* was split into two parts, a forward echelon and a rear echelon. The forward echelon comprised the Chief of the General Staff, the Operations Staff, the Director General of Signals, the Director of Training and part of the Intelligence Department. Code-named *'Robinson'*, this echelon was situated close to Hitler's war headquarters. In the course of the war the latter moved several times and its locations included Winiza, Goldap, Rosengarten, Insterburg and Berchtes-gaden. Wherever it went, *'Robinson'* went too. The rear echelon, code-named *'Kurfürst'*, comprised the other departments of the High Command with offices in and around Berlin. *'Robinson'* and *'Kurfürst'* kept in touch with each other by means of liaison officers and an excellent communications system.

Each day there were two major command conferences which decided the affairs of the *Luftwaffe*. The more important was the afternoon meeting at Hitler's headquarters, often presided over by the *Führer* in person and attended by the Chiefs of Staffs of each of the three services. There the conduct and progress of the war were discussed, and decisions of the highest importance were taken. The other conference took place each morning at *'Kurfürst'* and was chaired by the Chief of the *Luftwaffe* General Staff or his deputy. The decisions taken at the previous afternoon's *Führer* conference were discussed, and the necessary orders to implement these were issued direct to the *Luftflotte* and *Fliegerkorps* commanders.

The *Luftflotte*

At the beginning of the war almost all operational flying units in the *Luftwaffe* were divided between four *Luftflotten* (Air Fleets). *Luftflotte 1*, under *General der Flieger* Albert Kesselring, had its headquarters in Berlin and was responsible for units based in the north-east of Germany; *Luftflotte 2*, under *General der Flieger* Helmut Felmy, had its headquarters in Brunswick and controlled units in the north-west of Germany; *Luftflotte 3*, under *General der Flieger* Hugo Sperrle, had its headquarters in Munich and was responsible for units in south-west Germany; and *Luftflotte 4*, under *General der Flieger* Alexander Löhr, had its headquarters in Vienna and controlled units in south-east Germany as well as the newly acquired territories in Austria and Czechoslovakia. Each *Luftflotte* was a self-contained and balanced air force with its own fighter, bomber, reconnaissance and other units. They were, therefore, akin to the RAF or the USAAF overseas Commands or Air Forces, rather than to the RAF Home Commands which were organised functionally to operate in specific roles. As German troops occupied more and more territory, the areas covered by the original four *Luftflotten* were extended far beyond their original boundaries. To prevent over-extension, during the course of the war three new *Luftflotten* were formed: *Luftflotte 5*, covering Norway, Finland and northern areas in the Soviet Union; *Luftflotte 6*, covering the central area in the Soviet Union; and *Luftflotte Reich*, responsible for home air defence fighter and *Flak* units as well as all other flying units based permanently or temporarily at airfields in Germany itself.

The *Luftgau* and the *Fliegerkorps*

During its expansion in the 1930s the *Luftwaffe* was organised to exploit to the full the potential mobility of flying units. The aim was that these forces should be able to concentrate rapidly at points close to the battle front, as required by the evolving military situation. To facilitate the move between bases within their *Luftflotte* area, flying units were freed of their administrative and supply organisations. The area of responsibility of each *Luftflotte* was divided into a number of *Luftgaue* (Air Zones), each with a headquarters that provided personnel for administrative, supply and second-line servicing tasks at the airfields within their domain. Thus the *Luftgau* provided the necessary 'hotel facilities' at the airfields to enable incoming flying units to go into action from a new base with the minimum of delay. When a flying *Gruppe* took up residence at an airfield, its *Kommandeur* automatically took precedence over all other officers stationed there.

While the *Luftgau* organisation took care of administration in its set area, the parallel organisation for operational purposes was the *Fliegerkorps* (Air Corps). Typically a *Fliegerkorps* operated between 300 and 750 aircraft of all types, its strength depending upon the importance of its area and the nature of the operations it was called upon to fly. Usually a *Fliegerkorps* was subordinated to the *Luftflotte* covering that area, though on occasions they operated autonomously.

The Flying Units

The *Staffel*

During the early part of the war the *Staffel* (plural *Staffeln*) had a nominal strength of nine aircraft, and it was the smallest combat flying unit in general use in the *Luftwaffe*. The commander bore the title *Staffelkapitän* and was usually an *Oberleutnant* or a *Hauptmann*.

The number of flying personnel in the *Staffel* depended on the type of aircraft it operated. This varied between 10 in the case of single-seat aircraft and more than 40 in the case of multi-crew aircraft.

A *Staffel* usually possessed a few vehicles of its own and had a mobile repair shop able to carry out minor repairs to its aircraft. As a secondary duty, commissioned flying personnel would supervise the technical staff.

The number of ground personnel in a *Staffel* varied from 150 in the case of single-engined planes to 80 in the case of multi-engined planes. The multi-engined units possessed a smaller complement of ground staff, because much of their servicing and administration was carried out by detached personnel from the local *Luftgau* command.

The *Staffeln* within a *Geschwader* were designated using arabic numbers. Thus the 1st, 2nd and 3rd *Staffeln* belonged to the Ist *Gruppe*, the 4th, 5th and 6th belonged to the IInd *Gruppe* and the 7th, 8th and 9th belonged to the IIIrd *Gruppe*. The 10th, 11th and 12th *Staffeln* belonged to the IVth *Gruppe* (if there was one).

By the late war period the strength of a *Staffel* could be greater or smaller than that mentioned above, depending on the role of the unit and the availability of aircraft and crews. For example, following the expansion of the fighter force in the autumn of 1944, several fighter *Staffeln* were established at 16 aircraft and received corresponding increases in their complements of aircrew.

The *Gruppe*

The *Gruppe* (plural *Gruppen*) was the basic flying unit for operational and administrative purposes. When flying units were ordered to move between bases, they usually did so by *Gruppen*. Normally a *Gruppe* occupied one operational airfield, though the military situation in the area might dictate that more than one unit had to operate from the same base. From time to time individual *Staffeln* were detached from their parent *Gruppe* for operational reasons, or to re-equip or re-form. Initially the *Gruppe* was established at three *Staffeln* each with nine aircraft, plus a *Stab* (headquarters) unit with three, making 30 aircraft in all. After a period in action a *Gruppe* might have somewhat fewer aircraft, as can be seen from the actual *Luftwaffe* Orders of Battle that appear in the chapters that follow. From the mid-war period several fighter *Gruppen* operated a fourth *Staffel* and, if all four had a strength of 16 aircraft, those *Gruppen* were established at 67 aircraft.

The *Gruppe* commander carried the title of *Kommandeur* and was usually a *Hauptmann* or a *Major*. Under his command he had an adjutant, specialist technical officers and a medical officer. Depending on its function and the type of aircraft flown, the personnel strength of a *Gruppe* varied between 35 and 150 aircrew and 300 and 515 groundcrew.

The *Geschwader*

The *Geschwader* (plural *Geschwader*) was the largest flying unit in the *Luftwaffe* to have a fixed nominal strength. Initially it comprised three *Gruppen* with a total of 90 aircraft, and a *Stab* unit with four, making a total of 94 aircraft. Later in the war many fighter and bomber *Geschwader* received a fourth *Gruppe* and, exceptionally, a fifth. In bomber units the fourth *Gruppe* was an *Ergänzungs* (replenishment) unit, which provided training with an operational edge for new crews coming from the flying schools.

The *Geschwader* commander held the title of *Kommodore* and usually held the rank of *Major*, *Oberstleutnant* or *Oberst*. His staff included an adjutant, an operations officer, an Intelligence office, a navigation officer and such other specialists as might be necessary for the role of the unit.

The *Kommando*

As the *Luftwaffe* came under increasing pressure during the final year of the war, the formation of *Kommandos* (detachments) became increasingly common. These were small *ad hoc* fighting units, often named after their commanders, operating the latest types of aircraft. For example, *Kommando Welter* operated Me 262 jet fighters in the night fighting role while *Kommando Götz* operated Ar 234s in the reconnaissance role. Generally speaking, a *Kommando* had a strength of between three and six aircraft.

Designations of Flying Units

Within a *Geschwader* the aircraft were usually assigned to a single role, for example *Jagdgeschwader* (abbreviated to *JG*), day fighters; *Nachtjagd-* (*NJG*), night fighters; *Zerstörer-* (*ZG*), twin-engined fighters; *Kampf-* (*KG*), bombers; *Stuka-* (*StG*), single-engined dive-bombers; *Schlacht-* (*SG*), ground attack; and *Transportgeschwader* (*TG*).

The units belonging to the so-called *Lehrgeschwader* (*LG*), were organised rather differently. These *Geschwader*—there were two of them—were formed to test new aircraft types under operational conditions and to devise appropriate tactics. The *Lehrgeschwader* employed day fighter, bomber, single-engined dive-bomber and other types, with a separate *Gruppe* for each role.

Reconnaissance units usually operated as independent *Gruppen, Aufklärungsgruppen (Auflk. Gr)*. Other independent *Gruppen* were formed from time to time for specific tasks, for example *Kampfgruppe 100 (KGr 100)*, a specialist night and bad-weather bombing unit. A full list of unit prefixes is given at the end of this chapter.

All *Geschwader* and independent *Gruppen* were numbered with arabic numerals, for example *Kampfgeschwader 55, Jagdgruppe 106* and *Aufklärungsgruppe 124*.

Usually a *Gruppe* formed part of a *Geschwader* and was numbered in roman numerals before the *Geschwader* designation. Thus the fourth *Gruppe* of *KG 51* was written as *IV./KG 51* (a full point placed behind a numeral in German makes it an ordinal number, giving it same meaning as 'st', 'nd', 'rd' or 'th' in English). Similarly the *Stab* (Headquarters) flight of *Stukageschwader 3* would be abbreviated to *Stab/StG 3*.

As mentioned earlier, the *Staffeln* with a *Geschwader* were numbered consecutively using arabic numerals. Thus the third *Staffel* of *Kampfgeschwader 53* was abbreviated to *3./KG 53*, and it formed part of *I./KG 53*.

Luftwaffe Unit Prefixes

Aufklärungs	Reconnaissance
Bordflieger	Equipped with floatplanes for operation from warships
Ergänzungs	Replenishment
Erprobungs	Test
Fernaufklärungs	Long-Range Reconnaissance
Jagd	Fighter
Jagdbomber	Fighter-Bomber
Kampf	Bomber
Kampf zbV	*zur besonderen Verwendung*, literally 'Bomber for special purposes' (i.e. Transport)
Küstenflieger	Unit operating in cooperation with the Navy
Lehr	Tactical Development Unit
Luftlandes	Unit operating with airborne forces
Minensuchs	Mine Search (aircraft fitted with equipment to explode magnetic mines from the air)
Nachtjagd	Night Fighter
Nachtschlacht	Night Ground Attack
Nahaufklärungs	Short-Range Reconnaissance

Panzer	Anti-Tank (unit operating aircraft fitted with high-velocity cannon for use against tanks)
Schlepp	Glider Towing
Schnellkampf	High-Speed Bomber
Seeaufklärungs	Sea Reconnaissance
Seenot	Air–Sea Rescue
Seetransport	Floatplane Transport
Sturm	Operated Fw 190 fighters fitted with extra armour, to engage US heavy bombers from close range
Sturzkampf	Dive-Bomber
Transport	Transport
Träger	Unit formed to operate from aircraft carrier
Wettererkundungs	Weather Reconnaissance
Zerstörer	Twin-engined fighter (literally, 'destroyer')

Composition of the Main Operational Flying Units, 2 September 1939

The *Luftwaffe* Quartermaster General's records, now kept at the Bundesarchiv at Freiburg in Germany, give the number of aircraft held by each operational unit in that service. These figures were assembled and recorded at 10-day intervals, from before World War II until the system collapsed in the final weeks of the conflict.

This chapter gives the strength of the *Luftwaffe* operational units on 2 September 1939, the day after Germany invaded Poland and the day before Great Britain and France declared war. It will be seen that *Luftflotte 1* and *Luftflotte 4*, the two *Luftflotten* responsible for operations along Germany's eastern frontier, had been greatly strengthened before the attack on Poland. Nevertheless, strong forces of bombers and air defence fighters were held back in *Luftflotte 2* and *Luftflotte 3* in the west in readiness to counter any offensive moves by Great Britain and France.

The *Lehrdivision*, with *Lehrgeschwader 1* and *Lehrgeschwader 2*, detached several units to *Luftflotte 1* and *Luftflotte 4* for the period of the campaign in Poland to give crews operational experience.

On that day *Luftwaffe* front-line units possessed 3,659 serviceable aircraft, divided as follows:

Single-engined fighters	995
Twin-engined fighters	82
Ground-attack aircraft	37
Twin-engined bombers	1,020
Dive-bombers	319
Long-range reconnaissance aircraft	259
Short-range reconnaissance and army cooperation aircraft	293
Coastal aircraft	158
Transport aircraft	496
Total	**3,659**

Numerically the strongest element was the fighter force, with just over a thousand serviceable aircraft. The majority of units were equipped with the Bf 109E, though earlier versions of the fighter were still in front-line service and

Fig. 1. Operational Areas of the Luftflotten, *2 September 1939. At the outbreak of war the area of greater Germany was divided almost equally between the four* Luftflotten. *Luftflotte 1 (in north-east Germany and East Prussia) and* Luftflotte 4 *(in south-east Germany) controlled air operations during the campaign against Poland, though long-range units based outside their respective areas also flew operations.*

a few fighter units still operated the obsolescent Arado Ar 68 biplane. Due to delays in the production of the Bf 110 twin-engined fighter, the build-up of the *Zerstörergruppen* was behind schedule and only 82 serviceable aircraft were available. As can be seen in the detailed analysis below, several *Zerstörer* units had formed with Bf 109s, and would go into action with these fighters. As soon as the Bf 110 became available in quantity, these units were scheduled to re-equip.

The main striking power of the *Luftwaffe* came from the twin-engined bomber force, also with just over a thousand serviceable planes. The dive-bomber force was much smaller, with only 319 serviceable aircraft. However, this relatively meagre total would be sufficient to establish the *Stuka*'s legendary reputation over Poland. Each dive-bomber *Gruppe* was established with three Do 17s, to provide pre- and post-strike reconnaissance. As might be expected from a force created to support an army making rapid thrusts into enemy territory, the reconnaissance and army cooperation arms of the *Luftwaffe* were numerically very strong. The dedicated ground attack force, with 37 obsolescent Hs 123 biplanes, was a weak element. However, the tactics for this arm were still being developed and the method of its employment was far from clear. A noteworthy element was the air transport force of 496 serviceable planes, the largest in any air force in the world.

As it faced its first great test, the *Luftwaffe* was a well-balanced force and it had a fighting capability superior to any of those it was about to meet in action.

Lehrdivision[1]

Unit	Aircraft	Total	Serviceable
Lehrgeschwader 1			
Stab	He 111	10	4
I. (Z) Gruppe	Bf 110	32	29
II. (K) Gruppe	He 111	41	35
III. (K) Gruppe	He 111	40	34
IV. (St) Gruppe	Ju 87	39	36
	Do 17	3	3
Lehrgeschwader 2			
Stab	Bf 109	3	3
I. (J) Gruppe	Bf 109	36	34
10. Staffel JG 26	Bf 109	12	9
III. (A) Gruppe	Do 17	24	18
	He 46	2	2
	Hs 126	9	9
10. Staffel	He 111	9	8

Luftflotte 1

Jagdgeschwader 1			
I. *Gruppe*	Bf 109	54	54
Jagdgeschwader 2			
II. *Gruppe*	Bf 109	42	39
10. *(N) Staffel*[2]	Bf 109	9	9
Jagdgeschwader 3			
Stab	Bf 109	3	3
I. *Gruppe*	Bf 109	48	42
Jagdgeschwader 20			
I. *Gruppe*	Bf 109	21	20
Jagdgeschwader 21			
I. *Gruppe*	Bf 109	29	28
Zerstörergeschwader 1			
I. *Gruppe*	Bf 110	32	24
II. *Gruppe*	Bf 109[3]	36	36
Zerstörergeschwader 2			
I. *Gruppe*	Bf 109[3]	44	40
Kampfgeschwader 1			
Stab	He 111	7	1
I. *Gruppe*	He 111	38	32
Kampfgeschwader 2			
Stab	Do 17	11	10
I. *Gruppe*	Do 17	37	29
II. *Gruppe*	Do 17	35	33
Kampfgeschwader 3			
Stab	Do 17	9	7
II. *Gruppe*	Do 17	36	25
III. *Gruppe*	Do 17	39	38
Kampfgeschwader 4			
Stab	He 111	6	5
I. *Gruppe*	He 111	31	28
II. *Gruppe*	He 111	32	27

III. *Gruppe*	He 111	33	21
Kampfgeschwader 25			
I. *Gruppe*	Ju 88	18	15
Kampfgeschwader 152			
I. *Gruppe*	He 111	38	32
Sturzkampfgeschwader 1			
I. *Gruppe*	Ju 87	38	31
	Do 17	3	3
Sturzkampfgeschwader 2			
I. *Gruppe*	Ju 87	38	32
	Do 17	3	3
II. *Gruppe*	Ju 87	38	36
	Do 17	3	3
III. *Gruppe*	Ju 87	40	37
	Do 17	3	3
Lehrgeschwader 2			
II. *(Schlacht) Gruppe*	Hs 123	'40	37
Aufklärungsgruppe 10	Hs 126	23	22
	Do 17	12	12
Aufklärungsgruppe 11	Hs 126	9	9
	He 46	3	1
	Do 17	33	32
Aufklärungsgruppe 21	Hs 126	36	31
	He 45	9	8
Aufklärungsgruppe 41	Hs 126	32	26
	He 46	2	0
Aufklärungsgruppe 120	Do 17	13	12
Aufklärungsgruppe 121	Do 17	44	33

Luftflotte 2

Jagdgeschwader 26			
I. *Gruppe*	Bf 109	48	48
II. *Gruppe*	Bf 109	48	44
Zerstörergeschwader 26			
I. *Gruppe*	Bf 109[3]	52	46

II. Gruppe	Bf 109[3]	48	47
III. Gruppe	Bf 109[3]	48	44
Kampfgeschwader 26			
Stab	He 111	8	8
I. Gruppe	He 111	32	32
II. Gruppe	He 111	35	27
Kampfgeschwader 27			
Stab	He 111	6	3
I. Gruppe	He 111	34	28
II. Gruppe	He 111	26	18
III. Gruppe	He 111	28	20
Kampfgeschwader 28			
II. Gruppe	He 111	35	35
Aufklärungsgruppe 12	Hs 126	33	30
	He 46	10	8
	He 45	3	0
Aufklärungsgruppe 122	Do 17	30	27

Luftflotte 3

Jagdgeschwader 51			
I. Gruppe	Bf 109	47	39
Jagdgeschwader 52			
I. Gruppe	Bf 109	39	34
Jagdgeschwader 53			
I. Gruppe	Bf 109	51	39
II. Gruppe	Bf 109	43	41
Jagdgeschwader 70			
I. Gruppe	Bf 109	24	24
Jagdgeschwader 71			
I. Gruppe	Bf 109	39	18
Jagdgeschwader 72			
III. Gruppe	Ar 68	28	24

Zerstörergeschwader 52
I. Gruppe	Bf 109[3]	44	43

Kampfgeschwader 51
Stab	He 111	6	3
	Do 17	3	3
I. Gruppe	He 111	36	36
III. Gruppe	He 111	36	34

Kampfgeschwader 53
Stab	He 111	6	6
I. Gruppe	He 111	32	29
II. Gruppe	He 111	32	32
III. Gruppe	He 111	35	34

Kampfgeschwader 54
Stab	He 111	9	8
I. Gruppe	He 111	36	36

Kampfgeschwader 55
Stab	He 111	9	6
I. Gruppe	He 111	33	27
II. Gruppe	He 111	31	22

Sturzkampfgeschwader 51
III. Gruppe	Ju 87	40	34
	Do 17	3	3

Aufklärungsgruppe 13	Hs 126	53	49
	He 46	3	1
	He 45	3	2
Aufklärungsgruppe 22	Do 17	35	35
	Hs 126	12	12
Aufklärungsgruppe 23	Hs 126	12	8
	He 46	21	18
	He 45	3	1
Aufklärungsgruppe 123	Do 17	37	36

Luftflotte 4

Jagdgeschwader 76
I. Gruppe	Bf 109	49	45

Jagdgeschwader 77

I. Gruppe	Bf 109	50	43
II. Gruppe	Bf 109	50	36

Zerstörergeschwader 76

I. Gruppe	Bf 110	31	29
II. Gruppe	Bf 109[3]	40	39

Kampfgeschwader 76

Stab	Do 17	9	9
I. Gruppe	Do 17	36	33
III. Gruppe	Do 17	39	35

Kampfgeschwader 77

Stab	Do 17	6	6
I. Gruppe	Do 17	32	29
II. Gruppe	Do 17	32	32
III. Gruppe	Do 17	34	24

Sturzkampfgeschwader 76

I. Gruppe	Ju 87	39	32
	Do 17	·3	3

Sturzkampfgeschwader 77

Stab	Ju 87	3	3
I. Gruppe	Ju 87	39	32
	Do 17	3	3
II. Gruppe	Ju 87	39	34
	Do 17	3	3

Aufklärungsgruppe 14

	Hs 126	30	27
	He 46	6	1
	Do 17	11	9

Aufklärungsgruppe 31

	Hs 126	9	9
	He 46	17	17
	He 45	3	2
	Do 17	12	12

Aufklärungsgruppe 124

	Do 17	11	9

Units Assigned to the Navy

Various *Gruppen*	He 59	31	30
	He 60	81	66
	He 115	8	8
	Do 18	63	54
Trägergruppe 186[4]			
4. *Staffel*	Ju 87	12	12
5. and 6. *Staffeln*	Bf 109	24	24
Kampfgruppe 806	He 111	21	20

Transport Units

Kampfgeschwader zbV 1[5]			
Stab	Ju 52	3	3
I. *Gruppe*	Ju 52	53	53
II. *Gruppe*	Ju 52	53	53
III. *Gruppe*	Ju 52	53	52
IV. *Gruppe*	Ju 52	53	53
Kampfgeschwader zbV 2			
Stab	Ju 52	3	3
I. *Gruppe*	Ju 52	51	51
II. *Gruppe*	Ju 52	53	53
III. *Gruppe*	Ju 52	52	52
IV *Gruppe*	Ju 52	53	53
Kampfgruppe zbV 9	Ju 52	53	53
Kampfgeschwader zbV 172			
II. *Gruppe*	Ju 52	26	16
III. *Gruppe*	Ju 52	26	0
Special *Staffel*	Fw 200	2	0
	Ju 90	2	0
	Ju G.38	1	1

Notes

1. The *Lehrdivision* comprised units operating each of the main combat types and was responsible for developing tactics for use in each role.
2. Night fighter unit.

3. Although the *Zerstörergeschwader* designation implied that the unit operated twin-engined fighters, delays in production of the Messerschmitt Bf 110 resulted in several of these units being formed initially with Bf 109s.
4. *Trägergruppe 186* was formed to operate from the aircraft carrier *Graf Zeppelin*, then under construction (but never completed).
5. *KG zbV* = *Kampfgeschwader zur besonderen Verwendung* = Special Purpose Bomber *Geschwader*. This designation was applied to transport units during the early years of the war, to stress the operational importance of the role.

Composition of the Main Operational Flying Units, 17 August 1940

This chapter gives the strength of the *Luftwaffe* operational units on 17 August 1940, shortly after the Battle of Britain began in earnest. The main formations involved were *Luftflotte 2* in eastern France and Belgium, *Luftflotte 3* in western France and the newly created *Luftflotte 5* in Norway and Denmark. Of the fighter, bomber, dive-bomber and long-range reconnaissance units, about nine-tenths were committed to the attack on Great Britain.

On that day *Luftwaffe* front-line units possessed 3,157 serviceable aircraft, divided as follows:

Single-engined fighters	787
Twin-engined day fighters	219
Night fighters	63
Fighter-bombers	119
Dive-bombers	294
Twin-engined bombers	960
Four-engined bombers	7
Long-range reconnaissance aircraft	185
Short-range reconnaissance and army cooperation aircraft	135
Coastal aircraft	162
Transport aircraft	226
Total	**3,157**

Compared with the position eleven months earlier, the front-line strength of the *Luftwaffe* was smaller by some 500 aircraft. In reality, however, the reduction in its actual fighting strength was less than appeared at first sight. For the attack on Poland the force had deployed its maximum possible strength, and it had fielded several units equipped with obsolescent aircraft. This was not the case in August 1940. Moreover, during the campaign in Poland a large part of the flying training organisation had been shut down to release Ju 52s for the air transport force. In August 1940 these Ju 52s were back with the training schools and the front-line transport force comprised only 226 aircraft. That process could be reversed quickly: using aircraft from

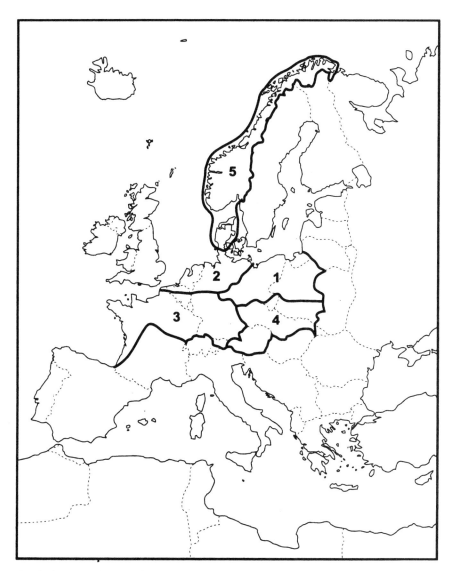

Fig. 2. Operational Areas of the Luftflotten, *17 August 1940:* Luftflotten *areas of responsibility during the Battle of Britain. Recently a new* Luftflotte, Luftflotte 5, *had been created to control operations from bases in Norway and Denmark, and each of the other* Luftflotten *had been given enlarged areas of responsibility.* Luftflotte 1 *and* Luftflotte 4 *had extended their areas eastwards into the German-occupied areas of Poland,* Luftflotte 2 *had extended its area to include Holland, Belgium and the north-east corner of France and* Luftflotte 3 *had extended its area to take in the rest of occupied France.*

training schools and instructor pilots, four additional *Geschwader* of Ju 52s could be reactivated in the transport role at short notice if required.

The reconnaissance units had suffered heavy losses during the campaign in the west and had not yet recovered their strength; several of these units had withdrawn to Germany to re-form. The single-engined fighter force was now re-equipped almost entirely with the Bf 109E, and the *Zerstörergruppen* were fully equipped with Bf 110s. Numerically, the twin-engined bomber force was slightly smaller than before, though the more effective Junkers Ju 88 had entered service in quantity and had started to replace the Do 17. The dedicated ground-attack force, though still small, was more than twice as large as before and had re-equipped with fighter-bomber versions of the Bf 109 and Bf 110. Other innovations were the small force of Focke Wulf Fw 200 four-engined bombers for long-range anti-shipping operations, and a small but growing force of night fighters for home defence. In August 1940 almost all front-line units in the *Luftwaffe* were equipped with modern aircraft. The force was geared for a long war, with the flying schools operating at full stretch to turn out replacement crews.

Luftflotte 2

Unit	Aircraft	Total	Serviceable
Jagdgeschwader 3			
Stab	Bf 109	2	2
I. Gruppe	Bf 109	30	24
II. Gruppe	Bf 109	34	30
III. Gruppe	Bf 109	34	25
Jagdgeschwader 26			
Stab	Bf 109	4	2
I. Gruppe	Bf 109	34	24
II. Gruppe	Bf 109	35	29
III. Gruppe	Bf 109	39	33
Jagdgeschwader 51			
Stab	Bf 109	4	2
I. Gruppe	Bf 109	29	23
II. Gruppe	Bf 109	25	25
III. Gruppe	Bf 109	39	39
Jagdgeschwader 52			
Stab	Bf 109	2	1
I. Gruppe	Bf 109	45	36
II. Gruppe	Bf 109	35	23

Jagdgeschwader 54			
Stab	Bf 109	4	3
I. Gruppe	Bf 109	34	24
II. Gruppe	Bf 109	38	36
III. Gruppe	Bf 109	36	29
Lehrgeschwader 2			
I. Gruppe	Bf 109	39	36[1]
II. Gruppe	Bf 109	39	34[1]
Erprobungsgruppe 210	Bf 109, Bf 110	30	15[1]
Zerstörergeschwader 26			
Stab	Bf 110	2	2
I. Gruppe	Bf 110	31	21
II. Gruppe	Bf 110	36	29
III. Gruppe	Bf 110	33	21
Zerstörergeschwader 76			
Stab	Bf 110	2	2
II. Gruppe	Bf 110	30	24
III. Gruppe	Bf 110	23	12
Nachtjagdgeschwader 1			
II. Gruppe	Ju 88, Do 17	28	14
Kampfgeschwader 1			
Stab	He 111	5	5
I. Gruppe	He 111	28	23
II. Gruppe	He 111	30	25
III. Gruppe	He 111	28	19
Kampfgeschwader 2			
Stab	Do 17	5	4
I. Gruppe	Do 17	28	21
II. Gruppe	Do 17	34	31
III. Gruppe	Do 17	29	24
Kampfgeschwader 3			
Stab	Do 17	6	5
I. Gruppe	Do 17	34	24
II. Gruppe	Do 17	34	27
III. Gruppe	Do 17	34	29

Kampfgeschwader 4
Stab	He 111	6	6
I. Gruppe	He 111	30	20
II. Gruppe	He 111	30	23
III. Gruppe	Ju 88	35	25

Kampfgeschwader 53
Stab	He 111	5	3
I. Gruppe	He 111	19	17
II. Gruppe	He 111	21	20
III. Gruppe	He 111	26	21

Kampfgeschwader 76
Stab	Do 17	5	3
I. Gruppe	Do 17	29	26
II. Gruppe	Ju 88	37	29
III. Gruppe	Do 17	30	23

Kampfgruppe 126	He 111	29	16

Sturzkampfgeschwader 1
II. Gruppe	Ju 87	36	26

Lehrgeschwader 1
IV. Gruppe	Ju 87	26	16

Küstenfliegergruppe 106	Ju 88, Do 18, He 115	30	23

Aufklärungsgruppe 11
3. Staffel	Do 17	5	5

Aufklärungsgruppe 13
2. Staffel	Hs 126	9	6

Aufklärungsgruppe 14
4. Staffel	Do 17	6	4
	Bf 110	6	6

Aufklärungsgruppe 31
3. Staffel	Do 17	10	5
4. Staffel	Hs 126	9	8

Aufklärungsgruppe 32			
4. *Staffel*	Hs 126	9	8
5. *Staffel*	Hs 126	9	8
Aufklärungsgruppe 41			
1. *Staffel*	Hs 126	9	5
2. *Staffel*	Hs 126	7	6
Aufklärungsgruppe 122			
2. *Staffel*	Ju 88	3	2
	He 111	7	6
3. *Staffel*	He 111	8	7
	Ju 88	3	3
4. *Staffel*	Ju 88	7	6
	He 111	3	2
Lehrgeschwader 2			
7. *Staffel*	Do 17, Bf 110	12	9 [2]

Luftflotte 3

Jagdgeschwader 2			
Stab	Bf 109	4	3
I. Gruppe	Bf 109	32	27
II. Gruppe	Bf 109	33	24
III. Gruppe	Bf 109	29	20
Jagdgeschwader 27			
Stab	Bf 109	5	5
I. Gruppe	Bf 109	39	39
II. Gruppe	Bf 109	39	27
III. Gruppe	Bf 109	39	32
Jagdgeschwader 53			
Stab	Bf 109	4	4
I. Gruppe	Bf 109	39	37
II. Gruppe	Bf 109	30	26
III. Gruppe	Bf 109	39	21
Zerstörergeschwader 2			
Stab	Bf 110	4	2
I. Gruppe	Bf 110	33	19
II. Gruppe	Bf 110	36	23

Lehrgeschwader 1			
V. Gruppe	Bf 110	36	24
Lehrgeschwader 1			
Stab	Ju 88	2	2
I. Gruppe	Ju 88	27	19
II. Gruppe	Ju 88	25	16
III. Gruppe	Ju 88	30	18
Kampfgeschwader 27			
Stab	He 111	5	3
I. Gruppe	He 111	30	12
II. Gruppe	He 111	34	18
III. Gruppe	He 111	25	23
Kampfgeschwader 40			
Stab	Ju 88	1	1
I. Gruppe	Fw 200	9	7
Kampfgeschwader 51			
I. Gruppe	Ju 88	25	18
II. Gruppe	Ju 88	30	17
III. Gruppe	Ju 88	27	20
Kampfgeschwader 54			
I. Gruppe	Ju 88	29	20
II. Gruppe	Ju 88	24	15
Kampfgeschwader 55			
Stab	He 111	5	3
I. Gruppe	He 111	32	27
II. Gruppe	He 111	32	26
III. Gruppe	He 111	34	23
Kampfgruppe 100	He 111	39	19
Kampfgruppe 806	Ju 88	32	23
Sturzkampfgeschwader 1			
Stab	Ju 87	3	2
	Do 17	4	3
I. Gruppe	Ju 87	36	28
II. Gruppe	Ju 87	30	23

Sturzkampfgeschwader 2

Stab	Ju 87	3	3
	Do 17	5	4
I. Gruppe	Ju 87	32	24
II. Gruppe	Ju 87	39	28

Sturzkampfgeschwader 3

Stab	Ju 87	1	1
	Do 17, He 111	6	4
I. Gruppe	Ju 87	38	24

Sturzkampfgeschwader 77

Stab	Ju 87	3	1
	Do 17	6	2
I. Gruppe	Ju 87	39	30
II. Gruppe	Ju 87	39	31
III. Gruppe	Ju 87	38	37

Lehrgeschwader 2

II. Gruppe	Bf 109	39	34[1]

Aufklärungsgruppe 11

2. Staffel	Do 17	5	4
	Bf 110	5	4

Aufklärungsgruppe 12

2. Staffel	Hs 126	4	1

Aufklärungsgruppe 22

1. Staffel	Do 17	6	5
	Bf 110	6	6
4. Staffel	Hs 126	10	7

Aufklärungsgruppe 31

2. Staffel	Hs 126	7	7

Aufklärungsgruppe 122

5. Staffel	He 111, Do 17	9	7

Aufklärungsgruppe 123

2. Staffel	Do 17	7	6
	Ju 88	2	2

3. Staffel	Ju 88	5	3
	Do 17	6	5

Luftflotte 5

Jagdgeschwader 77			
II. Gruppe	Bf 109	39	35
Zerstörergeschwader 76			
I. Gruppe	Bf 110	34	20
Kampfgeschwader 26			
Stab	He 111	5	5
I. Gruppe	He 111	28	28
III. Gruppe	He 111	20	19
Kampfgeschwader 30			
Stab	Ju 88	1	1
I. Gruppe	Ju 88	38	26
III. Gruppe	Ju 88	32	21
Küstenfliegergruppe 506	He 115	24	22
Aufklärungsgruppe 22			
2. Staffel	Do 17	6	2
Aufklärungsgruppe 121			
1. Staffel	He 111	5	4
	Ju 88	2	1
Aufklärungsgruppe 124			
1. Staffel	Hs 126	10	8

Unit Under the Direction of the *Luftwaffe* High Command

Aufklärungsgruppe der	Ju 86P, Ju 88,	47	28
Oberkommando der	He 111, He 116,		
Luftwaffe	Bf 110, Bv 142,		
	Do 215, Do 217		

Units Not Assigned to the *Luftflotten* Engaged in the Attack on Great Britain on this Date

Jagdgeschwader 52
III. Gruppe	Bf 109	31	23

Jagdgeschwader 77
Stab	Bf 109	4	4
I. Gruppe	Bf 109	36	30
III. Gruppe	Bf 109	29	20

Zerstörergeschwader 76
I. Gruppe	Bf 110	34	20

Nachtjagdgeschwader 1
Stab	Bf 110	3	2
I. Gruppe	Bf 110	33	24
III. Gruppe	Bf 110	33	20
	Bf 109	6	3

Kampfgeschwader 26
II. Gruppe	He 111	29	21

Kampfgeschwader 30
II. Gruppe	Ju 88	7	4

Kampfgeschwader 77
I. Gruppe	Ju 88	33	15
II. Gruppe	Ju 88	36	11
III. Gruppe	Ju 88	33	17

Sturzkampfgeschwader 2
III. Gruppe	Ju 87	39	20

Küstenfliegergruppe 406	Do 18	27	34
	Bv 139	1	1
Küstenfliegergruppe 606	Do 17	33	32
Küstenfliegergruppe 706	He 114, Ar 196	15	10
Küstenfliegergruppe 906	He 115, Do 18	28	21
Bordfliegergruppe 196	Ar 196	30	19[3]

Aufklärungsgruppe 12			
1. Staffel	Hs 126	10	8
Aufklärungsgruppe 13			
1. Staffel	Hs 126	6	4
3. Staffel	Hs 126	5	4
4. Staffel	Hs 126	6	3
5. Staffel	Hs 126	10	6
Aufklärungsgruppe 21			
1. Staffel	Hs 126	6	6
2. Staffel	Hs 126	6	6
4. Staffel	Hs 126	9	8
Aufklärungsgruppe 22			
3. Staffel	Do 17	6	4
Aufklärungsgruppe 23			
4. Staffel	Hs 126	6	4
Aufklärungsgruppe 32			
1. Staffel	Hs 126	10	8
2. Staffel	Hs 126	9	6
3. Staffel	Hs 126	8	8
Aufklärungsgruppe 120			
1. Staffel	He 111	1	1
	Ju 88	3	3
Aufklärungsgruppe 121			
3. Staffel	He 111	3	3
	Ju 88	4	2
4. Staffel	Ju 88	4	4
	Do 17	4	1
Aufklärungsgruppe 122			
1. Staffel	Ju 88	5	2
	He 111	4	4
Aufklärungsgruppe 123			
1. Staffel	Ju 88	7	3
	Do 17	5	5
Lehrgeschwader 2			
7. Staffel	Bf 110	9	8 [2]

Transport Units

Kampfgeschwader zbV 1			
Stab	Ju 52	3	3
I. Gruppe	Ju 52	47	42
II. Gruppe	Ju 52	43	13
III. Gruppe	Ju 52	53	32
IV. Gruppe	Ju 52	39	25
Kampfgruppe zbV 9	Ju 52	30	20
Kampfgruppe zbV 106	Ju 52	53	39
Kampfgruppe zbV 108	Ju 52, He 59, He 60, Do 24, Fw 200	27	18[4]
Kampfgruppe zbV 101, 102, 104, 105[5]			
Kampfgeschwader zbV 172			
I. Gruppe	Ju 52	45	34

Notes

1. Fighter-bomber unit.
2. Part of reconnaissance unit.
3. Unit operated floatplanes carried by warships.
4. This unit operated both landplane and floatplane transports.
5. These existed only as headquarters units, but could be formed into transport units at short notice after receipt of aircraft and instructor crews from flying schools.

Composition of the Main Operational Flying Units, 24 June 1941

This chapter gives the strength of the *Luftwaffe* operational units on 24 June 1941, three days after the opening of the attack on the Soviet Union. *Luftflotte 1* was supporting Army Group North in its advance along the southern shores of the Baltic towards Leningrad. *Luftflotte 2*, having transferred from the West, was supporting Army Group Centre. *Luftflotte 4* was supporting Army Group South in its advance towards Kiev and the Black Sea. *Luftflotte 5* expanded its area of operations eastwards, and moved units into airfields in Finland. In the West, *Luftflotte 3*, having lost many units to the Eastern Front, had expanded its area of responsibility to take in the whole of Holland, Belgium and the occupied part of France. In recognition of the growing threat to Germany itself, a new headquarters with *Luftflotte* status, *Luftwaffenbefehlshaber Mitte*, had been formed to direct units taking part in the air defence of the homeland, and in the far south another new formation, *Fliegerkorps X*, directed operations over the Mediterranean and in North Africa in conjunction with Italian forces.

On that day *Luftwaffe* front-line units possessed 3,428 serviceable aircraft, divided as follows:

Single-engined fighters	898
Twin-engined day fighters	105
Night fighters	148
Fighter-bombers	124
Dive-bombers	260
Twin-engined bombers	931
Four-engined bombers	4
Long-range reconnaissance aircraft	282
Short-range reconnaissance and army cooperation aircraft	388
Coastal aircraft	76
Transport aircraft	212
Total	**3,428**

Compared with the position ten months earlier, the *Luftwaffe* front-line strength was about 10 per cent greater. Its additional commitments far out-

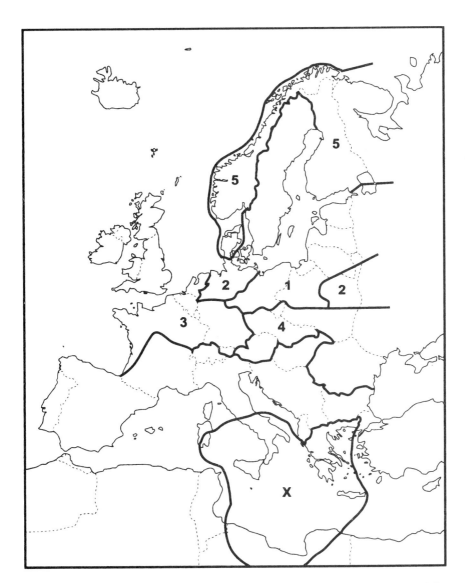

Fig. 3. Operational Areas of the Luftflotten, *24 June 1941:* Luftflotten *areas of responsibility at the time of the attack on the Soviet Union.* Luftflotte 5 *had extended its area of operations to take in Finland.* Luftflotte 1 *had extended its area eastwards to include air operations in support of the thrusts on Leningrad and Moscow.* Luftflotte 2 *had moved its main area of operations from the west to the east, and was now responsible for air operations on the central part of the Eastern Front.* Luftflotte 4 *in the south had extended its area of operations to include Rumania.* Fliegerkorps X *controlled air operations in the Mediterranean area.*

weighed this increase in fighting power, however. In the east the main battle front ran from the Black Sea to the Baltic, a distance of about 900 miles. To cover that frontage the *Luftwaffe* now found itself severely stretched. No longer could it concentrate the bulk of its forces to support a single campaign. Now, nearly a quarter of its front-line aircraft were tied down in theatres remote from the Eastern Front—in France and Belgium, in the Mediterranean and North Africa, and to defend the homeland.

Within the division of forces in the different roles there had been some important changes. The single-engined day fighter force was somewhat larger than before. The Bf 110 force had changed in its composition. While the twin-engined day fighter force was less than half its earlier size, many more of these aircraft were serving with fighter-bomber units and with the night fighter force. Due to the losses suffered, the twin-engined bomber force and the dive-bomber force continued their process of gradual reduction. As part of the preparation for the large-scale campaign in the east, the reconnaissance force had been greatly expanded and was now larger than ever before. The transport force had yet to recover from the losses suffered during the airborne invasion of Crete just over a month earlier, when it lost 170 Ju 52s destroyed or seriously damaged. The island was now in German hands but no sea lift had yet been established. As a result, a moderately large airlift was necessary to fly in essential supplies for the garrison. This restricted the size of the transport force available to support the campaign in the east.

Luftflotte 1

Unit	Aircraft	Total	Serviceable
Jagdgeschwader 54			
Stab	Bf 109	4	3
I. Gruppe	Bf 109	43	27
II. Gruppe	Bf 109	40	33
III. Gruppe	Bf 109	42	35
Kampfgeschwader 1			
II. Gruppe	Ju 88	29	27
III. Gruppe	Ju 88	30	29
Kampfgeschwader 76			
I. Gruppe	Ju 88	31	22
II. Gruppe	Ju 88	30	25
III. Gruppe	Ju 88	29	22
Kampfgeschwader 77			
Stab	Ju 88	1	1

I. Gruppe	Ju 88	30	23
II. Gruppe	Ju 88	31	23
III. Gruppe	Ju 88	29	20
Kampfgruppe 806	Ju 88	30	18
Aufklärungsgruppe 10			
1. Staffel	Fw 189	8	7
3. Staffel	Ju 88	6	5
	Bf 110	3	3
Aufklärungsgruppe 12			
1. Staffel	Fw 189	9	9
Aufklärungsgruppe 13			
1. Staffel	Hs 126	7	6
Aufklärungsgruppe 21			
2. Staffel	Hs 126	7	7
4. Staffel	Hs 126	6	5
7. Staffel	Hs 126	7	5
Aufklärungsgruppe 22			
1. Staffel	Ju 88	7	5
3. Staffel	Ju 88	9	6
Aufklärungsgruppe 23			
2. Staffel	Hs 126	7	7
3. Staffel	Hs 126	7	7
4. Staffel	Hs 126	5	4
Aufklärungsgruppe 31			
4. Staffel	Fw 189	9	9
Aufklärungsgruppe 32			
8. Staffel	Hs 126	7	6
Aufklärungsgruppe 33			
4. Staffel	Bf 110	9	9
Aufklärungsgruppe 41			
3. Staffel	Hs 126	7	5

Aufklärungsgruppe 122			
5. *Staffel*	Ju 88	9	8
Nachtaufklärungsstaffel 3	Do 17	10	3
Seeaufklärungsgruppe 125	He 60, He 114, Ar 95	27	22
Kampfgruppe zbV 106	Ju 52	44	8

Luftflotte 2

Jagdgeschwader 27			
Stab	Bf 109	4	4
II. Gruppe	Bf 109	40	31
III. Gruppe	Bf 109	40	14
Jagdgeschwader 51			
Stab	Bf 109	4	4
I. Gruppe	Bf 109	40	38
II. Gruppe	Bf 109	40	23
III. Gruppe	Bf 109	38	30
IV. Gruppe	Bf 109	38	26
Jagdgeschwader 53			
Stab	Bf 109	4	4
I. Gruppe	Bf 109	35	29
II. Gruppe	Bf 109	35	33
III. Gruppe	Bf 109	38	36
Lehrgeschwader 2			
II. (Schlacht) Gruppe	Bf 109	38	37[1]
	Hs 123	13	13
Zerstörergeschwader 26			
Stab	Bf 110	4	4
I. Gruppe	Bf 110	38	17
II. Gruppe	Bf 110	36	30
Kampfgeschwader 2			
Stab	Do 17	3	3
I. Gruppe	Do 17	38	21
III. Gruppe	Do 17	24	23

Kampfgeschwader 3

Stab	Ju 88, Do 17	2	2
I. Gruppe	Ju 88	38	32
II. Gruppe	Ju 88	38	32
III. Gruppe	Do 17	36	18

Kampfgeschwader 4

II. Gruppe	He 111	24	8

Kampfgeschwader 53

Stab	He 111	6	4
I. Gruppe	He 111	28	18
II. Gruppe	He 111	21	10
III. Gruppe	He 111	31	22

Schnellkampfgeschwader 210

Stab	Bf 110	5	4[1]
I. Gruppe	Bf 110	41	33[1]
II. Gruppe	Bf 110	37	37[1]

Sturzkampfgeschwader 1

Stab	Ju 87	3	2
	Bf 110	6	3
II. Gruppe	Ju 87	39	28
III. Gruppe	Ju 87	39	24

Sturzkampfgeschwader 2

Stab	Ju 87	3	3
	Bf 110	6	4
I. Gruppe	Ju 87	35	19
III. Gruppe	Ju 87	39	20

Sturzkampfgeschwader 77

Stab	Ju 87	3	1
	Bf 110	6	6
I. Gruppe	Ju 87	38	31
II. Gruppe	Ju 87	39	28
III. Gruppe	Ju 87	35	28

Aufklärungsgruppe 10

1. Staffel	Fw 189	8	8
2. Staffel	Hs 126	6	5

Aufklärungsgruppe 11

1. *Staffel*	Fw 189	6	6
4. *Staffel*	Ju 88	9	8

Aufklärungsgruppe 12

2. *Staffel*	Hs 126	7	6
3. *Staffel*	Hs 126	7	7
4. *Staffel*	Hs 126	10	10
5. *Staffel*	Fw 189	9	9
7. *Staffel*	Hs 126	6	5

Aufklärungsgruppe 13

1. *Staffel*	Hs 126	7	6
3. *Staffel*	Hs 126	9	8
6. *Staffel*	Hs 126	7	7
7. *Staffel*	Hs 126	7	7

Aufklärungsgruppe 14

3. *Staffel*	Fw 189	10	8
4. *Staffel*	Ju 88	9	6

Aufklärungsgruppe 21

1. *Staffel*	Hs 126	7	7

Aufklärungsgruppe 23

1. *Staffel*	Hs 126	7	7
5. *Staffel*	Hs 126	7	7

Aufklärungsgruppe 31

1. *Staffel*	Fw 189	8	9
3. *Staffel*	Bf 110	9	9

Aufklärungsgruppe 32

2. *Staffel*	Hs 126	6	5
6. *Staffel*	Hs 126	7	4
7. *Staffel*	Hs 126	7	7

Aufklärungsgruppe 33

1. *Staffel*	Ju 88	9	7

Aufklärungsgruppe 41

2. *Staffel*	Hs 126	7	5
5. *Staffel*	Fw 189	7	6

6. *Staffel*	Hs 126	8	7
Aufklärungsgruppe 122			
3. *Staffel*	Ju 88	8	3
	Bf 110	3	3
Lehrgeschwader 2			
9. *Staffel*	Hs 126	8	7 [2]
Nachtaufklärungsstaffel 2	Do 17	9	4
Kampfgeschwader zbV 1			
IV. *Gruppe*	Ju 52	40	38
Kampfgruppe zbV 102	Ju 52	43	8

Luftflotte 3

Jagdgeschwader 2			
Stab	Bf 109	4	4
I. *Gruppe*	Bf 109	36	30
II. *Gruppe*	Bf 109	40	36
III. *Gruppe*	Bf 109	37	32
Jagdgeschwader 26			
Stab	Bf 109	4	3
I. *Gruppe*	Bf 109	31	27
II. *Gruppe*	Bf 109	34	22
III. *Gruppe*	Bf 109	43	36
Zerstörergeschwader 76			
Stab	Bf 110	4	4
II. *Gruppe*	Bf 110	34	21
Kampfgeschwader 2			
II. *Gruppe*	Do 217	31	23
Kampfgeschwader 4			
I. *Gruppe*	He 111	29	19
III. *Gruppe*	He 111	25	15
Kampfgeschwader 40			
I. *Gruppe*	Fw 200	21	4

II. Gruppe	Do 217	12	5
	He 111	10	5
III. Gruppe	He 111	22	14
Kampfgruppe 100	He 111	19	14
Kampfgruppe 606	Ju 88	29	13
Küstenfliegergruppe 106	Ju 88	17	4
	He 115	9	5
Aufklärungsgruppe 123			
1. Staffel	Ju 88	9	6
	Bf 110	3	3
3. Staffel	Ju 88	4	4
	Bf 110	3	1

Luftflotte 4

Jagdgeschwader 3			
Stab	Bf 109	4	2
I. Gruppe	Bf 109	29	23
II. Gruppe	Bf 109	25	25
III. Gruppe	Bf 109	39	39
Jagdgeschwader 52			
Stab	Bf 109	1	3
I. Gruppe	Bf 109	38	28
II. Gruppe	Bf 109	39	37
III. Gruppe	Bf 109	43	41
Jagdgeschwader 77			
Stab	Bf 109	2	2
II. Gruppe	Bf 109	39	19
III. Gruppe	Bf 109	35	20
Lehrgeschwader 2			
I. Gruppe	Bf 109	40	20
Kampfgeschwader 27			
Stab	He 111	5	5
I. Gruppe	He 111	30	22

II. Gruppe	He 111	24	21
III. Gruppe	He 111	28	25

Kampfgeschwader 51

Stab	Ju 88	2	2
I. Gruppe	Ju 88	22	22
II. Gruppe	Ju 88	36	29
III. Gruppe	Ju 88	32	28

Kampfgeschwader 54

Stab	Ju 88	1	1
I. Gruppe	Ju 88	34	31
II. Gruppe	Ju 88	36	33

Kampfgeschwader 55

Stab	He 111	8	7
I. Gruppe	He 111	27	27
II. Gruppe	He 111	24	22
III. Gruppe	He 111	25	24

Aufklärungsgruppe 11

2. Staffel	Do 17	12	10
3. Staffel	Ju 88	6	5
	Bf 110	6	3
5. Staffel	Hs 126	6	6

Aufklärungsgruppe 12

6. Staffel	Hs 126	8	8

Aufklärungsgruppe 13

4. Staffel	Hs 126	8	8
5. Staffel	Hs 126	10	9

Aufklärungsgruppe 14

1. Staffel	Hs 126	9	8
5. Staffel	Hs 126	7	6

Aufklärungsgruppe 21

3. Staffel	Hs 126	8	8
5. Staffel	Hs 126	10	8
6. Staffel	Hs 126	9	9

Aufklärungsgruppe 22			
2. *Staffel*	Ju 88	9	8
4. *Staffel*	Hs 126	8	5
Aufklärungsgruppe 31			
2. *Staffel*	Fw 189	7	2
5. *Staffel*	Hs 126	7	6
Aufklärungsgruppe 32			
3. *Staffel*	Hs 126	11	11
4. *Staffel*	Hs 126	10	7
5. *Staffel*	Hs 126	8	7
Aufklärungsgruppe 33			
2. *Staffel*	Bf 110	9	8
3. *Staffel*	Ju 88	9	9
Aufklärungsgruppe 41			
3. *Staffel*	Fw 189	9	8
4. *Staffel*	Hs 126	7	7
6. *Staffel*	Hs 126	9	9
Aufklärungsgruppe 121			
3. *Staffel*	Ju 88	9	6
	Bf 110	3	3
4. *Staffel*	Ju 88	8	5
	Bf 110	1	0
Aufklärungsgruppe 122			
2. *Staffel*	Ju 88	9	7
	Bf 110	3	1
4. *Staffel*	Ju 88	8	8
	Bf 110	3	2
Lehrgeschwader 2			
7. *Staffel*	Bf 110	9	8 [2]
Nachtaufklärungsstaffel 1	Do 17	9	5
Kampfgruppe zbV 50	Ju 52	44	24
Kampfgruppe zbV 104	Ju 52	41	37

Luftflotte 5

Jagdgeschwader 77			
I. *Gruppe*	Bf 109	52	26
	Bf 110	12	7
Kampfgeschwader 26			
I. *Gruppe*	He 111	31	22
Kampfgeschwader 30			
I. *Gruppe*	Ju 88	34	19
II. *Gruppe*	Ju 88	31	22
Lehrgeschwader 1			
IV. *Gruppe*	Ju 87	42	39
Küstenfliegergruppe 406	Bv 138, Do 18,	24	14
	He 115		
Küstenfliegergruppe 506	He 115	9	8
Küstenfliegergruppe 706	Ar 196, He 115,	13	6
	He 114		
Küstenfliegergruppe 906	Do 18	9	5
Aufklärungsgruppe 32			
1. *Staffel*	Hs 126	10	9
Aufklärungsgruppe 120			
1. *Staffel*	Ju 88	12	6
Aufklärungsgruppe 124			
1. *Staffel*	Ju 88	9	4
	Do 215	2	2
Kampfgruppe zbV 108	Ju 52 floatplanes,	26	17
	Ju 52, Ju 90,		
	He 60, Do 18		

Luftwaffenbefehlshaber Mitte

Jagdgeschwader 1			
Stab	Bf 109	4	4

I. Gruppe	Bf 109	28	24
Nachtjagdgeschwader 1			
Stab	Bf 110	4	2
I. Gruppe	Bf 110	37	28
II. Gruppe	Bf 110	32	21
	Do 215	5	2
III. Gruppe	Bf 110	34	28
	Bf 109	11	9
Nachtjagdgeschwader 2			
Stab	Ju 88	4	4
I. Gruppe	Ju 88	32	15
	Do 17	6	4
Nachtjagdgeschwader 3			
Stab	Bf 110	3	3
I. Gruppe	Bf 110	37	32

Fliegerkorps X

Jagdgeschwader 27			
I. Gruppe	Bf 109	34	25
Zerstörergeschwader 26			
III. Gruppe	Bf 110	25	22
Lehrgeschwader 1			
Stab	Ju 88	1	1
I. Gruppe	Ju 88	35	4
II. Gruppe	Ju 88	25	11
III. Gruppe	Ju 88	27	11
Kampfgeschwader 26			
II. Gruppe	He 111	28	5
III. Gruppe	He 111	30	12
Kampfgeschwader 30			
III. Gruppe	Ju 88	15	6
Küstenfliegergruppe 506	Ju 88	11	4
Sturzkampfgeschwader 1			
I. Gruppe	Ju 87	25	21

Sturzkampfgeschwader 3

Stab	Ju 87	3	3
	Bf 110	4	0
I. Gruppe	Ju 87	30	13

Seeaufklärungsgruppe 126	He 60	23	16

Aufklärungsgruppe 14

2. Staffel	Hs 126	9	7
	Bf 110	3	3

Aufklärungsgruppe 121

1. Staffel	Ju 88	12	5

Aufklärungsgruppe 122

1. Staffel	Ju 88	7	7
	Bf 110	3	2

Aufklärungsgruppe 123

2. Staffel	Ju 88	6	2
	Bf 110	1	0

Kampfgeschwader zbV 1

Stab	Ju 52	2	1
I. Gruppe	Ju 52	27	14
II. Gruppe	Ju 52	39	19
III. Gruppe	Ju 52	41	29

Kampfgruppe zbV 9	Ju 52	25	9

Kampfgeschwader zbV 172

	Ju 52	44	8

Unit Under Direction of the *Luftwaffe* High Command

Aufklärungsgruppe der Oberkommando der Luftwaffe [3]	Ju 86P, Ju 88, He 111, Bf 109, Bf 110, Bv 142, Do 17, Do 215, Do 217	91	57

Notes

1. Fighter-bomber unit.
2. Reconnaissance unit.
3. This large reconnaissance unit operated under the direct control of the *Luftwaffe* High Command, and at this time it served mainly on the Eastern Front.

Composition of the Main Operational Flying Units, 27 July 1942

This chapter gives the strength of the *Luftwaffe* operational units on 27 July 1942, just over a year after the opening of the attack on the Soviet Union. The greater part of the *Luftwaffe*'s fighting strength was concentrated on the Eastern Front, where the German summer offensive was in full swing. The 6th Army had started out on the long advance that would take it into the city of Stalingrad. Meanwhile the Soviet Air Force had begun to recover from the heavy losses it had suffered during the previous year, and it was getting stronger with each month that passed.

Elsewhere the *Luftwaffe* faced intractable problems as it tried to meet the diverse range of threats that faced it. The RAF was mounting damaging attacks on the homeland, making it necessary for the German night fighter force to continue its expansion. Also in England the USAAF had started to build up its strength, but some months would elapse before it would make any impression on the balance of air power. In recognition of these developments, the fighter force assigned to *Luftwaffenbefehlshaber Mitte* had been expanded; in addition, that formation now acted more as a *Luftflotte*, taking operational responsibility for all bomber, ground-attack and other combat units based in metropolitan Germany or sent there to re-form or re-equip.

In North Africa the German advance had been halted at El Alamein, and the RAF had established air superiority over the weak *Luftwaffe* and Italian Air Force units in the area. Malta was still under blockade, though her fighter force was now strong enough to defend her against direct air attack. The main organisational change since the previous year concerned the strengthened presence in the Mediterranean area, where *Fliegerkorps X* had became *Luftflotte 2*. Meanwhile air operations on the central sector of the Eastern Front were now controlled by *Luftwaffenkommando Ost* with a status close to that of a *Luftflotte*.

On 27 July 1942 *Luftwaffe* front-line units possessed 3,500 serviceable aircraft, divided as follows:

Single-engined fighters	945
Twin-engined day fighters	58
Night fighters	203
Fighter-bombers	40

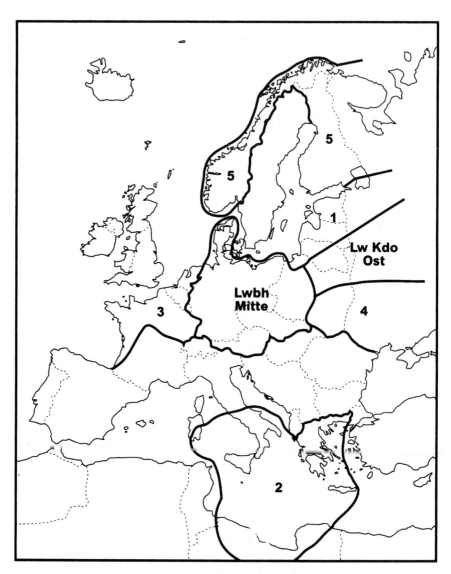

Fig. 4. Operational Areas of the Luftflotten, *27 July 1942:* Luftflotten *areas of responsibility at the time of the 1942 summer offensive in the Soviet Union. The main change since the previous year was that* Luftflotte *2 had moved yet again, this time to take control of air operations in the Mediterranean area. Its place in the central region of the Eastern Front was taken by* Luftwaffenkommando Ost, *which had a status close to that of a* Luftflotte. *In recognition of the greater threat to the homeland,* Luftwaffenbefehlshaber Mitte *had been expanded. That formation behaved in much the same way as a* Luftflotte, *assuming operational responsibility for bomber, ground-attack and other combat units based in metropolitan Germany or sent there to re-form or re-equip.*

Specialised ground-attack aircraft	19
Dive-bombers	249
Twin-engined bombers	1,119
Four-engined bombers	41
Long-range reconnaissance aircraft	188
Short-range reconnaissance and army cooperation aircraft	209
Coastal aircraft	64
Transport aircraft	365
Total	**3,500**

The force was little larger than in June of the previous year, and it was severely overstretched. *Luftflotte 2* in the Mediterranean and *Luftflotte 3* in the West retained relatively weak forces and were forced to fight holding actions. The Eastern Front drew the lion's share of the combat units, but even there the *Luftwaffe* could no longer be strong along the entire battle front. *Luftflotte 1* and *Luftflotte 5*, covering the northern sectors, possessed only moderate strength. The two strongest formations were *Luftflotte 4* and *Luftwaffenkommando Ost*, controlling the central and southern part of the front where the fiercest fighting was now taking place. Yet these two formations possessed only 348 serviceable single-engined fighters between them.

Another major problem facing the *Luftwaffe* was its ageing fleet of combat planes. Almost every combat type in front-line service was a developed version of an aircraft in service at the beginning of the conflict, nearly three years earlier. The only major exceptions were the Focke Wulf Fw 190 fighter and the Dornier Do 217 medium bomber and night fighter (and the latter type would be built only in moderate numbers). Two other new types on which the *Luftwaffe* had placed great hopes had run into severe difficulties. The He 177 heavy bomber was in production and one *Gruppe* had re-equipped with the type. It suffered severe teething troubles, however, and following a brief period in service it would be withdrawn for extensive modifications. The Messerschmitt Me 210 multi-role combat aircraft was intended to replace the Ju 87 dive-bomber and also the Bf 110 in its many roles. The type demonstrated poor handling characteristics, however, and would soon be abandoned. The Bf 109, Bf 110, Ju 88, He 111 and Ju 87 were fast approaching obsolescence, yet they would have to soldier on in service for some years longer.

Concerning unit organisation, the main change was that each multi-engined bomber *Geschwader* was now established with a IVth *Gruppe*. This provided training in the operational role of the *Geschwader* and also served as a holding unit for new crews. Most of these units were based in Germany, though in a few cases they were located closer to their operational *Gruppen*. Two single-engined fighter *Geschwader* had also acquired IVth *Gruppen*, though in each case these were normal fighting units. In another change, most of the reconnaissance and army cooperation *Staffeln* were assembled in twos and threes into *Nahaufklärungsgruppen*.

Luftflotte 1

Unit	Aircraft	Total	Serviceable
Jagdgeschwader 54			
I. *Gruppe*	Bf 109	40	25
II. *Gruppe*	Bf 109	40	28
III. *Gruppe*	Bf 109	22	18
Kampfgeschwader 1			
Stab	He 111	2	1
II. *Gruppe*	Ju 88	27	14
III. *Gruppe*	Ju 88	26	14
IV. *Gruppe*	Ju 88	33	21
Kampfgeschwader 53			
Stab	He 111	4	4
I. *Gruppe*	He 111	31	23
II. *Gruppe*	He 111	33	26
III. *Gruppe*	Ju 88	44	29
Sturzkampfgeschwader 1			
III. *Gruppe*	Ju 87	32	23
Aufklärungsgruppe der Überkommando der Luftwaffe			
3. *Staffel*	Ju 88	7	6
	Bf 109	3	3
Aufklärungsgruppe 122			
5. *Staffel*	Ju 88	10	5
Nachtaufklärungsstaffel 3	Do 17	12	5
Nahaufklärungsgruppe 11	Fw 189	9	6
	Hs 126	17	14

Luftflotte 2

Unit	Aircraft	Total	Serviceable
Jagdgeschwader 27			
Stab	Bf 109	3	2
I. *Gruppe*	Bf 109	23	15

II. Gruppe	Bf 109	24	16
III. Gruppe	Bf 109	20	7
Jagdgeschwader 53			
Stab	Bf 109	4	4
II. Gruppe	Bf 109	30	20
III. Gruppe	Bf 109	26	12
Jagdgeschwader 77			
2. and 3. Staffel	Bf 109	25	18
Zerstörergeschwader 26			
III. Gruppe	Bf 110	33	14
10. Staffel	Do 17	9	4
Nachtjagdgeschwader 2			
I. Gruppe	Ju 88	30	8
Lehrgeschwader 1			
Stab	Ju 88	1	0
I. Gruppe	Ju 88	28	11
II. Gruppe	Ju 88	26	13
IV. Gruppe	Ju 88	49	19
Kampfgeschwader 26			
I. Gruppe	He 111	36	27[1]
II. Gruppe	He 111	31	8[1]
III. Gruppe	Ju 88	29	20[1]
Kampfgeschwader 54			
Stab	Ju 88	2	1
I. Gruppe	Ju 88	28	6
Kampfgeschwader 77			
Stab	Ju 88	3	0
II. Gruppe	Ju 88	27	5
III. Gruppe	Ju 88	27	12
Kampfgeschwader 100			
II. Gruppe	He 111	25	12
Kampfgruppe 806	Ju 88	18	8

Sturzkampfgeschwader 3

Stab	Bf 110	4	2
I. Gruppe	Ju 87	22	11
II. Gruppe	Ju 87	29	14
III. Gruppe	Ju 87	32	17

Aufklärungsgruppe 121

1. Staffel	Ju 88	10	8

Aufklärungsgruppe 122

1. Staffel	Ju 88	10	3
	Bf 109	2	2
2. Staffel	Ju 88	9	5
3. Staffel	Ju 88	12	11

Aufklärungsgruppe 123

2. Staffel	Ju 88	9	6
	Ju 86	3	1

Aufklärungsgruppe 12

4. Staffel	Bf 110	12	5

Seeaufklärungsgruppe 125

2. Staffel	Ar 196	9	4

Seeaufklärungsgruppe 126

	He 111	9	3
	Ar 196	17	12
	He 60	1	0

Kampfgeschwader zbV 1

III. Gruppe	Ju 52	32	17
IV. Gruppe	Ju 52	50	26

Kampfgruppe zbV 400

	Ju 52	28	14

Kampfgruppe zbV 600

	Ju 52	38	29

Kampfgruppe zbV 800

	Ju 52	32	11

Luftflotte 3

Jagdgeschwader 2

Stab	Fw 190	4	3

I. Gruppe	Fw 190	36	29
II. Gruppe	Fw 190	37	34
III. Gruppe	Fw 190	39	31
10. Staffel	Fw 190	15	11 [2]
11. Staffel	Bf 109	9	8
Jagdgeschwader 26			
Stab	Fw 190	4	4
I. Gruppe	Fw 190	38	28
II. Gruppe	Fw 190	41	36
III. Gruppe	Fw 190	36	33
10. Staffel	Fw 190	15	12 [2]
Kampfgeschwader 2			
Stab	Do 217	2	2
I. Gruppe	Do 217	29	21
II. Gruppe	Do 217	26	15
III. Gruppe	Do 217	35	29
Kampfgeschwader 40			
I. Gruppe	He 177	30	16
II. Gruppe	Do 217	30	28
III. Gruppe	Fw 200	20	11
	Ju 88C	4	1
Kampfgruppe 106	Ju 88	31	23
Kampfgruppe 606	Ju 88	18	6
Aufklärungsgruppe 33			
1. Staffel	Ju 88	12	7
	Bf 109	3	3
	Fw 190	1	0
3. Staffel	Ju 88	7	6
Aufklärungsgruppe 123			
1. Staffel	Ju 88	7	3
	Bf 110	1	1
	Fw 190	1	0
3. Staffel	Ju 88	11	6
	Bf 110	1	0

Aufklärungsgruppe 13
1. Staffel	Hs 126	9	8

Aufklärungsgruppe 23	Hs 126	6	1

Luftflotte 4

Jagdgeschwader 3
Stab	Bf 109	3	2
I. Gruppe	Bf 109	24	9
II. Gruppe	Bf 109	22	10
III. Gruppe	Bf 109	25	12

Jagdgeschwader 52
Stab	Bf 109	4	4
II. Gruppe	Bf 109	40	24
III. Gruppe	Bf 109	35	20
15. Staffel	Bf 109	12	6 [3]

Jagdgeschwader 53
I. Gruppe	Bf 109	40	8

Jagdgeschwader 77
Stab	Bf 109	4	4
1. Staffel	Bf 109	9	6
II. Gruppe	Bf 109	23	16
III. Gruppe	Bf 109	27	21

Zerstörergeschwader 1
Stab	Bf 110	3	2
I. Gruppe	Bf 110	36	14
II. Gruppe	Bf 110	31	15
III. Gruppe	Bf 109	40	40
	Do 217	3	1

Zerstörergeschwader 2
7. Staffel	Bf 109	12	9

Lehrgeschwader 1
III. Gruppe	Ju 88	28	11

Kampfgeschwader 27
Stab	He 111	2	2

I. *Gruppe*	He 111	32	20
II. *Gruppe*	He 111	31	21
III. *Gruppe*	He 111	31	8
Kampfgeschwader 51			
Stab	Ju 88	2	0
I. *Gruppe*	Ju 88	30	17
II. *Gruppe*	Ju 88	33	8
III. *Gruppe*	Ju 88	28	8
Kampfgeschwader 55			
Stab	He 111	4	4
I. *Gruppe*	He 111	31	19
II. *Gruppe*	He 111	30	21
III. *Gruppe*	He 111	29	20
Kampfgeschwader 76			
Stab	Ju 88	3	2
I. *Gruppe*	Ju 88	27	13
II. *Gruppe*	Ju 88	33	14
III. *Gruppe*	Ju 88	38	12
Kampfgeschwader 100			
Stab	He 111	1	1
I. *Gruppe*	He 111	37	13
Sturzkampfgeschwader 1			
II. *Gruppe*	Ju 87	39	30
Sturzkampfgeschwader 2			
Stab	Ju 87	3	3
	Bf 110	6	4
I. *Gruppe*	Ju 87	28	20
II. *Gruppe*	Ju 87	31	19
III. *Gruppe*	Ju 87	18	11
Sturzkampfgeschwader 77			
Stab	Ju 87	3	1
	Bf 110	6	4
I. *Gruppe*	Ju 87	29	20
II. *Gruppe*	Ju 87	35	28
III. *Gruppe*	Ju 87	33	13

Schlachtgeschwader 1

Stab	Bf 109	2	1[1]
I. Gruppe	Bf 109	31	16[1]
II. Gruppe	Hs 129	28	13
	Hs 123	12	6

Aufklärungsgruppe der Oberkommando der Luftwaffe

2. Staffel	Ju 88	9	3
	Do 215	2	0

Aufklärungsgruppe 121

3. Staffel	Ju 88	10	5
4. Staffel	Ju 88	10	10

Aufklärungsgruppe 122

4. Staffel	Ju 88	10	5

Aufklärungsgruppe 10

3. Staffel	Ju 88	12	4

Aufklärungsgruppe 11

2. Staffel	Do 17	13	2

Aufklärungsgruppe 22

2. Staffel	Ju 88	9	8

Nachtaufklärungsstaffel 1	Do 17	12	8

Nahaufklärungsgruppe 1	Fw 189	8	6
	Bf 110	8	4

Nahaufklärungsgruppe 3	Fw 189	8	5
	Bf 110	5	4

Nahaufklärungsgruppe 4	Fw 189	15	11

Nahaufklärungsgruppe 6	Hs 126	7	5
	Bf 110	7	5

Nahaufklärungsgruppe 7	Fw 189	15	10

Nahaufklärungsgruppe 8	Fw 189	21	19

Nahaufklärungsgruppe 9	Fw 189	15	11
Nahaufklärungsgruppe 10	Fw 189	15	8
	Hs 126	11	7
Nahaufklärungsgruppe 12	Fw 189	9	8
	Bf 110	10	4
Nahaufklärungsgruppe 13	Hs 126	19	15
	Bf 110	7	3
Nahaufklärungsgruppe 14	Fw 189	11	10
	Bf 110	8	4
Nahaufklärungsgruppe 16	Fw 189	12	7
Seeaufklärungsgruppe 125			
1. Staffel	Bv 138	7	4
3. Staffel	Bv 138	15	7
Kampfgeschwader zbV 1			
II. Gruppe	Ju 52	35	2
Kampfgeschwader zbV 4			
	Ju 52	49	31
Kampfgeschwader zbV 5			
	Ju 52	52	22
Kampfgeschwader zbV 9			
	Ju 52	52	34
Kampfgruppe zbV 50	Ju 52	48	29
Kampfgruppe zbV 102	Ju 52	52	22
Kampfgruppe zbV 900	Ju 52	48	16

Luftwaffenkommando Ost

Jagdgeschwader 51			
Stab	Bf 109	2	1
I. Gruppe	Bf 109	31	15

II. Gruppe	Bf 109	34	30
III. Gruppe	Bf 109	37	22
IV. Gruppe	Bf 109	36	29
15. Staffel	Bf 109	10	6 [4]

Jagdgeschwader 54
Stab	Bf 109	4	3
I. Gruppe	Bf 109	43	27
II. Gruppe	Bf 109	40	33

Kampfgeschwader 3
Stab	Ju 88	2	2
I. Gruppe	Ju 88	34	15
II. Gruppe	Ju 88	27	16
III. Gruppe	Ju 88	27	19

Kampfgeschwader 4
Stab	He 111	3	3
I. Gruppe	He 111	26	23
II. Gruppe	He 111	25	19
III. Gruppe	He 111	35	18

Aufklärungsgruppe Oberkommando der Luftwaffe
1. Staffel	Ju 88	8	3
	Bf 110	1	1
	Bf 109	2	1
	Ju 86	1	1

Nachtaufklärungsstaffel 2	Do 17	12	9

Nahaufklärungsgruppe 2	Fw 189	8	5
	Hs 126	8	4

Nahaufklärungsgruppe 5	Fw 189	6	4
	Hs 126	15	13

Nahaufklärungsgruppe 15	Fw 189	15	12
	Hs 126	8	3

Kampfgruppe zbV 105	Ju 52	38	25

Kampfgruppe zbV 500	Ju 52	40	15

Kampfgruppe zbV 700	Ju 52	26	14

Luftflotte 5

Jagdgeschwader 5			
I. Gruppe	Fw 190	35	28
II. Gruppe	Bf 109	35	25
III. Gruppe	Bf 109	23	17
IV. Gruppe	Fw 190	26	20
13. Staffel	Bf 110	12	7
Kampfgeschwader 30			
I. Gruppe	Ju 88	35	29
II. Gruppe	Ju 88	37	26
III. Gruppe	Ju 88	36	32
Sturzkampfgeschwader 5			
I. Gruppe	Ju 87	43	39
Aufklärungsgruppe 120			
1. Staffel	Ju 88	12	10
Aufklärungsgruppe 124			
1. Staffel	Ju 88	11	7
Aufklärungsgruppe 32			
1. Staffel	Fw 189	8	6
	Hs 126	4	4
Küstenfliegergruppe 406	Bv 138	26	22
	He 115		
Küstenfliegergruppe 906	He 115	8	6
	Bv 138	6	6
Kampfgruppe zbV 108	Ju 52 floatplanes,	39	23
	Ju 52		

Luftwaffenbefehlshaber Mitte

Jagdgeschwader 1			
Stab	Fw 190	4	4
I. Gruppe	Fw 190	37	34

II. Gruppe	Fw 190	38	28
III. Gruppe	Fw 190	40	33
IV. Gruppe	Fw 190	39	28

Nachtjagdgeschwader 1
Stab	Bf 110	3	2
I. Gruppe	Bf 110	19	14
II. Gruppe	Bf 110	15	15
	Do 217	14	7
III. Gruppe	Bf 110	15	15
	Do 217	3	1

Nachtjagdgeschwader 2
Stab	Ju 88	3	1
II. Gruppe	Bf 110	23	17
	Do 217	10	1
	Do 215	6	5
III. Gruppe	Ju 88	20	13
	Do 217	15	7

Nachtjagdgeschwader 3
Stab	Bf 110	2	1
I. Gruppe	Bf 110	20	16
	Do 217	3	1
II. Gruppe	Bf 110	24	21
	Do 217	9	6
III. Gruppe	Bf 110	31	24
	Do 217	1	1

Nachtjagdgeschwader 4
Stab	Bf 110	1	1
II. Gruppe	Bf 110	15	8
III. Gruppe	Bf 110	19	13
	Do 217	7	5

Kampfgeschwader 2
IV. Gruppe	Do 217	35	30

Kampfgeschwader 3
IV. Gruppe	Ju 88	29	24

Kampfgeschwader 4
  IV. Gruppe   He 111   35   28

Kampfgeschwader 26
  IV. Gruppe   He 111   37   28

Kampfgeschwader 27
  IV. Gruppe   He 111   30   13

Kampfgeschwader 30
  IV. Gruppe   Ju 88   61   33

Kampfgeschwader 40
  IV. Gruppe   Fw 200   17   13
                         He 177   4   1

Kampfgeschwader 51
  IV. Gruppe   Ju 88   25   18

Kampfgeschwader 53
  IV. Gruppe   He 111   39   9

Kampfgeschwader 54
  IV. Gruppe   Ju 88   32   14

Kampfgeschwader 55
  IV. Gruppe   He 111   30   24

Kampfgeschwader 76
  IV. Gruppe   Ju 88   32   23

Kampfgeschwader 77
  IV. Gruppe   Ju 88   37   21

Kampfgeschwader 100
  IV. Gruppe   He 111   17   10

Kampfgeschwader zbV 1
  I. Gruppe   Ju 52   52   35

Kampfgeschwader zbV 172
                         Ju 52   52   10

Notes

1. Torpedo-bomber unit.
2. Fighter-bomber unit.
3. Croatian-flown unit.
4. Spanish-flown unit.

Composition of the Main Operational Flying Units, 17 May 1943

This chapter gives the strength of the *Luftwaffe* operational units on 17 May 1943, four days after the last of the Axis forces in North Africa had surrendered. For the *Luftwaffe* the end of the losing battle in that theatre brought a respite for the units involved, particularly the transport *Gruppen* which had suffered heavy losses.

The main German offensive on the Eastern Front that year, Operation 'Citadel', was scheduled to open in just over a month's time in the central sector. To keep the German intentions secret for as long as possible, the bulk of the fighter-bomber, ground-attack and dive-bomber units remained in other sectors until the last moment. In recognition of its enhanced importance, *Luftwaffenkommando Ost*, controlling operations over the central sector, had been upgraded to a full *Luftflotte*, *Luftflotte* 6; and a new formation, *Luftwaffenkommando Süd Ost*, had been formed to control air operations over Greece, Yugoslavia and Albania and to defend the important oil refineries at Ploesti in Romania. At this time *Luftwaffe* front-line units possessed 4,641 serviceable aircraft, divided as follows:

Single-engined fighters	980
Twin-engined day fighters	114
Night fighters	378
Fighter-bombers	216
Specialised ground-attack aircraft	61
Night harassment aircraft	148
Dive-bombers	413
Twin-engined bombers	1,269
Four-engined bombers	33
Long-range reconnaissance aircraft	215
Short-range reconnaissance and army cooperation aircraft	251
Coastal aircraft	149
Transport aircraft	414
Total	**4,641**

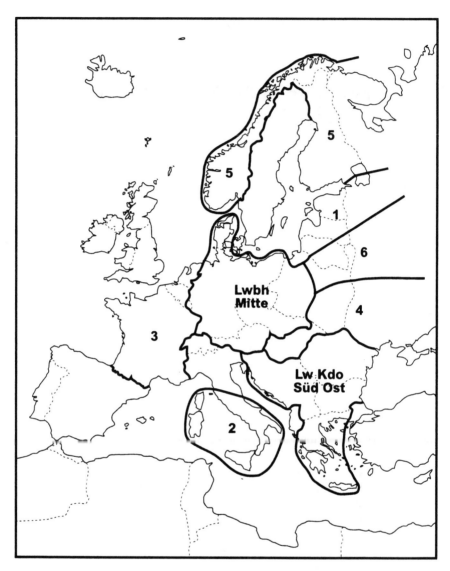

Fig. 5. Operational Areas of the Luftflotten, *17 May 1943:* Luftflotten *areas of responsibility shortly before the launching of Operation 'Citadel', intended as the decisive offensive on the Eastern Front during 1943. Since the planned action would take place on the central part of the front,* Luftwaffenkommando Ost *had been upgraded to* Luftflotte 6. *A few days earlier the last of the Axis forces in North Africa had surrendered.* Luftflotte 2, *at a low ebb after the heavy beating it had taken in previous months, was concentrated in Italy, where units were in the process of re-forming. In the Balkans a new formation,* Luftwaffenkommando Süd Ost, *had been formed to control air operations in the Balkans and defend the Rumanian oilfields.*

The front-line force was nearly one-third larger than in the previous July, and was close to the peak numerical strength it would attain. Even so, in each combat theatre it faced enemy air forces that were numerically far stronger. Moreover, since the previous census, most of the combat aircraft in the *Luftwaffe* had continued in their inexorable drift towards obsolescence. Now each opposing air force operated types that were more modern than their German counterparts.

Another serious deficiency now facing the *Luftwaffe* was the shortage of single-engined fighter units. For the defence of the homeland against the attacks by USAAF heavy bombers, the force had only 198 serviceable day fighters available—and to achieve that meagre figure it had been necessary to pull back some *Gruppen* from the battle fronts. The central and southern sectors of the Eastern Front were left with only 213 serviceable fighters, a reduction of about one-third since the previous July. In the south, *Luftflotte 2* was down to 170 serviceable fighters.

Despite its many problems, however, we can see that the *Luftwaffe* was girding itself to fight with renewed vigour in the coming summer. Four new bomber *Gruppen* were in the process of forming. Six *Gruppen* were re-equipping with new aircraft types or weapons—three with the He 177 heavy bomber, two with Do 217s modified to carry anti-shipping missiles and one with the Me 210 fighter-bomber. A further twenty-one *Gruppen* had withdrawn to re-form and retrain, and most of these would be ready to return to the fray in a few weeks.

Since the previous census *Luftflotten 1, 4* and *6* on the Eastern Front had each assembled a small number of *Störkampfstaffeln*. These units flew obsolete combat planes or training types modified for the light attack role. These aircraft now conducted night harassment missions over enemy territory. At relatively small cost, the move added an additional 148 planes to the *Luftwaffe*'s combat strength.

In a move intended to rationalise their status, the transport units had lost their unwieldy title of *Kampfgeschwader* (or *Kampfgruppen*) *zbV*. Instead, from now on they were known simply as *Transportgeschwader* or *Transportgruppen*. As the change came into force, several of these units received new identification numbers.

Luftflotte 1

Unit	Aircraft	Total	Serviceable
Jagdgeschwader 54			
Stab	Fw 190	4	4
I. Gruppe	Fw 190	36	30
II. Gruppe	Bf 109	40	40
10. Staffel	Fw 190	9	3 [1,2]

Nachtjagd Schwarm	Bf 109	5	1 [3]
Kampfgeschwader 53			
Stab	He 111	4	4
I. Gruppe	He 111	37	37
III. Gruppe	He 111	37	33
15. Staffel	Do 17	12	12 [4]
Sturzkampfgeschwader 5			
I. Gruppe	Ju 87	51	51
Aufklärungsgruppe 22			
3. Staffel	Ju 88	12	9
Aufklärungsgruppe 122			
5. Staffel	Ju 88	10	7
Nachtaufklärungsgruppe			
3. Staffel	Do 17	10	6
Nahaufklärungsgruppe 8	Bf 110	10	7
	Hs 126	11	9
Nahaufklärungsgruppe 11	Fw 189	12	12
	Hs 126	7	4
Seeaufklärungsgruppe 127	He 60, Ar 95	23	7
Störkampfstaffeln Luftflotte 1			
1. Staffel	Fw 58, He 46, Ar 66, Go 145	21	19
2. Staffel	Fw 58, He 46, Ar 66	20	13
3. Staffel	Fw 58, He 46, Ar 66, Go 145	21	15
4. Staffel	Fw 58, He 46, Ar 66	22	19

Luftflotte 2

Jagdgeschwader 27			
Stab	Bf 109	1	1

II. *Gruppe*	Bf 109	40	38
III. *Gruppe*	Bf 109	40	40
Jagdgeschwader 51			
II. *Gruppe*	Bf 109	40	29
Jagdgeschwader 53			
Stab	Bf 109	4	3
I. *Gruppe*	Bf 109	36	8
II. *Gruppe*	Bf 109	34	10
III. *Gruppe*	Bf 109	38	24
Jagdgeschwader 77			
Stab	Bf 109	4	3
I. *Gruppe*	Bf 109	22	3 [5]
II. *Gruppe*	Bf 109	27	11 [5]
III. *Gruppe*	Bf 109	23	0 [5]
Zerstörergeschwader 1			
II. *Gruppe*	Bf 110	32	8
III. *Gruppe*	Me 210	15	6 [6]
Zerstörergeschwader 26			
III. *Gruppe*	Bf 110	29	20
10. *Staffel*	Ju 88	12	12
Nachtjagdgeschwader 2			
Stab	Ju 88	1	0
I. *Gruppe*	Ju 88	18	8
II. *Gruppe*	Ju 88	11	10
Schlachtgeschwader 2			
II. *Gruppe*	Fw 190	22	4
	Hs 129	10	10
Schnellkampfgeschwader 10			
III. *Gruppe*	Fw 190	20	2
Lehrgeschwader 1			
Stab	Ju 88	1	1
I. *Gruppe*	Ju 88	37	29
II. *Gruppe*	Ju 88	31	10 [5]

Kampfgeschwader 1			
II. *Gruppe*	Ju 88	26	14
Kampfgeschwader 26			
II. *Gruppe*	He 111	37	20[7]
III. *Gruppe*	Ju 88	13	7[7]
Beleuchterstaffel	Ju 88	5	0[8]
Kampfgeschwader 30			
III. *Gruppe*	Ju 88	32	30
Kampfgeschwader 54			
Stab	Ju 88	1	1
I. *Gruppe*	Ju 88	20	11
II. *Gruppe*	Ju 88	22	10
III. *Gruppe*	Ju 88	34	16[5]
Kampfgeschwader 76			
Stab	Ju 88	2	2
I. *Gruppe*	Ju 88	36	2[5]
III. *Gruppe*	Ju 88	32	23
Kampfgeschwader 77			
II. *Gruppe*	Ju 88	26	20[5]
III. *Gruppe*	Ju 88	20	14
Aufklärungsgruppe 1??			
1. *Staffel*	Ju 88	9	2
	Bf 109	3	3
2. *Staffel*	Ju 88	6	2
	Me 410	5	2
	Me 210	1	0
Aufklärungsgruppe 12	Bf 109	12	8
Seeaufklärungsgruppe 126	Ar 196	30	21
Transportgeschwader 1			
III. *Gruppe*	Ju 52	35	13
IV. *Gruppe*	Ju 52	33	9
Transportgeschwader 5			
I. *Gruppe*	Me 323	21	10

II. Gruppe	Me 323	12	7
Transportgruppe 30	He 111	52	16
Savoy Staffel	SM.82	6	4 [9]
Seetransport Staffel	Ju 52 floatplanes	12	7
Ju 90/Ju 290 Staffel	Ju 90, Ju 290	7	3
Korps Transport Staffel	Ju 52	7	5

Luftflotte 3

Jagdgeschwader 2			
Stab	Fw 190	4	4
I. Gruppe	Fw 190	40	40
II. Gruppe	Fw 190	24	18
III. Gruppe	Fw 190	40	37
10. Staffel	Bf 109	13	8 [1]
11. Staffel	Bf 109	14	9 [1]
12. Staffel	Bf 109	15	12 [1]
Jagdgeschwader 26			
Stab	Fw 190	4	4
II. Gruppe	Fw 190	40	40
III. Gruppe	Fw 190	40	35
Jagdgeschwader 54			
11. Staffel	Fw 190	16	9 [1]
Schnellkampfgeschwader 10			
Stab	Fw 190	6	6
I. Gruppe	Fw 190	42	42
II. Gruppe	Fw 190	40	38
IV. Gruppe	Fw 190	30	23
Kampfgeschwader 2			
Stab	Do 217	2	2
I. Gruppe	Do 217	21	8
II. Gruppe	Do 217	26	26
	Me 410	9	3 [6]
III. Gruppe	Do 217	18	17

Kampfgeschwader 40

Stab	He 177	1	0
II. Gruppe	Do 217	21	19
V. Gruppe	Ju 88C	37	28 [10]

Kampfgeschwader 66

I. Gruppe	Do 217	23	7 [5]

Aufklärungsgruppe 33

1. Staffel	Ju 88	12	7
3. Staffel	Ju 88	12	8

Aufklärungsgruppe 122

3. Staffel	Ju 88	11	5

Aufklärungsgruppe 123

1. Staffel	Ju 88	12	6
3. Staffel	Ju 88	12	6
4. Staffel	Bf 109	10	7
	Fw 190	2	2
5. Staffel	Bf 109	12	9

Nahaufklärungsgruppe 13	Fw 190	31	25
Aufklärungsfliegerstaffel 222	Bv 222	4	1

Küstenfliegergruppe 196

5. Staffel	Ar 196	35	29

Korps Transport Staffel	LeO 451	6	1 [11]

Luftflotte 4

Jagdgeschwader 3

II. Gruppe	Bf 109	40	24
III. Gruppe	Bf 109	35	20

Jagdgeschwader 52

Stab	Bf 109	4	2
I. Gruppe	Bf 109	38	17
II. Gruppe	Bf 109	28	14
III. Gruppe	Bf 109	37	22
15. Staffel	Bf 109	10	6 [4]

Zerstörergeschwader 1			
10. Staffel	Bf 110	12	7 [3]
Schlachtgeschwader 1			
Stab	Fw 190	6	6
I. Gruppe	Fw 190	41	32
	Hs 129	10	9
II. Gruppe	Fw 190	25	17
	Hs 129	9	9
	Hs 123	12	8
Schlachtgeschwader 2			
Stab	Fw 190	3	1
I. Gruppe	Fw 190	8	4
	Hs 129	12	11
Jagdgeschwader 51			
Panzerjäger Staffel	Hs 129	16	14 [12]
Kampfgeschwader 3			
Stab	Ju 88	1	0
II. Gruppe	Ju 88	37	27
III. Gruppe	Ju 88	31	13
Kampfgeschwader 27			
Stab	He 111	2	0
I. Gruppe	He 111	34	13
III. Gruppe	He 111	23	15
14. Staffel	He 111	9	6 [13]
Kampfgeschwader 51			
III. Gruppe	Ju 88	21	11
Kampfgeschwader 55			
Stab	He 111	4	4
I. Gruppe	He 111	19	13
II. Gruppe	He 111	30	19
III. Gruppe	He 111	33	20
Kampfgeschwader 100			
I. Gruppe	He 111	37	35
Sturzkampfgeschwader 2			
Stab	Ju 87	3	2

	Ju 88	6	6
I. Gruppe	Ju 87	30	23
II. Gruppe	Ju 87	26	20
III. Gruppe	Ju 87	34	27
Sturzkampfgeschwader 3			
Stab	Ju 87	2	2
I. Gruppe	Ju 87	38	22
III. Gruppe	Ju 87	33	16
Sturzkampfgeschwader 77			
Stab	Ju 87	3	2
	Ju 88	6	6
I. Gruppe	Ju 87	39	33
II. Gruppe	Ju 87	39	30
III. Gruppe	Ju 87	39	24
Aufklärungsgruppe 22			
2. Staffel	Ju 88	12	8
Aufklärungsgruppe 100			
2. Staffel	Ju 88, Do 215	12	8
Aufklärungsgruppe 121			
3. Staffel	Ju 88	12	6
Aufklärungsgruppe 122			
4. Staffel	Ju 88	12	9
Nachtaufklärungsgruppe			
4. Staffel	Do 17, He 111,	11	3
	Do 217		
Nahaufklärungsgruppe 1	Fw 189	23	8
Nahaufklärungsgruppe 6	Fw 189	11	9
	Hs 126	12	10
	Bf 110	10	3
Nahaufklärungsgruppe 9	Fw 189	17	15
Nahaufklärungsgruppe 14	Fw 189	12	9
	Bf 110	7	4

Aufklärungsgruppe 23			
4. *Staffel*	Hs 126	9	6
Seeaufklärungsgruppe 125			
3. *Staffel*	Bv 138	15	12
Störkampfstaffeln Luftflotte 4			
1. *Staffel*	He 46, Do 17	13	5
2. *Staffel*	Ar 66, Ju 34, Fw 189	8	3
3. *Staffel*	Go 145	16	1
4. *Staffel*	Fw 58, Go 145, Ar 66	5	2
5. *Staffel*	Hs 126, He 46	14	7
6. *Staffel*	Go 145	16	15
Transportgeschwader 3			
I. *Gruppe*	Ju 52	53	48
Korps Transport Staffeln	Ju 52	32	26

Luftflotte 5

Jagdgeschwader 5			
Stab	Fw 190	2	2
I. *Gruppe*	Fw 190, Bf 109	35	23
II. *Gruppe*	Fw 190	23	20
III. *Gruppe*	Bf 109	26	24
IV. *Gruppe*	Fw 190, Bf 109	40	31
13. *Staffel*	Bf 110	12	8
14. *Staffel*	Fw 190	11	7
Kampfgeschwader 30			
I. *Gruppe*	Ju 88	37	32
Versuchsverband des Oberkommando der Luftwaffe			
1. *Staffel*	Ju 88	4	3 [14]
Aufklärungsgruppe 22			
1. *Staffel*	Ju 88	7	5
Aufklärungsgruppe 120			
1. *Staffel*	Ju 88	11	5

Aufklärungsgruppe 124			
1. *Staffel*	Ju 88	12	11
Aufklärungsgruppe 32			
1. *Staffel*	Fw 189	8	6
Küstenfliegergruppe 406	Bv 138	26	17
	He 115	9	9
Küstenfliegergruppe 196			
1. *Staffel*	Ar 196	28	25
Küstenfliegergruppe 706			
1. *Staffel*	Bv 138	6	5
	Ar 196	5	5
Küstenfliegergruppe 906	Bv 138	8	5
Seeaufklärungsgruppe 125			
1. *Staffel*	Bv 138	8	7
Transportgruppe 20	Ju 52 floatplanes	10	4
	Ju 52	36	27
Korps Transport Staffel	Ju 52	8	6
	He 111	1	1

Luftflotte 6

Jagdgeschwader 26			
I. *Gruppe*	Fw 190	36	30
Jagdgeschwader 51			
Stab	Fw 190	14	11
I. *Gruppe*	Fw 190	39	20
III. *Gruppe*	Fw 190	40	21
IV. *Gruppe*	Fw 190	28	20
15. *Staffel*	Bf 109	16	6[15]
Zerstörergeschwader 1			
Stab	Bf 110	2	2
I. *Gruppe*	Bf 110	38	30

Nachtjagd Schwarm	Ju 88	4	2[3]
Kampfgeschwader 1			
Stab	Ju 88	4	4
I. Gruppe	Ju 88	20	0[5]
III. Gruppe	Ju 88	37	18
Kampfgeschwader 4			
Stab	He 111	1	0
II. Gruppe	He 111	37	23
III. Gruppe	He 111	37	23
Kampfgeschwader 51			
II. Gruppe	Ju 88	37	28
Sturzkampfgeschwader 1			
Stab	Ju 87	1	1
	Bf 110	6	5
II. Gruppe	Ju 87	39	35
III. Gruppe	Ju 87	39	36
Aufklärungsgruppe 11			
4. Staffel	Ju 88	6	4
Aufklärungsgruppe 14			
4. Staffel	Ju 88	12	10
Aufklärungsgruppe 100			
1. Staffel	Ju 88	10	6
	Ju 86	2	1
	Do 215	1	1
Aufklärungsgruppe 121			
4. Staffel	Ju 88	9	6
Nachtaufklärungsgruppe			
2. Staffel	Do 17	2	1
	Do 217	6	3
Nahaufklärungsgruppe 3	Fw 189	18	13
Nahaufklärungsgruppe 4	Bf 109	23	18

	Bf 110	6	4
Nahaufklärungsgruppe 5	Bf 110	8	7
	Hs 126	17	13
Nahaufklärungsgruppe 10	Fw 189	12	9
	Hs 126	12	10
Nahaufklärungsgruppe 15	Fw 189	28	24
Störkampfstaffeln Luftflotte 6			
1. Staffel	Fw 58, He 46, Ar 66	19	18
2. Staffel	Go 145	20	18
3. Staffel	Fw 58, Ar 66	14	13
Korps Transport Staffel	Ju 52	8	4

Luftwaffenkommando Süd Ost

Jagdgeschwader 4			
I. Gruppe	Bf 109	40	40
Sturzkampfgeschwader 1			
IV. Gruppe	Ju 87	40	39
Luftwaffe Stab Kroatien			
Einsatzstaffel	Ju 88	37	32
Einsatzstaffel	He 46	15	11
Aufklärungsgruppe 123			
2. Staffel	Ju 88	12	7
Nahaufklärungsgruppe Kroatien	Hs 126	11	6
Seeaufklärungsgruppe 125			
2. Staffel	Ar 196	8	6

Luftwaffenbefehlshaber Mitte

Jagdgeschwader 1			
Stab	Fw 190	3	1
I. Gruppe	Fw 190	31	27

	Bf 109	7	0
II. Gruppe	Fw 190	39	31
Jagdgeschwader 3			
Stab	Bf 109	3	3 [5]
I. Gruppe	Bf 109	40	17 [5]
Jagdgeschwader 11			
I. Gruppe	Fw 190	40	27
II. Gruppe	Bf 109	54	27
Jagdgeschwader 27			
I. Gruppe	Bf 109	37	24
Jagdgeschwader 54			
III. Gruppe	Bf 109	45	41
Nachtjagdgeschwader 1			
Stab	Bf 110	4	4
I. Gruppe	Bf 110	27	20
	Do 215	1	0
II. Gruppe	Bf 110	26	17
	Do 217	6	3
III. Gruppe	Bf 110	23	20
IV. Gruppe	Bf 110	22	16
	Do 215	2	2
Nachtjagdgeschwader 3			
Stab	Bf 110	2	2
I. Gruppe	Bf 110	11	11
	Do 217	11	9
II. Gruppe	Do 217	29	20
III. Gruppe	Bf 110	23	18
IV. Gruppe	Ju 88	25	22
Nachtjagdgeschwader 4			
Stab	Bf 110	1	1
I. Gruppe	Bf 110	22	19
	Do 217	11	8
II. Gruppe	Bf 110	22	20
	Do 217	11	11
III. Gruppe	Bf 110	24	22
	Do 217	6	5
IV. Gruppe	Bf 110	23	23

	Do 217	3	3

Nachtjagdgeschwader 5
Stab	Bf 110	2	1
I. Gruppe	Bf 110	26	26
II. Gruppe	Bf 110	19	17
	Do 217	2	1
IV. Gruppe	Bf 110	18	18
	Ju 88	15	11

Lehrgeschwader 1
IV. Gruppe	Ju 88	42	17
	He 111	4	1

Kampfgeschwader 1
IV. Gruppe	Ju 88	78	41

Kampfgeschwader 2
IV. Gruppe	Do 217	38	27
	Do 17	7	3

Kampfgeschwader 3
I. Gruppe	Ju 88	37	29.[5]
IV. Gruppe	Ju 88	47	29

Kampfgeschwader 4
IV. Gruppe	He 111	42	34

Kampfgeschwader 6
I. Gruppe	Ju 88	31	21[2]
II. Gruppe	Ju 88	20	15[2]
III. Gruppe	Ju 88	34	28[2]
IV. Gruppe	He 111	53	35

Kampfgeschwader 26
I. Gruppe	He 111	19	10[5]
IV. Gruppe	He 111	26	7
	Ju 88	20	7

Kampfgeschwader 27
II. Gruppe	He 111	37	28[5]
IV. Gruppe	He 111	33	12

Kampfgeschwader 30			
IV. Gruppe	Ju 88	54	9
Kampfgeschwader 40			
I. Gruppe	He 177	12	10[6]
	Fw 200	6	1
III. Gruppe	He 177	12	12[6]
	Fw 200	11	2
IV. Gruppe	Fw 200	5	4
	He 177	3	0
	Ju 88	18	10
Kampfgeschwader 50			
I. Gruppe	He 177	29	4[2]
Kampfgeschwader 51			
IV. Gruppe	Ju 88	44	29
Kampfgeschwader 53			
II. Gruppe	He 111	13	0[5]
IV. Gruppe	He 111	41	30
Kampfgeschwader 54			
IV. Gruppe	Ju 88	33	20
	He 111	4	3
Kampfgeschwader 55			
IV. Gruppe	He 111	46	41
Kampfgeschwader 76			
II. Gruppe	Ju 88	5	3[5]
IV. Gruppe	Ju 88	37	13
Kampfgeschwader 77			
IV. Gruppe	Ju 88	44	34
Kampfgeschwader 100			
II. Gruppe	Do 217	37	0[16]
III. Gruppe	Do 217	35	11[17]
IV. Gruppe	Ju 88	28	8
Sturzkampfgeschwader 2			
IV. Gruppe	Ju 87	21	13

Sturzkampfgeschwader 3			
IV. *Gruppe*	Ju 87	20	16
Sturzkampfgeschwader 5			
IV. *Gruppe*	Ju 87	9	7
Sturzkampfgeschwader 77			
IV. *Gruppe*	Ju 87	18	14
Versuchsverband der Oberkommando der Luftwaffe			
2. *Staffel*	He 111, Ju 290, He 59, He 115, Fw 200	16	7 [14]
Nahaufklärungsgruppe 2	Bf 109	12	5 [6]
	Bf 110	9	9
Transportgeschwader 1			
I. *Gruppe*	Ju 52	22	16 [5]
II. *Gruppe*	Ju 52	49	34 [5]
Transportgeschwader 2			
II. *Gruppe*	Ju 52	20	8 [5]
III. *Gruppe*	Ju 52	24	12
Transportgeschwader 3			
II. *Gruppe*	Ju 52	50	39
III. *Gruppe*	Ju 52	52	37
IV. *Gruppe*	Ju 52	36	24
Transportgeschwader 4			
I. *Gruppe*	Ju 52	15	5 [5]
II. *Gruppe*	Ju 52	51	48 [5]

Notes

1. Fighter-bomber unit.
2. Unit forming.
3. Night fighter unit.
4. Croatian-flown unit.
5. Unit re-forming.
6. Unit re-equipping.

7. Torpedo-bomber unit.
8. Unit to illuminate enemy shipping, to facilitate night torpedo attacks.
9. Transport unit. The Savoia-Marchetti SM.82 was a three-engined Italian transport plane, some of which were transferred to the *Luftwaffe*.
10. Long-range fighter unit.
11. The LeO 451 was a French-built bomber. Several of these captured aircraft were converted into high-speed transports.
12. Anti-tank unit.
13. Railway attack unit.
14. Reconnaissance unit.
15. Spanish-flown unit.
16. Unit re-equipping with aircraft modified to carry the Hs 293 guided missile.
17. Unit re-equipping with aircraft modified to carry the Fritz-X guided missile.

Composition of the Main Operational Flying Units, 31 May 1944

This chapter gives the strength of the *Luftwaffe* operational units on 31 May 1944. Six days later Allied troops would land on the beaches of Normandy, to open up a new fighting front that would further extend the already over-stretched German forces. At the same time, on the Eastern Front the Soviet Army was making final preparations for its own massive summer offensive.

Since the previous May there had been two major organisational changes in the *Luftwaffe*. The formation controlling operations by units based in metropolitan Germany, *Luftwaffenbefehlshaber Mitte*, had been renamed *Luftflotte Reich*. Also there was a new formation, *Fliegerkorps XIV*, to control a centralised pool of air transport planes not allocated to individual *Luftflotten*.

At this time *Luftwaffe* front-line units possessed 4,928 serviceable aircraft, divided as follows:

Single-engined fighters	1,063
Twin-engined day fighters	151
Night fighters	572
Fighter-bombers	278
Ground-attack aircraft	352
Night harassment aircraft	305
Twin-engined bombers	840
Four-engined bombers	97
Long-range reconnaissance aircraft	153
Short-range reconnaissance and army cooperation aircraft	210
Coastal aircraft	123
Transport aircraft	719
Kampfgeschwader 200 (misc. aircraft)	65
Total	**4,928**

The front-line strength of the *Luftwaffe* was close to the peak it would attain, but even that was insufficient to meet its many commitments. On every battle front, and over the homeland, the force was under the most severe pressure.

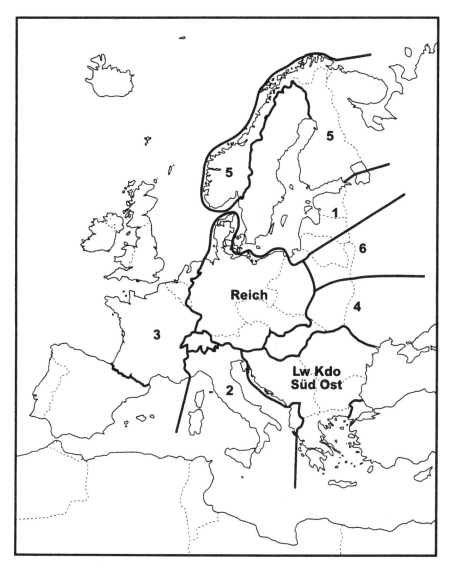

Fig. 6. Operational Areas of the Luftflotten, *31 May 1944:* Luftflotten *areas of responsibility just under a week before Allied forces landed in Normandy. Since the previous May the* Luftwaffe *had undergone two major organisational changes. The formation controlling operations by units based in metropolitan Germany,* Luftwaffenbefehlshaber Mitte, *had been upgraded to* Luftflotte *status and was now* Luftflotte Reich, *while a new formation,* Fliegerkorps XIV, *controlled the centralised pool of air transport units other than those allocated to individual* Luftflotten.

As at the time of the previous census, the most sorely felt shortage was in single-engined fighters. Between them the main formations responsible for the defence of the homeland, *Luftflotte Reich* and *Luftflotte 3*, had only 565 of these machines serviceable. That was far too few to defend targets from attacks by many hundreds of American heavy bombers accompanied by huge forces of escort fighters. Moreover, the available German fighter types, Bf 109Gs and Fw 190s, were outclassed by the latest versions of the P-47 Thunderbolt and the P-51 Mustang they were meeting in combat. A force of 82 twin-engined bomber-destroyers was also available to engage the daylight raiders, but these unwieldy aircraft, Bf 110s and Me 410s, suffered heavy losses whenever the American escorts caught up with them. Almost every incursion into Germany by the US Army Air Forces led to a full-scale air battle, during which the defenders usually took a fearful mauling.

To counter the RAF night attacks, the German night fighter force had 474 serviceable fighters deployed for the defence of the homeland. In addition there was *Jagdgeschwader 300*, designated as a day and night fighter unit and able to operate in either role.

Included in *Luftflotte Reich* were two special units, both under the control of the *Oberkommando der Luftwaffe*, with captured Allied aircraft on strength. One of these, *Versuchsverband Ob. d. L*, conducted trials and demonstration flights with captured aircraft. The other unit, *I./KG 200*, had the task of inserting agents into enemy territory and keeping them supplied. On some missions the unit employed Allied aircraft types, notably B-17 Flying Fortresses, Douglas DC-3s and French Lioré et Olivier 246 flying boats. These captured aircraft were used because they had superior range and/or load carrying abilities to the available German types rather than to deceive the enemy. Aircraft flown by *Versuchsverband Ob. d. L.* and *I./KG 200* carried *Luftwaffe* markings; contrary to what some accounts have suggested, they never flew on combat missions bearing Allied markings.

Luftflotte 3, responsible for air operations on the Western Front, was braced to meet the long-awaited Allied invasion of northern France. In addition to the specialised anti-shipping units, *Luftflotte 3* included several *Gruppen* of conventional bombers. Here, too, there was a serious shortage of single-engined day fighters, though there was an elaborate plan to transfer units from *Luftflotte Reich* when the invasion began. Several landing grounds had been pre-stocked with fuel and munitions to enable incoming units to go into action soon after arrival. The move would leave the homeland devoid of fighter protection but it was expected, correctly, that following the invasion the Allied heavy bombers would be used to provide support for the troops in the battle area.

In the Soviet Union the ground had not yet dried out after the spring thaw, and land operations were impossible over much of the area during May. There was no doubt, however, that the Red Army planned to launch a powerful offensive when the ground hardened. Due to the withdrawal of further fighter units for the defence of the homeland, by the end of May the four *Luftflotten* on the Eastern Front had only 372 serviceable single-engined fighters.

Although they were in the process of being replaced by ground-attack versions of the Fw 190 fighter, a substantial number of Ju 87s remained in service with *Schlachtgruppen* on the Eastern Front. The large-scale deployment of fast firing anti-aircraft guns (37mm and 40mm) made the tactic of dive-bombing too dangerous in most areas. Small numbers of Ju 87s had been converted for the anti-tank role, fitted with heavy cannon. The rest of those serving with *Schlacht* units flew as normal ground-attack planes. As *Stuka*s were replaced in day-flying units, they were handed to the night ground-attack force.

Operating in an area of secondary importance, *Luftflotte 2* had been starved of resources. It had only 75 day fighters, 48 bombers and an assortment of other aircraft.

Although the vast majority of combat units operated aircraft types that were either obsolete or were nearing obsolescence, some new designs were making their long-delayed entry into front-line service. Ten *Gruppen* had re-equipped, or were in the process of re-equipping, with the He 177 heavy bomber, and five *Gruppen* had re-equipped, or were in the process of re-equipping, with the Me 410 to operate the type in the bomber, bomber-destroyer or reconnaissance roles. One *Gruppe* was forming with Me 163 rocket fighters and another was about to re-equip with the Me 262 jet fighter.

Unit	*Luftflotte 1* Aircraft	Total	Serviceable
Jagdgeschwader 54			
Stab	Fw 190	4	4
I. Gruppe	Fw 190	44	36
II. Gruppe	Fw 190	52	48
Nachtjagdgeschwader 100			
II. Gruppe	Ju 88	29	23[1]
Kampfgeschwader 55			
14. Staffel	He 111	11	8
Schlachtgeschwader 3			
Stab	He 111	1	1
I. Gruppe	Ju 87	33	30
II. Gruppe	Ju 87	36	32
Nachtschlachtgruppe 1	Go 145, He 46	35	28

Nachtschlachtgruppe 3	Go 145, Ar 66	40	38
Nachtschlachtgruppe 11	He 50, Fokker C.V	22	19
Nachtschlachtgruppe 12	Ar 66	16	14
1. Ostfliegerstaffel	Go 145, Ar 66	9	8
Aufklärungsgruppe 22			
3. Staffel	Ju 188	6	2
	Ju 88	1	1
Aufklärungsgruppe 122			
5. Staffel	Ju 188	7	7
Nachtaufklärungsgruppe			
4. Staffel	Do 217	12	8
Nahaufklärungsgruppe 5	Bf 109	30	24
Nahaufklärungsgruppe 31	Fw 189	12	6 [2]
Seeaufklärungsgruppe 127	Ar 95, Hs 126	15	10

Luftflotte 2

Jagdgeschwader 4			
I. Gruppe	Bf 109	13	10
Jagdgeschwader 53			
III. Gruppe	Bf 109	17	13
Jagdgeschwader 77			
Stab	Bf 109	4	3
I. Gruppe	Bf 109	21	10
II. Gruppe	Bf 109	52	39
Nachtjagdgeschwader 6			
II. Gruppe	Bf 110	13	11 [1]
Lehrgeschwader 1			
Stab	Ju 88	1	1

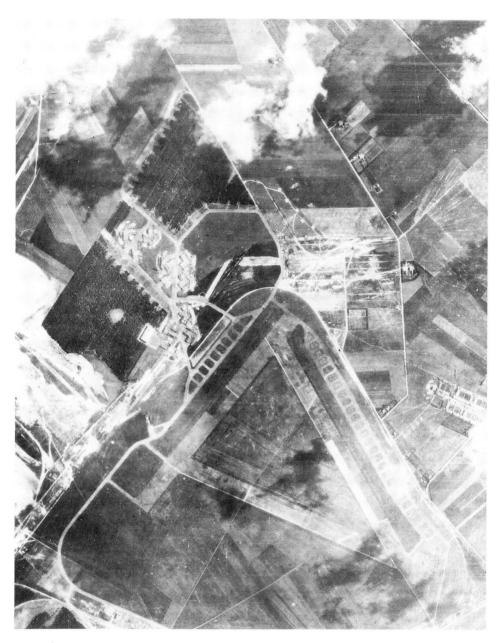

AIRFIELDS

(Above) During its pre-war expansionary phase the Luftwaffe *built several well-equipped main bases (*Fliegerhorste) *around Germany. This example, at Nordholz near Cuxhaven, shows the usual triangular pattern of runways and the distinctive 'ladder' parking aprons.*

The main bases had good permanent facilities, like the maintenance hangars (above) here seen at Schleswig, and air traffic control buildings (below) at Finsterwalde. (Via Schliephake)

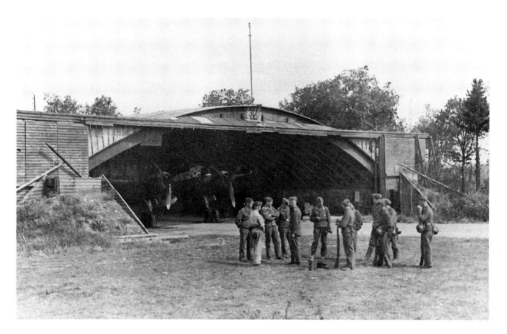

(Above) After the outbreak of war the Luftwaffe *set up large numbers of operational bases* (Einsatzhäfen) *in the occupied territories. These were characterised by dispersal and the camouflaging of facilities. This revetted hangarette at Chartres in northern France housed a Junkers Ju 88 of* Kampfgeschwader 66. *(Altrogge)*

(Above) Junkers Ju 87s of Stukageschwader 77 *at a forward landing ground during the campaign in France in 1940.*

FIGHTERS

(Above) The Messerschmitt Bf 109 was the most used German fighter type during the Second World War and more than 30,000 were produced. The example illustrated, a G model, carries on its nose the ace-of-spades badge of Jagdgeschwader 53; *the vertical bar on the rear fuselage indicates that the aircraft belonged to the* III. Gruppe. *(Via Schliephake)*

(Above) At the beginning of the war the Messerschmitt Bf 110 was the best twin-engined fighter in service in any air force, and it proved particularly effective in the bomber-destroyer and fighter-bomber roles. The aircraft nearest the camera carries the code 3U+HR. '3U' denoted Zerstörergeschwader 26 *and 'R' denoted the 7. Staffel. The 'H' was the individual letter of the aircraft within the unit.*

(Above) A Focke Wulf Fw 190A-8/R8 of II.(Sturm) Gruppe Jagdgeschwader 300. This sub-type carried considerable armour protection for the pilot and was fitted with a 3cm cannon just outboard of each main undercarriage leg. (Schröder)

(Left, upper) A close-up of a Sturmgruppe Fw 190, showing the toughened glass slabs on the sides of the canopy and, in the bottom left corner of the picture, the steel armour plating on the side of the cockpit. (Romm)

(Left, lower) Carrying extensive armouring, the Sturmgruppe Fw 190s were intended to move in close to American bombers before delivering the fatal burst with their heavy cannon. This B-24 is seen taking hits during such an attack.

(Left, top) The Messerschmitt Me 410 entered service in 1943 and was used in the heavy fighter role against USAAF bombers. This example carries four launchers for 21cm rockets under the wings.

(Left, centre and bottom) The heavily armed German twin-engined fighters, Bf 110s and Me 410s, were highly effective against American bomber formations. If they were caught by American escort fighters, however, they invariably suffered losses, as in this action where P-47s engaged Bf 110s. *(USAF)*

(This page, below) The Messerschmitt Me 163 rocket fighter, the first aircraft so powered to go into service anywhere, flew its first interception missions in May 1944. This example belonged to Jagdgeschwader 400, *the only unit to go into action with this type. (Via Ethell)*

(This page, bottom) A Messerschmitt Me 262 twin-jet fighter of the operational trials unit Erprobungskommando 262, *taking off in the summer of 1944. The* Luftwaffe *expected great things of this aircraft, but poor serviceability of its revolutionary new powerplants plagued the machine throughout its life.*

FIGHTER CONTROL

(Left) The best German long-range early warning radar was the Wassermann; this example was situated near Bergen in Holland. The radar operated on spot frequencies in the band 120–145MHz and had a maximum range of about 190 miles on high-flying aircraft. The aerial tower was 198 feet high, and the radar beam was electronically swept in the vertical plane to measure aircraft altitude.

(Right, top) Until neutralised by 'Window' metal strips dropped from RAF bombers in the summer of 1943, the Würzburg Reise was the most important German medium-range precision radar. Developed from the smaller Würzburg set used by Flak units, it was fitted with a parabolic reflector 7.5 metres (about 25 feet) in diameter and had a maximum range of about 50 miles.

(Right, centre) A typical Himmelbett night fighter control station, with a Freya radar in the foreground and two Würzburg Reise sets in the background. The Freya surveillance radar appeared in many forms. At the end of the conflict it operated on spot frequencies in the 50–190MHz band and had a maximum range of about 90 miles on high-flying aircraft. (Via Heise)

(Right, bottom) An artist's impression of the inside of a German fighter control bunker during an action. On the far right is the translucent screen used as a situation map, on which lights were projected from the rear to show the positions of hostile and friendly aircraft. The fighter controllers sat at the desks in the centre of the picture.

NIGHT FIGHTERS

(Top) The Messerschmitt Bf 110 was the most-used German night fighter type during the war, and several units still operated it in the spring of 1945. This example was fitted with Lichtenstein BC *airborne interception radar.*

(Above) A Junkers Ju 88G night fighter, with nose-mounted aerials for the SN-2 radar and a bulge above the cabin for the rotating Naxos *aerial.*

(Top) Twin 20mm cannon in an upwards-firing Schräge Musik *installation fitted to a Ju 88G.*

(Centre) The Heinkel He 219 served with the night fighter force in limited numbers during the latter half of the war. (Via Schliephake)

(Bottom) A Bf 109 operating in the Wilde Sau *single-seat night-fighting role.*

BOMBERS

(Left, upper) A typical bomber Gruppe *formation, flown by Heinkel He 111s of* Kampf-geschwader 53. *(Via Dierich)*

(Left, lower, and below) The He 111 was the mainstay of the German bomber force at the beginning of the war, and many were still in service in 1945. These examples belonged to I. Gruppe, Kampfgeschwader 100. *(Bätcher)*

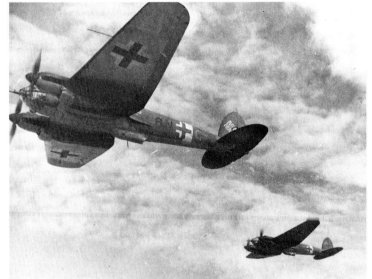

(Right, upper) The Dornier Do 17 was in service in large numbers at the beginning of the war, but from the summer of 1940 it was being replaced by the Ju 88. This example belonged to KG 76.

(Right, lower) Just entering service when the war began, the Junkers Ju 88 went on to become the most important bomber type. This example is seen taking off with a 500kg and a 250kg bomb on its external racks.

(Below) The Junkers Ju 188 was intended as a replacement for the Ju 88 but it was built in far smaller numbers and never saw large-scale service.

(Left, upper) Although it had the appearance of a twin-engined aircraft, the Heinkel 177 was a four-engined heavy bomber employing powerplants coupled in pairs. This example belonged to Kampfgeschwader 1, which operated the type on the Eastern Front in the summer of 1944. (Von Riesen)

(Below) The Messerschmitt Me 262 began operations in July 1944, flying as a fighter-bomber with Kampfgeschwader 51. Each aircraft in the photograph carries a pair of 250kg bombs under the nose. (Via Dierich)

(Below) Much was expected of the Arado Ar 234 jet bomber, but only one Gruppe of Kampfgeschwader 76 had equipped fully with the type when Soviet forces overran the Arado factories and production ceased. (KG 76 Archiv)

GROUND-ATTACK AIRCRAFT, DIVE BOMBERS

(Below) Junkers 87 dive-bombers were used in large numbers during the initial part of the war, and came to symbolise the concept of air support for Blitzkrieg *attacks by army* Panzer *units. These examples belonged to* Sturzkampfgeschwader 5 *serving on the Eastern Front. (Schmid)*

(Left) The SD-2 fragment-ation bomb was unleashed at the beginning of the invasion of the USSR. A Ju 88 or a Do 17 could carry up to 360 of these weapons, a Bf 109 or a Ju 87 up to 96. Nicknamed the 'Butterfly Bomb' by the Allies, the weapon was very effective against personnel in the open, against soft-skinned vehicles or against aircraft on the ground.

(Above) The Henschel Hs 129 armoured ground-attack aircraft was widely used on the Eastern Front from the spring of 1942. The type proved difficult to keep serviceable in battlefield conditions, however, and it was only moderately successful. (Scheffel)

(Left, upper) A close-up view of a Junkers Ju 87 anti-tank aircraft, fitted with two 3.7cm high-velocity automatic cannon. (Via Obert)

(Left, lower) From 1943 the Focke Wulf Fw 190 replaced the Ju 87 in most ground-attack units. This example, an Fw 190F-8 of Schlachtgeschwader 10, was operating in Hungary during the winter of 1944/ 45. (Via Obert)

I. Gruppe	Ju 88	20	17
II. Gruppe	Ju 88	21	17
Kampfgeschwader 76			
II. Gruppe	Ju 88	25	13[1]
Schlachtgeschwader 4			
Stab	Fw 190	3	2
I. Gruppe	Fw 190	14	4[2]
II. Gruppe	Fw 190	27	9[2]
Nachtschlachtgruppe 9	Ju 87, CR.42	37	23
Aufklärungsgruppe 122			
2. Staffel	Me 410, Ju 88	8	4
Aufklärungsgruppe 123			
1. Staffel	Ju 88	5	3
Nahaufklärungsgruppe 11	Bf 109	15	8
Bordfliegergruppe 196			
2. Staffel	Ar 196	6	5
Transportgeschwader 1			
II. Gruppe	SM 82	46	35

Luftflotte 3

Jagdgeschwader 2			
Stab	Fw 190	3	0
I. Gruppe	Fw 190	19	14
II. Gruppe	Bf 109	13	11
III. Gruppe	Fw 190	29	19
Jagdgeschwader 26			
Stab	Fw 190	2	2
I. Gruppe	Fw 190	33	23
II. Gruppe	Fw 190	32	25
III. Gruppe	Bf 109	37	21
Zerstörergeschwader 1			
I. Gruppe	Ju 88	30	25

III. Gruppe	Ju 88	23	12
Nachtjagdgeschwader 4			
Stab	Bf 110	2	0
I. Gruppe	Ju 88	16	7
II. Gruppe	Ju 88, Bf 110, Do 217	20	12
III. Gruppe	Bf 110, Do 217	19	10
Nachtjagdgeschwader 5			
I. Gruppe	Bf 110	15	9
III. Gruppe	Bf 110	18	8
Nachtjagdgeschwader 6			
II. Gruppe	Bf 110	13	11[1]
Kampfgeschwader 2			
I. Gruppe	Ju 188	12	9
II. Gruppe	Ju 188	5	0
III. Gruppe	Do 217	7	1
IV. Gruppe	Ju 188, Do 217	31	15
Kampfgeschwader 6			
Stab	Ju 188	1	1
I. Gruppe	Ju 188	22	15
II. Gruppe	Ju 88	3	2
III. Gruppe	Ju 188	25	5[3]
IV. Gruppe	Ju 88	33	18
Kampfgeschwader 26			
II. Gruppe	Ju 88	37	27
III. Gruppe	Ju 88	35	14
Kampfgeschwader 30			
I. Gruppe	Ju 88	2	1[2]
Kampfgeschwader 40			
I. Gruppe	He 177	20	11[1]
II. Gruppe	He 177	30	26[2]
III. Gruppe	Fw 200	29	1[2]
IV. Gruppe	He 177, Fw 200	17	7

Kampfgeschwader 51			
II. *Gruppe*	Me 410	24	17
Kampfgeschwader 54			
Stab	Ju 88	1	1
I. *Gruppe*	Ju 88	11	5
III. *Gruppe*	Ju 88	14	8
Kampfgeschwader 66			
I. *Gruppe*	Ju 188	31	12[3]
Kampfgeschwader 76			
6. *Staffel*	Ju 88	12	3
Kampfgeschwader 77			
I. *Gruppe*	Ju 88	28	17
II. *Gruppe*	Ju 88	25	8
Kampfgeschwader 100			
III. *Gruppe*	Do 217	31	13
Schlachtgeschwader 4			
III. *Gruppe*	Fw 190	40	36
Schnellkampfgeschwader 10			
I. *Gruppe*	Fw 190	33	19
Fernaufklärungsgruppe 5	Ju 290	11	4
	Do 217	2	0
	He 111	1	0
Aufklärungsgruppe 33			
1. *Staffel*	Ju 188, Ju 88	7	3[3]
Aufklärungsgruppe 121			
1. *Staffel*	Me 410	9	3
Aufklärungsgruppe 122			
3. *Staffel*	Ju 188, Ju 88	8	2
Aufklärungsgruppe 123			
3. *Staffel*	Ju 88	9	3
4. *Staffel*	Bf 109	10	6

5. Staffel	Bf 109	7	6
	FW 190	4	2
	He 111	1	0
6. Staffel	Ju 88, Ju 188, Do 217	5	0
Nahaufklärungsgruppe 13	Bf 109	42	24
Seeaufklärungsgruppe 128 2. *Staffel*	Ar 196	12	10
Seeaufklärungsgruppe 129	Bv 222	4	2
Transportgeschwader 4 IV. *Gruppe*	LeO 451	31	13
Korps Transport Staffeln	LeO 451	11	4
	Ju 52	22	14

Luftflotte 4

Jagdgeschwader 51 IV. *Gruppe*	Bf 109	35	22
Jagdgeschwader 52 Stab	Bf 109	1	1
I. *Gruppe*	Bf 109	29	10
II. *Gruppe*	Bf 109	23	18
III. *Gruppe*	Bf 109	23	20
Jagdgeschwader 53 I. *Gruppe*	Bf 109	33	30
Jagdgeschwader 77 III. *Gruppe*	Bf 109	31	28
Jagdgeschwader 301 II. *Gruppe*	Bf 109	11	10[1]
Nachtjagdgeschwader 6 IV. *Gruppe*	Bf 110	27	22

Nachtjagdgeschwader 100

2. *Staffel*	Bf 110	16	10

Kampfgeschwader 4

I. *Gruppe*	He 111	34	27

Kampfgeschwader 27

14. *Staffel*	He 111	12	7

Schlachtgeschwader 2

Stab	Ju 87	1	1
I. *Gruppe*	Ju 87	47	34
II. *Gruppe*	Fw 190	42	20[3]
III. *Gruppe*	Ju 87	39	27
10. *Staffel*	Ju 87	12	12[4]

Schlachtgeschwader 3

10. *Staffel*	Ju 87	12	12[4]

Schlachtgeschwader 9

IV. *Gruppe*	Hs 129	67	66

Schlachtgeschwader 10

Stab	Fw 190	5	2
I. *Gruppe*	Fw 190	32	16
II. *Gruppe*	Fw 190	31	15
III. *Gruppe*	Fw 190	40	24

Schlachtgeschwader 77

I. *Gruppe*	Fw 190	34	32[3]
II. *Gruppe*	Fw 190	33	21
III. *Gruppe*	Ju 87	39	35
10. *Staffel*	Ju 87	12	12[4]

Nachtschlachtgruppe 4

	Go 145	30	28

Nachtschlachtgruppe 5

	Go 145	58	42
	Ar 66		

Aufklärungsgruppe 11

2. *Staffel*	Ju 88	10	7

Aufklärungsgruppe 22 *2. Staffel*	Ju 88	10	8
Aufklärungsgruppe 100 *2. Staffel*	Ju 188	11	8
Aufklärungsgruppe 121 *3. Staffel*	Ju 188	6	5
Nachtaufklärungsgruppe *1. Staffel*	Do 217 He 111	12	8
Nahaufklärungsgruppe 1	Fw 189	12	7
Nahaufklärungsgruppe 2	Bf 109	23	15
Nahaufklärungsgruppe 6	Fw 189	11	6[2]
Nahaufklärungsgruppe 14	Bf 109	29	23
Seeaufklärungsgruppe 125	Bv 138	15	10
Transportgeschwader 2 *III. Gruppe*	Ju 52	45	43
Transportgeschwader 3 *III. Gruppe*	Ju 52	43	42
Korps Transport Staffeln	Ju 52	24	19

Luftflotte 5

Jagdgeschwader 5			
III. Gruppe	Bf 109	31	31
IV. Gruppe	Bf 109	31	28
13. Staffel	Bf 110	16	16
Kampfgeschwader 40 *3. Staffel*	He 177	10	10
Schlachtgeschwader 5 *I. Gruppe*	Ju 87	13	13

	Fw 190	15	12[3]
Nachtschlachtgruppe 8	Ju 87	24	22
Aufklärungsgruppe 22			
1. Staffel	Ju 88	12	12
Aufklärungsgruppe 32	Fw 189	12	8
Aufklärungsgruppe 120			
1. Staffel	Ju 188	6	5
Aufklärungsgruppe 124			
1. Staffel	Ju 88, Ju 188	12	11
Seeaufklärungsgruppe 130	Bv 138	21	15
Seeaufklärungsgruppe 131	Bv 138	7	5
	Ar 196	2	2
Bordfliegergruppe 196	Ar 196	20	20
Küstenfliegerstaffel 406	He 115	8	7
Transportgruppe 20	Ju 52	32	28
Seetransportstaffel 2	Ju 52	10	9
Korps Transport Staffel	Ju 52	10	6
	He 111	2	2

Luftflotte 6

Jagdgeschwader 51			
Stab	Bf 109	4	4
	Fw 190	16	16
I. Gruppe	Bf 109	44	34
III. Gruppe	Bf 109	40	32
Nachtjagdgeschwader 100			
I. Gruppe	Ju 88, Do 217	32	21[1]

Kampfgeschwader 4			
Stab	He 111	1	0
II. Gruppe	He 111	35	28
III. Gruppe	He 111	37	26
Kampfgeschwader 3			
14. Staffel	Ju 88	12	8
Kampfgeschwader 27			
I. Gruppe	He 111	37	37
III. Gruppe	He 111	37	33
Kampfgeschwader 53			
Stab	He 111	1	1
I. Gruppe	He 111	37	27
II. Gruppe	He 111	34	28
III. Gruppe	He 111	37	24
Kampfgeschwader 55			
I. Gruppe	He 111	35	27
II. Gruppe	He 111	32	20
III. Gruppe	He 111	34	29
Schlachtgeschwader 1			
I. Gruppe	Ju 87	39	35
II. Gruppe	Ju 87	30	24
	Fw 190	10	3[3]
III. Gruppe	Fw 190	42	33
10. Staffel	Ju 87	12	12[4]
Nachtschlachtgruppe 2	Ju 87, Ar 66	75	58
Aufklärungsgruppe 11			
4. Staffel	Ju 188, Ju 88	11	7
Aufklärungsgruppe 14			
4. Staffel	Ju 188, Ju 88	8	6
Aufklärungsgruppe 31	Fw 189	5	3
Aufklärungsgruppe 100			
1. Staffel	Ju 88	12	5

Nachtaufklärungsgruppe			
2. *Staffel*	Do 217	12	8
Nahaufklärungsgruppe 4	Bf 109, Fw 189, Hs 126	38	24
Nahaufklärungsgruppe 10	Hs 126, Bf 109, Fw 189	27	20
Nahaufklärungsgruppe 15	Fw 189	19	16
Transportgeschwader 3			
I. Gruppe	Ju 52	48	44
Korps Transport Staffeln	Ju 52	22	14

Luftflotte Reich

Jagdgeschwader 1			
Stab	Fw 190	2	2
I. Gruppe	Fw 190	43	15
II. Gruppe	Fw 190	42	20
III. Gruppe	Bf 109	48	21
Jagdgeschwader 3			
Stab	Bf 109	4	2
I. Gruppe	Bf 109	26	9
II. Gruppe	Bf 109	29	23
III. Gruppe	Bf 109	31	9
IV.(Sturm) Gruppe	Fw 190	54	1 [3]
Jagdgeschwader 5			
I. Gruppe	Bf 109	43	36
II. Gruppe	Bf 109	44	36
Jagdgeschwader 11			
Stab	Bf 109	4	3
I. Gruppe	Fw 190	28	20
II. Gruppe	Bf 109	31	14
III. Gruppe	Fw 190	28	11
10. Staffel	Fw 190, Bf 109	10	7

Jagdgeschwader 27			
Stab	Bf 109	4	4
I. Gruppe	Bf 109	44	34
II. Gruppe	Bf 109	24	12 [2]
III. Gruppe	Bf 109	26	20
IV. Gruppe	Bf 109	22	16
Jagdgeschwader 53			
II. Gruppe	Bf 109	31	14
Jagdgeschwader 54			
III. Gruppe	Fw 190	23	8
Jagdgeschwader 300			
Stab	Fw 190	2	1
I. Gruppe	Bf 109	29	19
II. Gruppe	Fw 190	32	23
III. Gruppe	Bf 109	27	25
Jagdgeschwader 301			
I. Gruppe	Bf 109	25	21
Jagdgeschwader 302			
I. Gruppe	Bf 109	27	11
Jagdgeschwader 400			
I. Gruppe	Me 163	10	0 [5]
Einsatzstaffel JG 104	Bf 109	4	4 [6]
Einsatzstaffel JG 106	Bf 109	5	3 [6]
Einsatzstaffel JG 108	Bf 109	12	6 [6]
Zerstörergeschwader 1			
II. Gruppe	Bf 110	30	15
Zerstörergeschwader 26			
I. Gruppe	Me 410	20	6
II. Gruppe	Me 410	50	24
III. Gruppe	Me 262	6	1 [3]
	Bf 110	9	9

Zerstörergeschwader 76
I. Gruppe	Me 410	47	25
II. Gruppe	Me 410	33	0 [3]
	Bf 110	3	2

Nachtjagdgeschwader 1
Stab	He 219	2	1
	Bf 110		
I. Gruppe	He 219, Me 410	33	26
II. Gruppe	He 219, Bf 110	21	11
III. Gruppe	Bf 110	17	17
IV. Gruppe	Bf 110	23	14

Nachtjagdgeschwader 2
Stab	Ju 88	4	4
I. Gruppe	Ju 88	31	21
II. Gruppe	Ju 88	33	19
III. Gruppe	Ju 88	28	18

Nachtjagdgeschwader 3
Stab	Ju 88, Bf 110	3	3
I. Gruppe	Bf 110	26	22
II. Gruppe	Ju 88	37	13
III. Gruppe	Bf 110	29	20
IV. Gruppe	Ju 88, Bf 110	32	21

Nachtjagdgeschwader 5
Stab	Bf 110	3	1
II. Gruppe	Bf 110	19	13
IV. Gruppe	Bf 110	18	8

Nachtjagdgeschwader 6
Stab	Bf 110	2	1
I. Gruppe	Bf 110, Do 217	24	21
II. Gruppe	Bf 110	10	8 [1]
III. Gruppe	Bf 110	18	13
IV. Gruppe	Bf 110	27	22

Nachtjagdgeschwader 7
I. Gruppe	Ju 88	21	9 [7]

Nachtjagdgeschwader 101
I. Gruppe	Bf 110, Ju 88	39	39

II. *Gruppe*	Do 217	38	28

Nachtjagdgeschwader 102
I. *Gruppe*	Bf 110	39	14
II. *Gruppe*	Bf 110	39	16

Nachtjagdgruppe 10	Bf 109, Fw 190, He 219, Ta 154, Ju 88, Bf 110	23	14

Lehrgeschwader 1
IV. *Gruppe*	Ju 88	30	18

Kampfgeschwader 1
Stab	He 177	2	1[3]
I. *Gruppe*	He 177	30	11[3]
II. *Gruppe*	He 177	29	0[3]
III. *Gruppe*	He 177	30	12[3]
IV. *Gruppe*	He 177	34	12[3]
	Ju 88	12	9

Kampfgeschwader 3
III. *Gruppe*	He 111	35	21[3]
IV. *Gruppe*	Ju 88	23	14

Kampfgeschwader 4
IV. *Gruppe*	He 111	37	22

Kampfgeschwader 26
IV. *Gruppe*	Ju 88	34	15

Kampfgeschwader 27
II. *Gruppe*	He 111	15	12[2]
IV. *Gruppe*	He 111	58	33

Kampfgeschwader 30
IV. *Gruppe*	Ju 88	22	12

Kampfgeschwader 51
IV. *Gruppe*	Me 410	12	5

Kampfgeschwader 53
IV. *Gruppe*	He 111	39	21

Kampfgeschwader 54
IV. Gruppe	Ju 88	13	9

Kampfgeschwader 55
IV. Gruppe	He 111	34	17

Kampfgeschwader 76
IV. Gruppe	Ju 88	28	10

Kampfgeschwader 77
II. Gruppe	Ju 88	31	21 [2]
IV. Gruppe	Ju 88	38	24

Kampfgeschwader 100
II. Gruppe	He 177	30	0 [3]
IV. Gruppe	He 177	21	6
	Do 217	17	7

Schlachtgeschwader 3
III. Gruppe	Fw 190	34	31 [3]

Aufklärungsgruppe 122
1. Staffel	Me 410	6	0 [3]
	Bf 110	2	3
4. Staffel	Ju 188	11	0 [3]

Nahaufklärungsgruppe 8
	Bf 109	2	2 [2]

Nahaufklärungsgruppe 14
3. Staffel	Bf 109	2	0 [2]

Transportgeschwader 2
II. Gruppe	Ju 52	12	9

Versuchsverband Oberkommando der Luftwaffe

Mosquito	1	0
P-38 Lightning	1	1
P-47 Thunderbolt	1	1
Spitfire	2	0
P-51 Mustang	3	0
Typhoon	1	1
Misc. German types	16	6

Kampfgeschwader 200

I. Gruppe	Ju 290, Ju 252, Ju 352	5	1
	Ar 232	1	1
	Bloch 160–162	2	0
	Ju 188, He 111	19	12
	He 59, He 115	4	4
	Boeing B-17	6	0
	Douglas DC 3	1	0
	Misc. German types	31	22
II. Gruppe	Misc. German types	25	25

Luftwaffenkommando Süd Ost

Jagdgeschwader 51

II. Gruppe	Bf 109	52	43

Jagdgeschwader 301

II. Gruppe	Bf 109	9	8[1]

Zerstörergeschwader 26

11. Staffel	Ju 88	16	16

Nachtjagdgeschwader 100

6. Staffel	Do 217	15	11

Schlachtgeschwader 151

13. Staffel	Ju 87	7	7

Nachtschlachtgruppe 7	CR.42, Ca 314, Ju 87, He 46	29	25

Aufklärungsgruppe 2

3. Staffel	Bf 110	12	10

Aufklärungsgruppe 33

3. Staffel	Ju 188, Ju 88	6	5

Aufklärungsgruppe 123

2. Staffel	Ju 88	8	3
	Ju 86	2	1

	Bf 109	1	0
Nahaufklärungsgruppe 12	Bf 109	15	5
Nahaufklärungsstaffel Kroatien	Hs 126 Do 17, Do 215	8	5
Seeaufklärungsgruppe 126	Ar 196	48	37
Transportgeschwader 1 IV. Gruppe	Ju 52	45	41
Transportgeschwader 4 II. Gruppe	Ju 52	39	36
Transportgeschwader 5 I. Gruppe	Me 323	21	13
Seetransportstaffel 1	Ju 52	12	11
Seetransportstaffel 3	Ju 52	8	7

Fliegerkorps XIV

Transportgeschwader 1 I. Gruppe	Ju 52	48	39 [2]
III. Gruppe	SM.82	16	5 [3]
Transportgeschwader 3 II. Gruppe	Ju 52	43	38 [3]
IV. Gruppe	SM.82	41	33
Transportgeschwader 4 I. Gruppe	Ju 52	47	47 [3]
III. Gruppe	Ju 52	46	45
Transportgeschwader 5 II. Gruppe	Me 323	21	9
Transport Gruppe 10	SM.81	35	25
Transport Gruppe 30	He 111	33	32

Transport Gruppe 110	SM.82	35	0[5]
Transportgruppe Bronkow	Ju 52	41	38
4. Transport Staffel	Fiat G.12	16	11[5]
5. Transport Staffel	Ju 90, Ju 252	12	7[2]

Notes

1. Part unit.
2. Unit re-forming.
3. Unit re-equipping.
4. Anti-tank unit.
5. Unit forming.
6. Operational flight from training school, using instructor pilots.
7. Illuminating unit, to drop flares to assist night fighters to locate RAF bomber streams. The idea was not a success and would soon be dropped.

Composition of the Main Operational Flying Units, 10 January 1945

This chapter gives the strength of *Luftwaffe* operational flying units on 10 January 1945, during the lull in operations immediately following the failure of the major German offensive in the Ardennes. Due to the rapidly deteriorating military situation, the various *Luftflotten* were now squeezed into an area little greater than metropolitan Germany. The notional boundaries separating these formations were constantly changing, and because of this no map has been provided. Two major formations, *Luftwaffenkommando Süd Ost* and *Fliegerkorps XIV*, had been disbanded.

For the Ardennes offensive *Luftflotte 3*, now based in western Germany, had been strengthened by the transfer of several single-engined fighter *Gruppen* from *Luftflotte Reich*. It was responsible for providing day fighter protection for western areas of Germany. *Luftflotte Reich*, for its part, had assumed control of the bulk of the night fighter force.

Since the previous May, *Luftflotten 1, 4, 5* and *6* on the Eastern Front had suffered varying degrees of misfortune. Worst off was *Luftflotte 1*, now cut off in the Courland pocket in Lithuania and unable to mount sustained air operations. *Luftflotte 4* had withdrawn to Hungary and Yugoslavia, where it assumed the tasks previously carried out by *Luftwaffenkommando Süd Ost*. *Luftflotte 5* had withdrawn from Finland and was confined to Norway. *Luftflotte 6*, the strongest formation on the Eastern Front, operated from bases in East Prussia and western Poland.

In Italy *Luftflotte 2* retained its once-renowned title for historic reasons only. After further drains on its remaining strength during the previous seven months, it was reduced to fifty serviceable combat aircraft.

At this time the *Luftwaffe* front-line units possessed 4,566 serviceable aircraft, divided as follows:

Day fighters	1,462
Night fighters	808
Ground-attack aircraft	613
Night harassment aircraft	302
Multi-engined bombers	294
Anti-shipping aircraft	83
Long-range reconnaissance aircraft	176

Short-range reconnaissance and army cooperation aircraft	293
Coastal aircraft	60
Transport aircraft	269
Kampfgeschwader 200 (misc. aircraft)	206
Total	**4,566**

The number of serviceable aircraft deployed in combat units was slightly lower than in May 1944. However, since then the fighting posture of the *Luftwaffe* had changed greatly. Following repeated attacks by Allied strategic bombers on the German synthetic oil industry, there was a severe shortage of aviation fuel. This caused a sharp reduction in flying, except by home defence fighter units and those operating jet aircraft. Several bomber *Gruppen* had already disbanded, and that process was continuing. The only unit engaged in strategic offensive action was *Kampfgeschwader 53*, whose He 111s air-launchedV.1 flying-bombs at targets in England on moonless nights when the weather was bad.

With the force now firmly on to the defensive, the day and night fighter arms received the highest priority for resources. These were now at the greatest strength they would ever attain.

Three types of jet aircraft were in service—the Messerschmitt Me 163, the Me 262 and the Arado Ar 234. Less than a hundred of these advanced machines were in service with front-line units, however, and they had yet to make any serious impact on operations.

Luftflotte 1

Unit	Aircraft	Total	Serviceable
Jagdgeschwader 51			
Stab	Bf 109	20	16
	Fw 190	1	1
I. Gruppe	Fw 190	35	32
II. Gruppe	Fw 190	40	41
Schlachtgeschwader 3			
III. Gruppe	Fw 190	39	35
Nachtschlachtgruppe 3	Go 145	34	26
	Ar 66		
Nahaufklärungsgruppe 5	Bf 109	29	22
	Fw 189		

Transportgeschwader 1
I. Gruppe   Ju 52   45   42

Luftflotte 2

Nachtschlachtgruppe 3   Ju 87   23   14

Aufklärungsgruppe 122   Me 410   16   13
                                   Ju 88, Ju 188

Nahaufklärungsgruppe 11   Bf 109   29   23
                                   Fw 190

Luftflotte 3

Jagdgeschwader 1
Stab   Fw 190   5   4
I. Gruppe   Fw 190   27   22
II. Gruppe   Fw 190   40   30
III. Gruppe   Fw 190   40   35

Jagdgeschwader 2
Stab   Fw 190   4   3
I. Gruppe   Fw 190   28   23
II. Gruppe   Fw 190   3   2
III. Gruppe   Fw 190   19   6

Jagdgeschwader 3
I. Gruppe   Bf 109   31   22
III. Gruppe   Bf 109   32   26
IV. (Sturm) Gruppe   Fw 190   35   24

Jagdgeschwader 4
Stab   Fw 190   2   1
I. Gruppe   Bf 109   41   33
II. (Sturm) Gruppe   Fw 190   25   18
III. Gruppe   Bf 109   13   10
IV. Gruppe   Bf 109   26   17

Jagdgeschwader 11
Stab   Fw 190   7   6
I. Gruppe   Fw 190   23   20
II. Gruppe   Bf 109   37   31
III. Gruppe   Fw 190   42   26

Jagdgeschwader 26			
Stab	Fw 190	3	3
I. Gruppe	Fw 190	60	36
II. Gruppe	Fw 190	64	42
III. Gruppe	Fw 190	56	28
Jagdgeschwader 27			
Stab	Fw 190	2	2
I. Gruppe	Bf 109	33	24
II. Gruppe	Bf 109	25	20
III. Gruppe	Bf 109	28	23
IV. Gruppe	Bf 109	24	22
Jagdgeschwader 53			
Stab	Bf 109	4	1
II. Gruppe	Bf 109	46	29
III. Gruppe	Bf 109	39	25
IV. Gruppe	Bf 109	46	34
Jagdgeschwader 54			
III. Gruppe	Fw 190	47	31
IV. Gruppe	Fw 190	50	39
Jagdgeschwader 77			
Stab	Bf 109	2	1
I. Gruppe	Bf 109	43	24
II. Gruppe	Bf 109	32	20
III. Gruppe	Bf 109	10	7
Lehrgeschwader 1			
Stab	Ju 88	1	1
I. Gruppe	Ju 88	29	25
II. Gruppe	Ju 88	34	26
Kampfgeschwader 51			
Stab	Me 262	1	0
I. Gruppe	Me 262	51	37
Kampfgeschwader 53			
Stab	He 111/V.1	1	1
I. Gruppe	He 111/V.1	37	25
II. Gruppe	He 111/V.1	33	29
III. Gruppe	He 111/V.1	30	24

Kampfgeschwader 66			
I. Gruppe	Ju 88	29	17
Kampfgeschwader 76			
III. Gruppe	Ar 234	12	11
Schlachtgeschwader 4			
Stab	Fw 190	49	17
I. Gruppe	Fw 190	29	24
II. Gruppe	Fw 190	40	36
III. Gruppe	Fw 190	34	24
Nachtschlachtgruppe 1	Ju 87	44	37
Nachtschlachtgruppe 2	Ju 87	39	26
Nachtschlachtgruppe 20	Fw 190	28	21
Kommando Sperling	Ar 234	4	4 [1]
Kommando Hecht	Ar 234	1	1 [1]
Kommando Braunegg	Me 262	5	2 [1]
Nahaufklärungsgruppe 1	Bf 109	15	8
Nahaufklärungsgruppe 13	Bf 109	51	39
	Fw 190		
Transportgeschwader 3			
II. Gruppe	Ju 52	50	48
Transportgeschwader 4			
III. Gruppe	Ju 52	51	46
Transportgruppe 30	He 111	10	5

Luftflotte 4

Jagdgeschwader 51			
II. Gruppe	Bf 109	36	26
Jagdgeschwader 52			
II. Gruppe	Bf 109	34	30

Jagdgeschwader 53			
I. *Gruppe*	Bf 109	19	18
Jagdgeschwader 76			
Stab	Bf 109	4	4
Kampfgeschwader 4			
Stab	He 111	1	1
I. *Gruppe*	He 111	25	22
II. *Gruppe*	He 111	23	12
III. *Gruppe*	He 111	24	11
Kampfgeschwader 27			
IV. *Gruppe*	He 111	14	10
Schlachtgeschwader 2			
Stab	Fw 190	10	7
	Ju 87		
I. *Gruppe*	Fw 190	32	23
II. *Gruppe*	Fw 190	34	29
III. *Gruppe*	Ju 87	35	29
10. *Staffel*	Ju 87	10	9 [2]
Schlachtgeschwader 9			
IV. *Gruppe*	Hs 129	59	45
Schlachtgeschwader 10			
Stab	Fw 190	3	1
I. *Gruppe*	Fw 190	22	17
II. *Gruppe*	Fw 190	23	19
III. *Gruppe*	Fw 190	21	20
Nachtschlachtgruppe 5	Go 145	47	39
	Ar 66		
Nachtschlachtgruppe 7	Hs 126	54	37
	CR.42		
Nachtschlachtgruppe 10	Ju 87	30	25
Fernaufklärungsgruppe 2	Ju 88	25	17
	Ju 188		

Aufklärungsgruppe 33	Ju 88	13	10
Aufklärungsgruppe 121	Ju 188	8	5
Fernaufklärungsgruppe Nacht	Do 217 Ju 88	7	6
Nahaufklärungsgruppe 12	Bf 109 Ju 88	23	16
Nahaufklärungsgruppe 14	Bf 109 Fw 189	46	35
Nahaufklärungsstaffel Kroatien	Bf 109 Hs 126	24	16
Transportgeschwader 2			
II. Gruppe	Ju 52	11	11
III. Gruppe	Ju 52	28	16
Transportgeschwader 3			
III. Gruppe	Ju 52	31	22

Luftflotte 5

Jagdgeschwader 5			
Stab	Bf 109	4	4
III. Gruppe	Bf 109	55	43
IV. Gruppe	Bf 109 Fw 190	45	35
Zerstörergeschwader 26			
IV. Gruppe	Me 410	41	35
Nachtjagdstaffel Norwegen	Bf 110 Ju 88 He 219	10	9
Kampfgeschwader 26			
Stab	Ju 88	11	4[3]
I. Gruppe	Ju 88	30	22[3]
II. Gruppe	Ju 88	37	32[3]
III. Gruppe	Ju 88	37	25[3]

Nachtschlachtgruppe 8	Ju 87	33	30
Aufklärungsgruppe 32	Fw 190 Bf 109	9	6
Aufklärungsgruppe 120	Ju 88 Ju 188	19	17
Aufklärungsgruppe 124	Ju 88 Ju 188	12	8
Seeaufklärungsgruppe 130	Bv 222 Bv 138	2 21	1 19
Transportgruppe 20	Ju 52	50	47
Seetransportstaffel 2	Ju 52 floatplanes	7	5

Luftflotte 6

Jagdgeschwader 51			
I. Gruppe	Bf 109	36	26
III. Gruppe	Bf 109	38	28
IV. Gruppe	Bf 109	34	24
Jagdgeschwader 52			
Stab	Bf 109 Fw 190	10	5
I. Gruppe	Bf 109	34	30
III. Gruppe	Bf 109	42	40
Nachtjagdgeschwader 5			
I. Gruppe	Bf 109 Ju 88	43	35
Nachtjagdgeschwader 100			
I. Gruppe	Bf 109 Ju 88	51	41
Kampfgeschwader 55			
IV. Gruppe	He 111	14	10
Schlachtgeschwader 1			
Stab	Fw 190	5	5

II. Gruppe	Fw 190	39	38
III. Gruppe	Fw 190	38	36
Schlachtgeschwader 3			
Stab	Fw 190	9	8
I. Gruppe	Fw 190	47	43
II. Gruppe	Fw 190	34	31
Schlachtgeschwader 77			
Stab	Fw 190	6	6
I. Gruppe	Fw 190	40	34
II. Gruppe	Fw 190	38	31
III. Gruppe	Fw 190	38	30
10. Staffel	Ju 87	19	16 [2]
Nachtschlachtgruppe 4	Ju 87	60	47
	Si 204		
Seeaufklärungsgruppe 126	Ar 196	21	11
	Bv 138	9	6
Fernaufklärungsgruppe 1	Ju 188	25	17
	Me 410		
Fernaufklärungsgruppe 3	Ju 188	22	15
	Me 410		
Aufklärungsgruppe 22	Ju 188	13	10
Aufklärungsgruppe 122	Ju 88	28	23
	Me 410		
Aufklärungsgruppe Nacht	Ju 88	36	23
	Ju 188, Do 217		
Nahaufklärungsgruppe 2	Bf 109	35	30
	Fw 189		
Nahaufklärungsgruppe 3	Bf 109	57	46
	Fw 189		
Nahaufklärungsgruppe 4	Bf 109	23	21
	Fw 189		

Nahaufklärungsgruppe 8	Bf 109	24	16
	Fw 189		
Nahaufklärungsgruppe 15	Bf 109	20	13
	Fw 189		
Seeaufklärungsgruppe 126	Ar 196	21	11
	Bv 138	6	6
Transportgeschwader 3			
I. Gruppe	Ju 52	36	27

Luftflotte Reich

Jagdgeschwader 300			
Stab	Fw 190	6	4
I. Gruppe	Bf 109	57	37
II. (Sturm) Gruppe	Fw 190	41	28
III. Gruppe	Bf 109	44	38
IV. Gruppe	Bf 109	53	39
Jagdgeschwader 301			
Stab	Fw 190	5	5
I. Gruppe	Fw 190	38	26
II. Gruppe	Fw 190	40	38
III. Gruppe	Fw 190	26	20
Jagdgeschwader 400			
I. Gruppe	Me 163	46	19
Nachtjagdgeschwader 1			
Stab	Bf 110	20	18
	He 219		
I. Gruppe	He 219	64	45
II. Gruppe	Bf 110	37	24
III. Gruppe	Bf 110	37	31
IV. Gruppe	Bf 110	33	24
Nachtjagdgeschwader 2			
Stab	Ju 88	8	7
I. Gruppe	Ju 88	41	26
II. Gruppe	Ju 88	28	20

III. Gruppe	Ju 88	49	26
IV. Gruppe	Ju 88	36	29

Nachtjagdgeschwader 3

Stab	Ju 88	6	3
I. Gruppe	Bf 110	48	40
II. Gruppe	Ju 88	30	23
III. Gruppe	Ju 88	37	22
IV. Gruppe	Ju 88	37	19

Nachtjagdgeschwader 4

Stab	Bf 110	5	5
	Ju 88		
I. Gruppe	Ju 88	34	17
II. Gruppe	Ju 88	23	18
III. Gruppe	Ju 88	28	19

Nachtjagdgeschwader 5

Stab	Ju 88	10	8
I. Gruppe	Bf 110	43	29
	Ju 88		
III. Gruppe	Bf 110	66	60
	Ju 88		
IV. Gruppe	Bf 110	51	24
	Ju 88		

Nachtjagdgeschwader 6

Stab	Bf 110	29	23
	Ju 88		
I. Gruppe	Bf 110	26	12
	Ju 88		
II. Gruppe	Ju 88	26	18
III. Gruppe	Bf 110	23	19
	Ju 88		
IV. Gruppe	Bf 110	37	29
	Ju 88		

Nachtjagdgeschwader 11

I. Gruppe	Bf 109	43	30
	Ju 88		
II. Gruppe	Bf 109	41	23
	Me 262		

Nachtjagdgeschwader 100			
II. Gruppe	Ju 88	25	18
Nachtjagdgruppe 10	Ju 88	17	14
Kampfgeschwader 100			
II. Gruppe	He 177	44	32
Bordfliegergruppe 196	Ar 196	25	23
Aufklärungsgruppe 122	Ju 188	9	7
Kampfgeschwader 200	Various types	295	206

Notes

1. Reconnaissance unit.
2. Anti-tank unit.
3. Torpedo-bomber unit.

Composition of the Main Operational Flying Units, 9 April 1945

This chapter gives the strength of the *Luftwaffe* operational flying units on 9 April 1945, less than a month before the end of the war and the last date for which a reasonably comprehensive set of figures is available.

Since January there had been further major organisational changes, and there were clear signs of impending collapse on all fronts. In recognition of their current weakness, four once-mighty *Luftflotten* had been downgraded in status. *Luftflotte 1*, cut off in Lithuania and bypassed by the Soviet advance, had become *Luftwaffenkommando Courland*. *Luftflotte 2* in the south had become *Luftwaffe General Italy*. *Luftflotte 3* had become *LuftwaffenkommandoWest*, and *Luftflotte 5* had become *Luftwaffe General Norway*. Between them, these four new formations possessed fewer than 450 serviceable combat planes.

With the general breakdown of communications, in a few cases units' figures were omitted from the Quartermaster General's census. In these cases, the author has included approximate figures.

At this time the *Luftwaffe* front-line units possessed approximately 3,331 serviceable aircraft, divided as follows:

Day fighters	1,305
Night fighters	485
Ground-attack aircraft	712
Night harassment aircraft	215
Multi-engined bombers	37
Long-range reconnaissance aircraft	143
Short-range reconnaissance and army cooperation aircraft	309
Coastal aircraft	45
Transport aircraft	10
Kampfgeschwader 200 (misc. aircraft)	70
Total	**3,331**

The number of serviceable aircraft deployed in combat units was more than one-quarter less than in January. The reduction was not spread evenly throughout the various arms, however, resulting in a grossly unbalanced force. The bomber arm was reduced to a mere 37 aircraft, and its main striking force comprised a few dozen Mistel pick-a-back aircraft with Fw 190s mounted on explosive-carrying Ju 88s. There were few transport units, and the anti-shipping arm had been disbanded. Only the ground-attack force had undergone a significant expansion in the past year and it now comprised 712 serviceable aircraft.

Several aircraft production centres and storage parks had already been overrun by Allied ground forces. Others were under threat and were being hastily evacuated. Given those problems, it is remarkable that the strength of the combat units had not fallen much further. Two factors contributed to the maintenance of *Luftwaffe* strength, at least on paper. First, following the surge in production during the previous year, there were large numbers of aircraft in storage parks available to replace losses, and secondly the crippling shortage of fuel meant that units equipped with piston-engined aircraft flew relatively low sortie rates. As a result their loss rates fell considerably. Many of these aircraft would sit out the rest of the war in relative safety, hidden in camouflaged dispersals some distance from their airfields.

Me 262 jet fighters were at last going into action in moderate numbers, but they were far too few and far too late. For the defence of the homeland, *Luftflotte Reich* was down to 389 serviceable day fighters, of which just over 100 were jet-propelled. In action against American raiding forces the jet fighters were often outnumbered by as many as ten to one, and it is not surprising that they were able to achieve little. The night fighter force possessed 485 serviceable aircraft, but the fuel shortage curtailed flying and its operational capability was far lower than the numerical strength would suggest.

Luftflotte 4

Unit	Aircraft	Total	Serviceable
Jagdgeschwader 51			
II. *Gruppe*	Bf 109	7	5
Jagdgeschwader 52			
II. *Gruppe*	Bf 109	43	29
Jagdgeschwader 53			
I. *Gruppe*	Bf 109	27	27
Jagdgeschwader 76			
Stab	Bf 109	1	1
Schlachtgeschwader 2			
I. *Gruppe*	Fw 190	33	21

Schlachtgeschwader 9

10. *Staffel*	Hs 129	6	6
14. *Staffel*	Hs 129	13	9

Schlachtgeschwader 10

Stab	Fw 190	6	4
I. Gruppe	Fw 190	23	21
II. Gruppe	Fw 190	24	15
III. Gruppe	Fw 190	30	17

Nachtschlachtgruppe 5	Go 145 Ar 66	69	52
Nachtschlachtgruppe 10	Ju 87	14	9
Aufklärungsgruppe 11	Ju 88	12	12
Aufklärungsgruppe 33	Ju 188 Ju 88	10	10
Aufklärungsgruppe 121	Ju 188	12	12
Aufklärungsgruppe Nacht	Do 217	11	10[1]
Nahaufklärungsgruppe 12	Bf 109 Hs 126	30	26
Nahaufklärungsgruppe 14	Bf 109 Bf 110	42	19
Nahaufklärungsgruppe 16	Fw 189	10	7
Nahaufklärungsstaffel Kroatien	Bf 109 Hs 126	17	16

Luftflotte 6

Jagdgeschwader 3

Stab	Fw 190	4	4
II. Gruppe	Bf 109	51	49
III. Gruppe	Bf 109	47	46
IV. Gruppe	Fw 190	61	56

Jagdgeschwader 6

Stab	Fw 190	4	4
	Bf 109		
I. Gruppe	Fw 190	72	59
II. Gruppe	Fw 190	48	45
III. Gruppe	Bf 109	21	17

Jagdgeschwader 11

Stab	Fw 190	4	4
I. Gruppe	Fw 190	55	53
III. Gruppe	Fw 190	54	51

Jagdgeschwader 52

Stab	Bf 109	8	7
I. Gruppe	Bf 109	40	37
III. Gruppe	Bf 109	32	30

Jagdgeschwader 77

Stab	Bf 109	1	1
I. Gruppe	Bf 109	30	26
II. Gruppe	Bf 109	36	30
III. Gruppe	Bf 109	34	25

Ergänzungs Jagdgeschwader 1

	Bf 109	109	97

Kampfgeschwader 4

Stab	He 111	1	1
I. Gruppe	He 111	27	17
8. Staffel	He 111	5	1

Kampfgeschwader 53

7. Staffel	He 111	4	1

Schlachtgeschwader 1

Stab	Fw 190	3	2
I. Gruppe	Fw 190	40	39
II. Gruppe	Fw 190	44	38
III. Gruppe	Fw 190	42	36

Schlachtgeschwader 2

Stab	Fw 190	6	6

II. Gruppe	Fw 190	44	38
III. Gruppe	Ju 87	30	25
10. Staffel	Ju 87	21	21
Schlachtgeschwader 3			
Stab	Fw 190	8	4
II. Gruppe	Fw 190	47	43
Schlachtgeschwader 4			
I. Gruppe	Fw 190	30	24
II. Gruppe	Fw 190	39	39
III. Gruppe	Fw 190	24	20
Schlachtgeschwader 9			
I. Gruppe	Fw 190	59	54
Schlachtgeschwader 77			
Stab	Fw 190	8	8
I. Gruppe	Fw 190	34	34
II. Gruppe	Fw 190	34	27
III. Gruppe	Fw 190	47	46
10. Staffel	Ju 87	14	12
Schlachtgeschwader 151			
13. Staffel	Fw 190	18	17
Nachtschlachtgruppe 4	Ju 87	45	36
	Si 204		
Nachtschlachtgruppe 5	Ar 66	16	11
	Go 145		
Nachtschlachtgruppe 8	Ar 66	48	39
	Go 145, Ju 87		
Fernaufklärungsgruppe 2	Ju 188	1	0 [1]
Fernaufklärungsgruppe 3	Me 410	2	2 [1]
Aufklärungsgruppe 11	Ju 188	10	10

Aufklärungsgruppe 22	Me 410 Ju 88, Ju 188, Si 204	26	12
Aufklärungsgruppe 100	Ju 188	8	5
Fernaufklärungsgruppe 121	Me 410	13	4
Fernaufklärungsgruppe 122	Me 410	23	16
Nacht Aufklärungsgruppe	Do 217 Ju 88, Ju 188	25	10[1]
Nahaufklärungsgruppe 2	Bf 109	30	20
Nahaufklärungsgruppe 3	Bf 109	37	22
Nahaufklärungsgruppe 4	Bf 109	2	2[1]
Nahaufklärungsgruppe 8	Bf 109	35	21
Nahaufklärungsgruppe 11	Fw 189	10	8[1]
Nahaufklärungsgruppe 13	Bf 110 Fw 189, Si 204	13	8[1]
Nahaufklärungsgruppe 15	Bf 109	31	26
Nahaufklärungsgruppe 31	Fw 190 Si 204	15	12
Panzer Reconnaissance Units	Fi 156	33	26
Seeaufklärungsgruppe 126	Ar 196 Bv 138	18	11
Bordfliegergruppe	Ar 196	29	29

Luftflotte Reich

Jagdgeschwader 2 *I. Gruppe*	Fw 190	5	3

II. Gruppe	Fw 190	8	4
III. Gruppe	Fw 190	12	9
Jagdgeschwader 4			
Stab	Fw 190	6	4
II. Gruppe	Fw 190	50	34
III. Gruppe	Bf 109	61	56
Jagdgeschwader 7			
Stab	Me 262	5	4
I. Gruppe	Me 262	41	26
II. Gruppe	Me 262	30	23
Jagdgeschwader 26			
Stab	Fw 190	4	3
I. Gruppe	Fw 190	44	16
II. Gruppe	Fw 190	57	29
III. Gruppe	Fw 190	35	15
Jagdgeschwader 27			
I. Gruppe	Bf 109	29	13
II. Gruppe	Bf 109	48	27
III. Gruppe	Bf 109	19	15
Kampfgeschwader (Jäger) 54			
I. Gruppe	Me 262	37	21
Jagdgeschwader 301			
Stab	Ta 152	3	2
I. Gruppe	Fw 190	35	24
II. Gruppe	Fw 190	32	15
Jagdgeschwader 400			
II. Gruppe	Me 163	38	22
Jagdgruppe 10	Fw 190	15	9
Jagdverband 44	Me 262	ca30	ca15 [2]
Nachtjagdgeschwader 1			
Stab	He 219	29	25
	Bf 110		
1. Staffel	He 219	22	19

4. Staffel	Bf 110	16	15
7. Staffel	Bf 110	16	14
10. Staffel	Bf 110	17	15

Nachtjagdgeschwader 2

Stab	Ju 88	2	2
I. Gruppe	Ju 88	25	22
II. Gruppe	Ju 88	24	21
III. Gruppe	Ju 88	29	27

Nachtjagdgeschwader 3

Stab	Ju 88	4	4
1. Staffel	Ju 88	14	12
7. Staffel	Ju 88	19	16
10. Staffel	Ju 88	20	17

Nachtjagdgeschwader 4

Stab	Ju 88	4	4
	Bf 110		
1. Staffel	Ju 88	17	9
4. Staffel	Ju 88	28	23
7. Staffel	Ju 88	14	11

Nachtjagdgeschwader 5

Stab	Ju 88	16	10
	Bf 110		
1. Staffel	Ju 88	17	10
4. Staffel	Ju 88	28	25
	Bf 110		
7. Staffel	He 219	34	32
	Ju 88, Bf 110		
10. Staffel	Ju 88	12	11

Nachtjagdgeschwader 6

Stab	Ju 88	17	17
	Bf 110		
1. Staffel	Ju 88	17	17
4. Staffel	Ju 88	14	11
7. Staffel	Bf 110	15	12
10. Staffel	Ju 88	15	8

Nachtjagdgeschwader 11

1. Staffel	Bf 109	16	15

4. *Staffel*	Bf 109	14	9
7. *Staffel*	Bf 109	21	19
10. *Staffel*	Me 262	9	7

Nachtjagdgeschwader 100

I. *Gruppe*	Ju 88	23	20
	Fw 58		

Kommando Bonow	Ar 234	2	1 [4]
Nachtschlachtgruppe 1	Ju 87	8	1
Nachtschlachtgruppe 2	Ju 87	5	5
Nachtschlachtgruppe 20	Fw 190	27	11
Nahaufklärungsgruppe 1	Bf 109	16	9
Nahaufklärungsgruppe 6	Me 262	7	3
Nahaufklärungsgruppe 14	Fw 189	4	4

Kampfgeschwader 200

I. *Gruppe*	Various transport types		
II. *Gruppe*	Mistel, Ju 88, Ju 188		
III. *Gruppe*	Fw 190	31	21
KG 200 total		ca100	ca60 [2]

Luftwaffenkommando West

Jagdgeschwader 53

Stab	Bf 109	1	1
II. *Gruppe*	Bf 109	39	24
III. *Gruppe*	Bf 109	40	24
IV. *Gruppe*	Bf 109	54	27

Kampfgeschwader 51

I. *Gruppe*	Me 262	15	11
II. *Gruppe*	Me 262	6	2

Kampfgeschwader 76

Stab	Ar 234	2	2
II. Gruppe	Ar 234	5	1
III. Gruppe	Ar 234	5	1
Fernaufklärungsgruppe 100	Ar 234	6	1
Fernaufklärungsgruppe 123	Ar 234	12	7
	Ju 188		
Nahaufklärungsgruppe 13	Bf 109	39	26

Luftflottenkommando East Prussia

Jagdgeschwader 51

Stab	Fw 190	20	11
I. Gruppe	Bf 109	10	8
III. Gruppe	Bf 109	23	7

Schlachtgeschwader 3

I. Gruppe	Fw 190	27	24
Nahaufklärungsgruppe 4	Bf 109	26	17
	Fw 189		

Luftwaffe General Denmark

Aufklärungsgruppe 33	Ar 234	13	8
	Ju 188		

Luftwaffe General Norway [5]

Jagdgeschwader 5

Stab	Bf 109		
II. Gruppe	Me 410		
III. Gruppe	Bf 109		
IV. Gruppe	Bf 109, Fw 190		
Day fighter total		ca50	ca35 [2]
Nachtjagdstaffel Norwegen	Bf 110, Ju 88,	ca10	ca5 [2]
	He 219		
Aufklärungsgruppe 32	Fw 190, Bf 109	ca10	ca5 [2]

Aufklärungsgruppe 124	Ju 88, Ju 188	ca20	ca10 [2]
Seeaufklärungsgruppe 130	Bv 222, Bv 138	ca10	ca5 [2]
Transportgruppe 20	Ju 52	ca10	ca5 [2]
Seetransportstaffel 2	Ju 52	ca10	ca5 [2]

Luftwaffenkommando Courland

Jagdgeschwader 54			
Stab	Fw 190	5	5
I. Gruppe	Fw 190	38	33
II. Gruppe	Fw 190	41	38
Schlachtgeschwader 3			
III. Gruppe SG 54	Fw 190	43	41
Nachtschlachtgruppe 3	Go 145	18	16
Nahaufklärungsgruppe 5	Bf 109	25	18
	Fw 190		

Luftwaffe General Italy

Nachtschlachtgruppe 9	Fw 190	38	35
	Ju 87		
Fernaufklärungsgruppe 122	Ju 188	14	12
Kommando Sommer	Ar 234	3	2 [3]
Nahaufklärungsgruppe 11	Fw 190	24	14
	Bf 109		

Notes

1. Part unit.
2. Approximate figure.
3. Reconnaissance unit.
4. Night fighter unit.
5. The records for *Luftwaffe General Norway* were not included in the census return; probably they were lost in the general chaos at the end of the war.

The Fighter Force

Fighter-versus-Fighter Tactics

In the *Luftwaffe* fighter-versus-fighter tactics depended on aggressive manoeuvring and exploiting known performance advantages over enemy fighter types. The basic fighter unit was the *Rotte* (cell), comprising a leader (*Rottenführer*) and his wing-man (*Katchmarek*). During cruising flight the two aircraft flew almost in line abreast about 200 yards (metres) apart. Each pilot concentrated his search inwards to cover his partner's blind area behind and below. When in combat against enemy fighters the wing-man kept guard on his leader's tail, allowing the latter to concentrate on the task of setting up his attack.

Two *Rotten* made up a *Schwarm*, with the leading *Rotte* to one side and slightly ahead of the other and the aircraft stepped down into the sun. A *Staffel* formation comprised three *Schwärme* stepped up in line astern.

While operating in areas where contact with the enemy was likely, the fighters maintained a high cruising speed. With its component aircraft spaced about 200 yards apart, the *Schwarm* formation was approximately 600 yards wide. That meant it was almost impossible for the aircraft to hold position during a tight turn at high speed. The answer was the 'cross-over' turn: each aircraft turned as tightly as it could, and swapped sides in the formation.

In determining the effectiveness of a combat formation for fighters there are three factors to consider: first, the ability of the formation to manoeuvre while maintaining cohesion; secondly, the ability of the pilots to cover each others' blind areas and thus prevent a surprise attack; and thirdly, the ease with which an aircraft in the formation could receive support if it came under attack. On each of these three criteria, the German tactical formation was greatly superior to any of those used by other air forces early in the war.

Using the 'cross-over' turn, the *Schwarm* could turn as tightly as each aircraft was able. In cruising flight, every pilot in the *Schwarm* kept watch over his comrades' blind areas. If an aircraft in a *Rotte* or a *Schwarm* came under attack from behind, a simple turn placed the attacker under threat of attack.

Over Poland, France and during the early part of the Battle of Britain, the German fighters' tactics outclassed those of their opponents. Also, during this period, the altitude performance of the Messerschmitt Bf 109E was superior to that of any of the opposing fighter types. In general, therefore, the German tactics were to move into position above their opponents and 'bounce' them, if possible from out of the sun. After a single firing pass, the German fighters would use the speed gained in the dive to zoom back into position above their opponent. If necessary, the process was then repeated. Since the opposing fighters were usually slower and more manoeuvrable than the Bf 109, the German pilots preferred to avoid turning fights.

If the German fighters were themselves 'bounced' from above, if there was time each would turn independently to face the attackers. If there was not time, the German fighters would often bunt into high-speed dives. That exploited the advantages of the direct injection fuel system fitted to their Daimler Benz or BMW engines. If an enemy fighter fitted with an engine with the normal float carburettor tried to follow, that engine would cut out due to fuel starvation. An alternative was the *Abschwung* (American 'Split-S') manoeuvre—a half roll pulled through into a steep dive at full throttle. However, this tactic produced a considerable altitude loss—between 10,000 and 15,000 feet—which precluded its use except as a measure of desperation.

These tactics served the German fighter force well, provided units were allowed the tactical freedom to exploit the performance of their aircraft. Often during bomber escort missions this was not the case, however. During the Battle of Britain part of the fighter force was tasked with providing a close escort for each individual bomber *Gruppe*. In this case fighter pilots had strict orders not to engage enemy fighters unless they or their assigned bomber formation came under direct threat of attack. The fighter pilots hated this duty, for it meant they surrendered the initiative to the enemy. Given free rein, fighter commanders preferred to range aggressively ahead of the bombers and sweep the area clear of enemy fighters.

Fighter-versus-Bomber Tactics

Up to the autumn of 1942 the standard German tactics against enemy day bombers involved quarter or stern attacks by *Rotten* or *Schwärme*. When engaging American bomber formations, however, German fighters attacking from the rear often suffered losses from the powerful defensive crossfire.

The first major change in tactics was to deliver the attacks from head-on, where the bombers' defensive armament was less powerful and their armour protection less effective. The bombers cruised at speeds around 175 mph and the fighters ran in at about 300 mph, so their closing speed was nearly 500 mph. That allowed time for only a brief half-second burst before the fighter pilot had to break away to avoid colliding with his prey. To bring down a heavy bomber with such a brief firing pass called for exceptionally good shooting. A few skilful pilots built up large victory scores using this method, but the average German fighter pilot achieved little. On the other hand, during a *Staffel* attack there was a good chance of damaging one or two bombers and forcing them to leave the relative safety of the formation. Aircraft flying alone could then be finished off at leisure.

HEAD-ON ATTACK ON A B-17

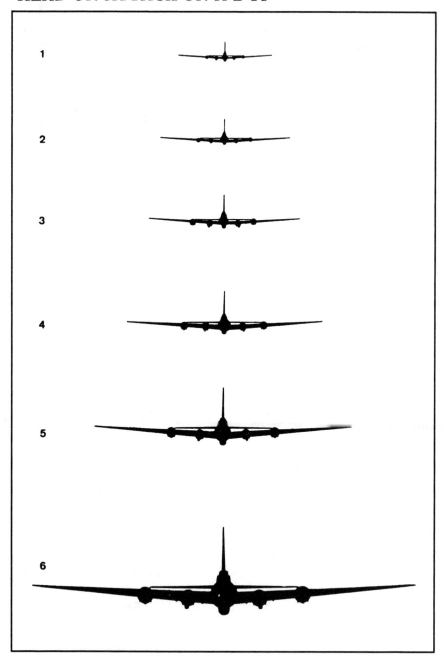

During the spring and summer of 1943 the *Luftwaffe* experimented with air-to-air bombing attacks, and attacks with large unguided rockets from outside the range of the bombers' defensive fire. Again, the intention was to damage aircraft and force them to leave formation, so that they could be picked off. The bombs and the unguided rockets proved to be inaccurate weapons, however. Although they achieved a few spectacular successes, for the most part they detonated too far from the bombers to inflict serious damage.

In the autumn of 1943 two *Zerstörergeschwader*, 26 and 76, returned to the homeland to buttress the fighter defences. The twin-engined bomber-destroyers, Messerschmitt Bf 110s and Me 410s, carried a forward-firing armament of four 20m cannon, two 30mm cannon and four 21cm rocket launchers. Against unescorted bomber formations the twin-engined fighters proved highly effective. Their fire-power was sufficient to inflict lethal damage on the American heavy bombers, and they carried enough fuel and ammunition to permit repeated attacks on the enemy formations.

The extending reach of the US escorts quickly imposed constraints on the twin-engined fighters' operations, however. During an attack on Frankfurt am Main on 4 October 1943, P-47 Thunderbolts caught a *Gruppe* of Bf 110s as it was moving into position to launch rockets into a bomber formation. In the ensuing combat the escorts shot down more than ten of the unwieldy twin-engined fighters, without loss to themselves. From then on bomber-destroyers tried to keep beyond the reach of the US escorts, and initially they restricted their operations to east of the line Bremen–Kassel–Frankfurt. During the months that followed the US escorts penetrated progressively deeper into Germany and eventually, after suffering heavy losses, the twin-engined fighter units were forced to cease operations.

In the spring of 1944 the increasing strength, reach and performance of the American escort fighters led to a further change in tactics. German fighter units would assemble into large attack formations comprising three or four

Fig. 7 (left). A head-on attack on a B-17. Hold the page a comfortable arm's length (about two feet) from your eyes to see the apparent size of a B-17 at the various ranges. During a head-on attack, the closing speed of the two aircraft was about 500 mph, or more than 200 yards per second.

1. *Range 800 yards. At this distance the bomber had to be centred in the fighter's gunsight graticule if it was to be hit.*
2. *One second later, range 600 yards: fighter about to open fire.*
3. *Half a second later, range 500 yards: the fighter commenced firing.*
4. *Half a second later, range 400 yards: the fighter ceased firing.*
5. *Half a second later, range 300 yards: the fighter pilot eased up his nose to move out of the path of the bomber.*
6. *Half a second later, range 200 yards: if the fighter was not out of the bomber's path by this time, a collision was almost inevitable.*

Gruppen, sometimes with more than a hundred fighters, to punch through the escorts and attack the bombers. However, in such actions the German fighters faced a fundamental problem. To stand a good chance of knocking down the rugged American bombers, the German fighters needed to carry batteries of heavy cannon and rockets, but any fighter carrying such a heavy weapons load was easy meat for the fast and nimble American escort fighters.

To overcome this problem *Generalmajor* Galland, the Inspector of Fighters, devised a new tactic. Special units, *Sturmgruppen,* were formed with heavily armoured Fw 190s fitted with heavy 30mm cannon. These were to engage the bombers. Lightly armed fighter *Gruppen* were to escort each *Sturmgruppe* and hold off the American escorts while the Focke Wulfs delivered their attacks. The *Sturmgruppe* with its two covering 'light' *Gruppen* made up a *Gefechtsverband* (battle formation) with a strength of up to a hundred aircraft.

During the summer and autumn of 1944 individual *Gefechtsverbände* sometimes engaged bomber formations with considerable success. The huge German fighter formations needed a long time to form up and climb to the raiders' altitude, however, and they were most unwieldy. Frequently the wide-ranging American fighters were able to engage the German attack formations and break them up before they could get close to the bombers.

During the final nine months of the war the *Luftwaffe* sent small forces of Me 262 jet fighters against the American heavy bombers, although there were never enough of these fighters airborne to achieve a significant success. The jet fighters were fast enough to operate successfully without escorts, and their armament of four 30mm cannon was powerful enough to knock down the bombers.

When they attacked bombers from astern, the jet fighters' high overtaking speeds allowed their pilots only a brief firing pass. To overcome this problem, jet fighters would dive past the escorts at speeds around 500 mph, aiming for a position about one mile behind and 1,500 feet below the bombers. When they reached that point they made a high-G pull-up to 'dump' speed, then they levelled off behind the bombers. At the end of the manoeuvre the jet fighters were in an ideal position to attack—inside the screen of escort fighters, behind the bombers and closing at about 100 mph. If the fighter carried rockets it would fire those first, then, unless the bomber had obviously suffered fatal damage, it would attack the same target with its cannon. When about 100 yards from the bomber the jet pilot would pull up and break away over the target, to avoid falling debris.

Night Fighter Tactics

From the beginning of the war until May 1940 the night air defence of the German homeland was left mainly to the *Flak* arm of the *Luftwaffe.* The night fighter force comprised a few single-seater fighters, mainly Bf 109s, whose pilots relied on searchlights in the target area to illuminate the enemy bombers for attack. This tactic was termed *Helle Nachtjagd* (illuminated night fighting). Due to their small numbers, and the small numbers of RAF aircraft operating over Germany (mostly on leaflet-dropping missions), the night fighters achieved few victories. The searchlights were situated around the more important towns and cities, and night fighters orbiting over the gun-defended areas were often illuminated and then engaged by 'friendly' anti-aircraft gunners.

The RAF night offensive against German industrial targets began in earnest in May 1940. This revealed the ineffectiveness of the night defences, and Göring ordered *Oberst* Josef Kammhuber to set up a specialised night fighter force with its associated fighter control organisation. Kammhuber was soon promoted to *Generalmajor* and by mid-August 1940 his force comprised *Nachtjagdgeschwader 1* with two *Gruppen* of Bf 110s for home air defence. *Nachtjagdgeschwader 2*, with a single *Gruppe* equipped with Ju 88s and Do 17s, flew intruder missions against RAF bomber bases in England.

To overcome this problem of misidentification and engagement by *Flak* batteries, Kammhuber repositioned the night fighter engagement zones away from German cities—and therefore clear of their gun defences. Initially there were only a few *Freya* radars, early warning sets with a maximum range of about 100 miles. These sets provided warning of the approach of enemy aircraft, but their indications were not precise enough to provide for the accurate ground control of fighters. A better radar was needed, and it was not long in coming.

In 1941 the Telefunken company began mass production of the Giant *Würzburg* radar, a precision tracking equipment with a maximum range of 50 miles. A pair of these radars and one *Freya* formed the basis of the *Himmelbett* (Four-Poster Bed) system of fighter control. The wide-beam *Freya* radar provided area surveillance and directed the narrow-beam Giant *Würzburg* sets on to their targets: one Giant *Würzburg* tracked the enemy bomber while the other tracked the German night fighter. The ranges, bearings and altitudes of the two aircraft were displayed on a special plotting table, from which the fighter control officer vectored the night fighter into position to attack the bomber.

Under Kammhuber's direction a line of *Himmelbett* stations, each with two Giant *Würzburgen* and one *Freya*, was erected at 20-mile intervals across northern Europe. This created a defensive barrier through which raiders had to pass on their flights to and from targets in Germany. The barrier was shaped like a huge inverted sickle. The 'handle' ran through Denmark from north to south, and the 'blade' curved through northern Germany, Holland, Belgium and eastern France to the Swiss frontier.

As the raiders were detected approaching the defensive barrier, the night fighters were scrambled and headed for their assigned ground control stations. They then orbited, waiting for an enemy bomber to come within range of the ground station's Giant *Würzburg* radar. Once the controller had both aircraft in view on his plotting table, the interception would begin. These actions were closely controlled one-on-one affairs. Unless in hot pursuit of a bomber, a night fighter rarely moved outside the 50-mile range of the Giant *Würzburg* radars controlling it.

Meanwhile German long-range night fighters conducted intruder missions against RAF night bomber bases thought likely to be active. Any ground activity seen was bombed and/or strafed, and any aircraft seen were attacked. The intruders did not shoot down many bombers, but their activities caused considerable disruption. Many more bombers were destroyed in accidents, as their tired crews tried to land at airfields whose lights were dimmed so as not to attract enemy planes.

Once he had established a viable fighter control system using radar, Kammhuber was ordered to concentrate all his available night fighters to work within it in the home defence role. Thus, in October 1941, the night intruder operations against RAF bomber airfields ceased.

During 1942 the German night defences were further improved with the introduction of a lightweight airborne interception radar, the *Lichtenstein BC*, which had a maximum range of five miles. This equipment was fitted to the Bf 110s and Ju 88s.

As the night fighter force increased in strength and capability, it posed an increasingly severe threat to Bomber Command's operations. During 1941 and the first part of 1942 the RAF bombers penetrated the defensive barrier on a broad front and over an extended period. As the RAF learned more about the German system, however, its main weakness became clear. A single fighter control station directed only one interception at a time, or a maximum of about six interceptions per hour. The easiest way to degrade the system was for raiders to penetrate the defensive line on a narrow front in a concentrated mass, in a so-called 'bomber stream'. Thus the three or four *Himmelbett* stations astride the bombers' path had far more targets than they could handle, and the rest of the stations (and their orbiting night fighters) could play no part in the action. The same applied to the *Flak* batteries that lay along the bombers' route and at the target. Bomber Command first used its 'bomber stream' tactic in the spring of 1942. In reply, Kammhuber constructed additional *Himmelbett* sites in front of and behind the original defensive barrier, to thicken the latter.

Kammhuber's defensive line was situated some distance to the north and west of the main targets, and the close defence of the latter was left to the *Flak* batteries. In the spring of 1943 *Major* Hajo Herrmann asked to be allowed to employ a small force of single-engined fighters, Bf 109s and Fw 190s, to engage RAF night bombers over their target. Herrmann's plan did not call for the use of radar. He argued that over the target the light from searchlights, fires on the ground and the Pathfinders' marker flares would

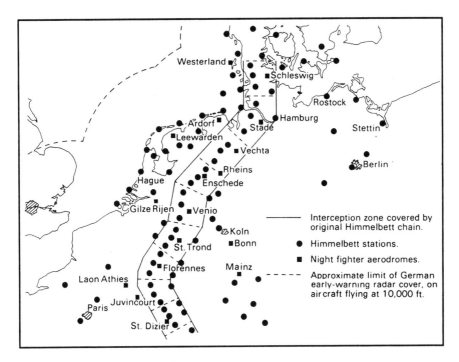

Fig. 8. Layout of the German system of close-controlled night fighting at the end of 1942.

illuminate the bombers. Then the fighters could pick them off delivering visual attacks. *Flak* batteries would engage bombers below a certain briefed altitude, typically 5,500 metres (18,000 feet), and fuse their shells to explode below that altitude. Any bomber found above that altitude could thus be engaged safely by the fighters. In July Herrmann conducted a small-scale operational trial of his aptly named *Wilde Sau* (Wild Boar) tactics. When this proved a success, Herrmann received permission to expand his unit into a full *Geschwader*.

Until the summer of 1943 the precision radars on which German night fighters depended, the Giant *Würzburg* and the *Lichtenstein*, had operated without hindrance. But now the RAF had prepared a counter to these radars—'Window', strips of thin aluminium foil 30cm long and just over 1.5cm wide. Two thousand such strips, tied in a bundle which broke up in the slipstream, produced an echo on radar similar to that from a heavy bomber.

In July 1943 RAF bombers used 'Window' to neutralise the defences during a series of attacks on Hamburg. Each bomber released one bundle of foil per minute. The clouds of fluttering strips effectively saturated the defences with thousands of spurious targets. For the RAF the new tactic was a complete success, and its losses fell dramatically.

At a stroke, 'Window' nullified the *Himmelbett* system of control on which the German night fighter force had depended. Kammhuber was ousted from his post as commanding *General* of night fighters and his replacement, *General* Josef Schmid, began a far-reaching reorganisation of the force's tactical methods. As a temporary expedient, Herrmann's *Wilde Sau* target defence tactics were pushed hard: since they did not rely on radar, they were impervious to radar jamming. The formation of the first *Geschwader* of *Wilde Sau* fighters, *JG 300*, was rushed ahead and there were plans to create two more.

Under Schmid's direction the twin-engined night fighter force adopted a variation of the Wild Boar tactic code-named *Zähme Sau* (Tame Boar). Under this system, large numbers of night fighters were scrambled as the raiding force approached. The fighters operated under radio broadcast control, with the aim of setting up long running battles. At the target, the twin-engined night fighters engaged bombers in the same way as the *Wilde Sau* fighters.

During the autumn of 1943 *Luftwaffe* ground tracking stations developed considerable expertise in exploiting the emissions from the bombers' radars. The culprits were the H2S ground-mapping radar and the 'Monica' tail warning radar, whose signals could be detected from great distances. Further to exploit these emissions, night fighters began carrying airborne homing equipment, the *Naxos* set to home on H2S radiations and *Flensburg* to home on emissions from 'Monica'. At the same time the *Luftwaffe* introduced a new airborne interception radar for night fighters—the *SN-2* equipment, with a range of four miles. Since the new radar operated on a longer wavelength than did *Lichtenstein*, it was little affected by the 'Window' strips then in use.

For several months the new German airborne systems escaped discovery by the British intelligence service. *SN-2* operated in the same part of the frequency spectrum as *Freya* ground early warning radars and for a long time its emissions went unrecognised. Being passive systems, *Naxos* and *Flensburg* emitted no tell-tale radiations.

It took some time for the night fighter force to become familiar with its new tactics and equipment. When it did, at the end of 1943, the force emerged from the traumas of the previous summer more effective than ever.

To show the operation of the new German tactics, let us take a close look at a typical night operation during the early part of 1944. While at readiness the night fighter crews relaxed in dimly lit huts close to their aircraft. Usually there was enough warning of the approach of the bombers for the crews to walk out to their machines and strap in without undue haste. As they taxied into position for take-off, the crews tuned their radios to the broadcast frequency for the latest information on the raiders' position, heading and probable target. The broadcasts also informed each *Gruppe* of the radio beacon to head for when airborne.

The night fighters orbited over their assigned assembly beacon, spiralling up to altitudes around 20,000 feet. At a single beacon there might be as many as 50 night fighters orbiting in the darkness. In peacetime such a hazard would be considered unacceptable, but in the event there were remarkably few collisions.

As the bomber stream moved deeper into German-occupied territory, its intentions became clearer to those tracking it. The controllers ordered the night fighter *Gruppen* from beacon to beacon, each step calculated to bring them closer to the raiding force. Finally, the night fighters were ordered to fly on a set heading to seek out the bombers using radar, homing receivers and visual search. Sometimes a crew's first indication of the 'stream' was the bucking of their plane as it hit the turbulent wakes from the heavy bombers. Once in contact with the enemy, the night fighter crew's first duty was to inform Divisional control of the bombers' location and heading. This information would be relayed to other night fighter units, to bring them into action.

Once the night fighter pilot had a bomber in sight, his usual tactic was to close in from behind and slightly below. This silhouetted the bomber against the light background of the stars, while the fighter was much more difficult to see against the darker ground. If the bomber crew was vigilant and detected the threat in time, the bomber pilot would commence a violent 'corkscrew' manoeuvre and was usually able to escape. If, however, the bomber crew failed to detect the night fighter before it entered the blind zone beneath their aircraft, their chances of escape were slim. From that position the night fighter pilot could ease up the nose of his aircraft, and rake the bomber with cannon-fire as it flew past. If the fighter carried upward-firing cannon (code-named *Schräge Musik*), he would manoeuvre into position and attack with these. Most German night fighter pilots aimed to hit the wing between the engines: there lay a fuel tank with hundreds of gallons of inflammable petrol. Because they usually engaged from short range—often within 75 yards—night fighter pilots did not like to fire into the fuselage and risk detonating the bomb load.

Early in 1944 RAF Bomber Command launched several deep-penetration attacks into Germany, suffering heavy losses during some of them. A particularly hard night was that of 19/20 February, when 78 aircraft were lost out of 823 attacking Leipzig. This phase of the battle culminated on the night of 30/31 March when the German night fighter force achieved its greatest success ever. Bomber Command lost 95 aircraft that night out of 795 attacking Nuremberg, and it is believed that 79 fell to attacks from night fighters.

Following that success, however, the German night fighter force entered a long period of decline. A few months later the RAF captured a Ju 88 night fighter with *SN-2* radar and a *Flensburg* homer, and also discovered the existence of *Naxos*. Tests with the *SN-2* radar revealed that longer strips of metal foil, code-named 'Rope', were effective against it. As a counter to *Flensburg*, 'Monica' was removed from most Bomber Command aircraft. At the same time there were strict orders restricting the use of H2S. In rapid succession the three German airborne systems were rendered far less effective.

That was a serious setback for the German night fighter force, but it was only one of four major reverses suffered in the summer of 1944. The second, and equally serious, blow was the entry into action of No 100 Group of Bomber Command. Formed to support the night bombing raids, the Group began operations with a dozen squadrons. Half the units were equipped with specialised jamming aircraft to disrupt the German radar network; the other half operated Mosquito night fighters to harass their German counterparts in the air and on the ground.

The third reverse suffered by the German night fighter force stemmed from the Allied advance through France, which created a huge gap in the German early warning radar cover. The RAF exploited this gap, during attacks on western and southern Germany, by routing its bombers across France. The *Luftwaffe* redeployed ground radars to fill the void, but the days when the night fighters could provide defence in depth had gone for ever.

The fourth calamity to afflict the night fighter force, and the most serious of all, stemmed from the Allied strategic bomber offensive on the German oil industry. Following a series of devastating raids on refineries, monthly pro-

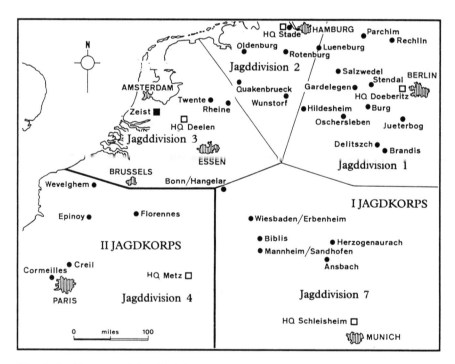

Fig. 9. Jagdkorps *and* Jagddivision *boundaries, Reich Air Defence fighter units, March 1944.*

Key: ■ Jagdkorps *headquarters;* □ Jagddivision *headquarters;* ● *fighter airfield*

duction of aviation fuel slumped. The resultant fuel famine imposed harsh operational constraints on every part of the *Luftwaffe*, including the night fighter force.

Delivered in rapid succession, those body-blows left the German night fighter force stunned and reeling. As a result, during the final seven months of the war, it was able to mount little more than a token opposition.

Organisation of Reich Air Defence

During the war the organisation of units assigned to Reich air defence underwent several changes, as the Allied air attacks became more of a menace. This section describes the organisation as it stood in March 1944, as the defenders were about to face their most severe test.

Luftflotte Reich controlled all home defence flying and *Flak* units located in Holland and Germany. Day and night fighter units were subordinated to I. *Jagdkorps* with its headquarters in Zeist in Holland. The *Korps* was divided into four *Jagddivisionen*. *Jagddivision 1*, with its headquarters at Döberitz near Berlin, controlled the defence of north-eastern Germany; *Jagddivision 2*, headquartered at Stade near Hamburg, controlled the defence of north central Germany; *Jagddivision 3*, headquartered at Deelen in Holland, controlled the defence of north-western Germany; and *Jagddivision 7*, with its headquarters at Schleissheim near Munich, controlled the defence of southern Germany. *Jagddivision 4*, with its headquarters at Metz in France, controlled the fighter units based in that country and in Belgium. This *Jagddivision* lay outside the area controlled by *Luftflotte Reich*, but the latter could call on it to assist in the defence of the homeland.

On 6 March 1944 the five *Jagddivisionen* had the following aircraft serviceable:

Jagddivisionen	1	2	3	4	7	Total
Single-engined day fighters (Bf 109, Fw 190)	78	128	54	116	182	558
Twin-engined day fighters (Bf 110, Me 410)	21	5	–	–	66	92
Single-engined night fighters (Bf 109, Fw 190)	41	–	17	–	30	88
Twin-engined night fighters (Bf 110, Ju 88, Do 217, He 219)	74	67	46	32	41	260
Others	8	15	3	–	–	26
Totals	**222**	**215**	**120**	**148**	**319**	**1,024**

By this stage of the war *Luftflotte Reich* had to make use of every fighter it had available. The figures given above include 31 single-seat fighters operated by factory defence units. These used new machines just off the production line, flown into action by production test pilots from the factory. There were also fifteen single-engined fighters kept available for action at fighter training schools, to be flown by instructors. The 26 aircraft in the 'Others' column belonged to trials units, airborne tracking units and the Illumination *Gruppe* (to drop flares to show the current whereabouts of a bomber stream); these aircraft would not normally engage enemy aircraft directly. Night fighter units, with both single-engined and twin-engined fighter types, regularly took part in actions against American daylight raiding forces.

Day and night fighter operations were directed from the headquarters bunkers of the five fighter *Divisionen*. These bunkers served as clearing houses for information on the movements of hostile and friendly aircraft supplied by radar stations, ground observer posts, raid tracking aircraft and fighter crews. Inside the large operations room was a vertical translucent screen etched with a gridded map of the *Division's* area. Plots on friendly and hostile aircraft were projected on the rear of the screen, by women auxiliaries using special narrow-beam torches. In his book *The First and the Last*, Adolf Galland described the mood inside one of these headquarters, nicknamed 'Battle Opera Houses', during an engagement:

> On entering one was immediately infected by the nervous atmosphere reigning there. The artificial light made faces appear even more haggard than they really were. Bad air, cigarette smoke, the hum of ventilators, the ticking of Teletypes and the subdued murmur of countless telephone operators gave one a headache. The magic centre of attraction in this room was a huge frosted-glass panel on which were projected the position, altitude, strength and course of the enemy as well as of our own formations. The whole was reminiscent of a huge aquarium lit up, with a multitude of water-fleas scuttling madly behind the glass walls. Each single dot and each change to be seen here was the result of reports and observations from radar sets, aircraft-spotters, listening posts, reconnaissance and contact planes, or from units in action. They all merged together by telephone or wireless in this centre to be received, sorted and within a few minutes transposed into transmittable messages. What was represented here on a giant map was a picture of the air situation in the sector of a fighter *Division*, with about one minute's delay.

In front of the screen sat the Divisional operational officer and his fighter controllers. Close by them sat the liaison officers in contact with the fighter airfields by telephone and with the aircraft airborne by radio. This allowed the controller to get his fighters into the air in good time, assemble his force and direct it into action to inflict maximum damage.

To show how the German air defence system worked in practice, here are translated entries from the War Diary of *I. Jagdkorps* describing a major daylight operation and one by night. In each case the entries were written within a few hours of the action described.

Action Against USAAF attack on Anklam, Danzig, Marienburg, Gotenhafen, 9 October 1943

The approach flight for the attack on aircraft armament plants in eastern Germany was via the North Sea and the Baltic. Several hundred American four-engined bombers flew in three large formations, without fighter escort, at altitudes between 4,500 and 6,000 m. The distance from Great Britain to Marienburg in East Prussia and back totalled about 2,500 km.

At 09.09 hours, two forces of enemy bombers comprising two hundred aircraft were observed about 100 to 150 km north-west of Texel island. These crossed the west coast of Jutland between the island of Sylt and Esbjerg and, flying over the islands of Fyn and Lolland, they reached the Neubrandenburg–Anklam area. At 11.50 hours they began their return flight, on a north-westerly heading, leaving the coast of Denmark near Esbjerg. The last position obtained on the bombers was at 13.46 hours, when they were 80 km north of the island of Vlieland.

At 14.00 hours a force of about 80 enemy fighters made a rendezvous with the returning bombers to the north of the island of Texel.

A third bomber force, with a total strength of about 300 aircraft, crossed over Jutland, Fyn, and Zealand flying on south-easterly heading. These aircraft bombed shipyards, harbour installations and aircraft factories at Danzig, Marienburg and Gotenhafen. They commenced their return flights at 13.18 hours. The bombers passed over Husum and Esbjerg and their last recorded position was at 15.50 hours when they were 70 km west of Esbjerg.

Other Events on 9 October 1943

At 05.36 hours a Mosquito reconnaissance plane flew over the western part of the Baltic, via Westerland. Presumably it was conducting a weather reconnaissance. Morning weather reconnaissance flights often provided headquarters *I. Jagdkorps* with an indication of the penetration route to be taken by an American raiding force coming in later.

From 07.00 hours to 12.00 hours a total of 22 aircraft, all flying singly, appeared off the Dutch coast. During the period between 16.25 hours and 16.48 a force of 30 to 40 American fighters flew across Texel island and up to Terschelling island.

At 14.50 hours an enemy force comprising about a hundred Marauders, Bostons and Spitfires attacked Woensdrecht airfield in Holland. The raiders flew at altitudes between 2,000 m and 4,000 m, and withdrew via the Scheldt estuary.

From 11.40 hours, 15 to 20 Mosquito reconnaissance aircraft crossed the coast between the estuaries of the Somme and the Scheldt, flying on south-easterly headings. These continued to the Frankfurt am Main–Mannheim–Stuttgart region, presumably conducting pre-strike reconnaissance for future raids. The aircraft withdrew to the north-west and the last position report, at 15.55 hours, indicated a flight above Le Treport.

Weather
Cloud-free skies, good visibility.

Effects of the Raids

Anklam: Buildings at the Arado aircraft factory set on fire and several fires started in the city. Casualties: 150 dead, 150 wounded.

Gotenhafen: Four ships and one floating dock damaged, some installations partially destroyed. Torpedo experimental station and arsenal damaged, heavy damage to buildings in the city. Casualties: 100 dead, 1,500 homeless.

Marienburg: Focke Wulf plant heavily damaged. Casualties: 70 dead, 100 wounded, 500 homeless

Danzig: Light damage to buildings. Casualties: 4 dead, 2 missing.

Woensdrecht Airfield: Heavy damage to the taxiways. Airfield out of commission for one week.

Commitment of *I. Jagdkorps*

The long detour by the enemy force over the North Sea, Jutland and the Baltic made it difficult to commit day fighter units, since most of these were based in Holland and north-west Germany. Nevertheless, it was possible to bring large numbers of fighters into contact and so inflict heavy losses on the American force. The action developed as follows:

Jagddivision 1 units took off from Holland and headed over the North Sea. These fighters were unable to make contact with the bomber force, and they landed on airfields in the Hamburg–Schleswig Holstein area. After refuelling, *Jagddivision 1* units successfully attacked the bombers during their withdrawal.

Day fighter units of *Jagddivision 2* engaged the enemy bombers during their approach and return flights. Single-engined and twin-engined fighters entered the fray over the German Bight and Jutland.

A weak force of fighters from *Jagddivision 3*, which included factory defence units, attacked the bomber formations over the coast and at the western end of the Baltic. For the action over the Bay of Danzig, only night fighters from bases in Pomerania and East Prussia were available.

Aircraft from two *Geschwader* of *Jagddivision 5* were flown to airfields in the German Bight, where they refuelled. These forces were successfully committed against American bombers during their withdrawal flight.

All the night fighters available for daylight operations (between 80 and 100) were sent into action. These successfully attacked enemy bombers on their approach and withdrawal flights, over the western Baltic, Jutland and over the North Sea.

Total Commitment from *I. Jagdkorps*:

566 sorties, which included those by night fighters and aircraft flying double sorties.

Enemy losses:
53 planes definitely shot down.
11 planes probably shot down, mostly over the sea.
Most of the enemy losses occurred during the withdrawal phase.

Additional aircraft shot down by Flak:
1 Mosquito east of Gent.
1 Mosquito north of Gent.

1 Mosquito near Antwerp.
1 Marauder bomber crashed near Shooten.

Own losses:
10 aircraft (5 Bf 109, 3 Fw 190, 2 Ju 88).
14 aircraft damaged.
Casualties: 1 dead, 1 wounded, 10 missing.

The operations on 9 October 1943 represented a considerable victory for the units of *I. Jagdkorps*, achieved in return for minimal losses. These successes were due to the superior armament of the German planes when engaging four-engined bombers, and because the enemy chose to attack on a cloudless autumn day without fighter protection. Because of the deep penetration into German territory, the defenders had plenty of time to deliver attacks on the bomber formations.

Author's Comments

American records give the strength of the raiding forces that day, and the losses suffered, as follows:

Anklam: 115 B-17s, of which 106 attacked. 18 planes lost, 52 damaged.

Marienburg: 100 B-17s, of which 96 attacked. 2 planes lost, 13 damaged.

Gotenhafen: 112 B-17s, of which 109 attacked. 6 planes lost, 63 damaged.

Danzig. and Gotenhafen: 51 B-24s, of which 41 attacked. 2 planes lost, 20 damaged.

Woensdrecht Airfield: 72 B-26s, of which 66 attacked. No planes lost, 26 damaged.

It can be seen that the defenders greatly exaggerated the scale of their success that day. *I. Jagdkorps* claimed 53 planes definitely shot down and 11 probably shot down, compared with an actual American loss of 28 planes. However, the War Diary account was written within a few hours of the event, and it is important to note that it gave the total of *unverified* victory claims submitted by fighter units. Verification would weed out many overclaims, but this was a painstaking process that would take several months to complete.

I. Jagdkorps War Diary Account of RAF attack on Frankfurt am Main on the night of 22/23 March 1944

During the first half of the night, the RAF opened its operations with a force of 100 Mosquito bombers. These came in over the Dutch coast and attacked the airfields at Leeuwarden, Twente, Deelen and Venlo in Holland, and well as targets in the Ruhr area and the city of Frankfurt am Main. During the Mosquito attack, a bomber stream of some 600 aircraft took off and came in over the southern part of the North Sea.

A force of minelaying aircraft detached itself from the main force and flew over Jutland to drop mines in areas of the Baltic. After completing this task these aircraft returned to Great Britain. The main force of bombers altered course to the south, over the sea north of Ameland, and continued into the Osnabrück area. At this point a force of Mosquitos left the stream. These headed for Berlin, where they dropped bombs in an attempt to disguise the bombers' main target. Meanwhile the heavy bombers continued in a tight stream towards their target, Frankfurt am Main. After bombing, the attackers withdrew to the north-west, flying over Belgium and northern France and leaving the continent between Ostende and Dieppe. Whereas the Mosquito attacks were barely effective, the heavy attack on Frankfurt caused considerable damage to industrial installations. The enemy minelaying action in the western Baltic caused some dissipation of the German night fighter effort, and this must be regarded as a successful British diversionary tactic.

Besides the attacks described above, the RAF carried out the following actions during the second half of the night:
Several long-range night fighters carried out strafing attacks on the airfields at Stade and Langendiebach.
Three courier aircraft were observed crossing the Skagerrak on their way between Great Britain and Sweden.

Commitment of *I. Jagdkorps*

The following forces were committed by *I. Jagdkorps* in night pursuit operations:
Jagddivision 3. Bf 110 units, reinforced by units from *Jagddivision 4*, assembled over radio beacon *Ludwig* [near Osnabrück] and were directed into the bomber stream over Lippstadt and Paderborn. Ju 88 units were directed from their airfields (at Twente, Quakenbrück, Langensalza and St Trond) to radio beacon *Quelle* [near Hamburg] via radio beacon *Ludwig* and into the bomber stream. The twin-engined fighter *Gruppe* from Mainz-Finthen was sent towards Kassel, then it flew via radio beacons *Marie* and *Ludwig* before being directed into the bomber stream.
Jagddivision 2. The twin-engined fighter *Gruppe* from Vechta assembled over radio beacon *Quelle*, then flew via radio beacon *Ludwig* and was directed into the bomber stream. The twin-engined fighter *Gruppe* from Westerland assembled over radio beacon *Hummer*, was then guided towards Bremen and was directed into the bomber stream west of Quackenbrück.
Jagddivision 1. The twin-engined fighter *Gruppen* from Werneuchen and Erfurt were directed via radio beacon *Ludwig* and entered the bomber stream east of Münster. The twin-engined fighter *Gruppen* from Parchim and Stendal assembled over radio beacon *Marie* [north-east of Hanover]. After the attack on Frankfurt started, these aircraft were ordered to land.

Target Defence [*Wilde Sau*] Operations

Jagddivision 3. The single-engined fighter *Gruppen* from Rheine and Wiesbaden-Erbenheim assembled over the light beacon at Brunswick. The *Gruppe* from Rheine was recalled because it did not have the range to reach the target. The *Gruppe* from Wiesbaden went into action over Frankfurt am Main.
Jagddivision 2. The single-engined fighter *Gruppe* from Oldenburg assembled over Bremen and was directed past Soltau in the direction of Frankfurt. Because these aircraft lacked the range to reach Frankfurt, they were ordered to land.

Himmelbett [Close Controlled Night Fighter Operations] against Mosquitos and the bomber stream during its withdrawal: several twin-engined fighters from *Jagddivision 3.*

The Illumination *Gruppe* based at Münster-Handorf assembled over radio beacon *Marie* and was directed via Hanover to Frankfurt. The weather conditions prevented it participating in the action by dropping flares.

I. Jagdkorps employed a total of 243 single-engined and twin-engined fighters, besides the aircraft from the Illumination *Gruppe*.

The two alterations in course by the bomber stream, coupled with the diversionary actions by the minelaying force and the Mosquitos, complicated the direction of the German night fighter force. This led to many last-minute changes of plan, and accounts for the fact that the successes achieved were unremarkable in spite of the excellent weather conditions for the defence.

Allied losses
38 bombers certainly brought down.

German losses
8 aircraft. Casualties: 2 dead, 6 wounded, 12 missing.

Weather Conditions
Scattered areas of nimbus cloud, base 600 to 800 m and extended as high as 2,000 m. Over the target area the skies were clear with good visibility at high altitude.

Remarks
The damage caused by British long-range fighters was as follows:
Stade: 1 Bf 110 destroyed, 1 damaged. 4 personnel wounded.
Langendiebach: 1 Bf 110 damaged, 1 aircrewman slightly injured.
One of our fighters was shot down over Frankfurt by our own *Flak*. The pilot escaped by parachute.

Author's Comments

RAF records give the strength of the raiding forces that night, and the losses suffered, as follows:
Frankfurt am Main: 816 Lancasters, Halifaxes and Mosquitos. 33 planes lost.
Minelaying operation in the Baltic: 128 Halifaxes and Stirlings. 1 plane lost.
Diversionary and harassing attacks: 22 Mosquitos
Long-range night fighter patrols: 16 Mosquitos

As was usually the case when air actions took place over German-held territory, and the aircraft wrecks could be counted, the defenders' claims were reasonably accurate on this occasion. *I. Jagdkorps* made an unverified claim of 38 planes certainly shot down, compared with an actual RAF loss of 34.

The Bomber Force

Horizontal Bombing Tactics

The tactics used during bombing attacks were governed by the nature of the target and the strength of its defences. For horizontal attacks, the *Lotfe* tachometric bomb sight was the standard type fitted to *Luftwaffe* multi-engined bombers during the war. To carry out an attack with this sight the aircraft had to fly a straight and level bombing run of about 40 seconds, at medium or high altitude. Alternatively the crew could attack from low level, in which case the pilot released the bombs 'by eye'.

Against the easiest targets—those lacking any form of defence—bombers could make accurate attacks from below 10,000 feet. In that case the aircraft would attack individually, making two or more deliberate runs and releasing the bombs only when the crews were satisfied they would hit the target. However, the *Luftwaffe* had few opportunities to carry out such attacks, and these became even fewer as the war progressed.

If there were strong anti-aircraft gun defences at a target, crews would make only one bombing run from high altitude, where they were less vulnerable to return fire. But this additional safety for the aircraft and crew was bought at some cost in bombing accuracy.

If attacks from enemy fighters were expected, the bombers flew in mutually protecting formations. If the latter were engaged by anti-aircraft fire, they would open out and the aircraft would follow their leaders as the latter flew a meandering course to prevent accurate predicted fire.

When a fighter escort was available, the latter cruised somewhat faster than the bomber formation. To maintain station on their charges, fighters assigned to close escort duties usually flew a weaving path to match the bombers' rate of advance. The fighters' comparatively short endurance meant that often the bombers had to fly the most direct route to the target. Whenever possible, the rendezvous point with the fighters was chosen so that a direct route from there to the target did not take the force through a major gun-defended area.

When the bombers reached the target, if crews had been briefed to make individual bomb runs, the formation would widen out slightly. This gave the individual planes room to make slight heading changes without getting in each other's way. Alternatively, the aircraft might deliver a pattern-bombing attack, in which the aircraft flew in close formation and all released their bombs when the leader was seen to release his. If specialist types of bomb were employed, these often determined the attack altitude. For example, armour-piercing bombs had to be released from high altitude or they would not attain sufficient velocity to punch their way into the target.

When the strength of enemy defences was such that daylight attacks might incur unacceptably heavy losses, the bombers would revert to night attacks. During its night attacks on Britain from the summer of 1940 until the late spring of 1941, the *Luftwaffe* employed the so-called 'Crocodile' tactic. This was the opposite of the 'bomber stream' in that aircraft flew very widely spaced. It was a tactic that was permissible only so long as the British night fighter and gun defences were relatively weak. Aircraft of the same *Gruppe* or *Geschwader* flew along the same route at about four-minute (12-mile) intervals. Sometimes units had orders to string out their attacks over a longer period, to cause disruption over as long a period as possible. On occasions, these night raids lasted from just after dusk until shortly before dawn.

Radio Beam Systems

At the outbreak of the war, only the *Luftwaffe* possessed radio systems to assist bomber crews to find targets at night or in bad weather. The simplest was code-named *Knickebein* (Bent Leg). This employed two radio beams, one to delineate the track to the target and a second which crossed the first over the target. The standard radio receiver used for airfield-approach signals also picked up the beam signals, so the aircraft did not need to carry special equipment to use the system. Using beams from *Knickebein* transmitters in Holland and France, the bombers could navigate with reasonable accuracy over central and southern England.

In July 1940, following the discovery of *Knickebein*, the RAF formed a countermeasures organisation to jam the German beam transmissions. As a means of masking the beam signals, the primitive British jamming was often ineffective. However, the jamming had an important secondary effect in showing that the defenders were fully aware of the presence of the beams. Fearing that British fighters might be patrolling the beams, German bomber crews became increasingly reluctant to use them. As a result, *Knickebein* fell into disuse over British territory.

Quite separate from *Knickebein*, the *Luftwaffe* introduced two electronic systems to aid bombing: the *X-Gerät* used by *Kampfgruppe 100*; and the *Y-Gerät* used by *III./Kampfgeschwader 26*. These systems were more accurate than *Knickebein*, but they were also more complex and they required special equipment in the aircraft.

On occasions the *Luftwaffe* used its precision beam attack units as pathfinders, to lead attacks and start fires at the target to guide the main force of bombers. For example, *Kampfgruppe 100* used these tactics during the large and destructive attack on Coventry on the night of 14/15 November 1940.

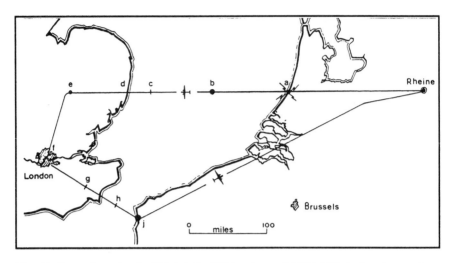

Fig. 10. Route flown by the Heinkel He 177 bombers of I./KG 100 *during the attack on London on the night of 18/19 April 1944.*

(a) *Radio Beacon Noordwijk, over which the German bomber force funnelled into the bomber stream.*

(b) *En-route fixing point, marked by six flame floats dropped into the sea by pathfinder aircraft.*

(c) *Position where aircraft commenced dropping* Düppel *radar reflective foil.*

(d) *Coast-in just north of Orfordness at altitudes around 17,000 feet.*

(e) *Turning point just east of Newmarket, marked by red parachute flares dropped by pathfinders.*

(f) *Just before reaching the target, the bombers commenced a descent and began to release* Düppel *at maximum rates. They levelled off for the bombing run, then resumed the descent after bomb release.*

(g) *During their withdrawal the bombers descended at about 000ft/min, making a high-speed dash for the coast.*

(h) *At mid-channel cease dropping* Düppel.

(j) *Cross French coast at altitudes around 2,500 feet.*

As in the case of *Knickebein*, the Royal Air Force soon learned of the existence of the bombing systems and introduced special equipment to jam them. Recent research has shown that, as with the earlier system, the British jamming had remarkably little direct effect.

In fact, compared with those in later years, the early German target-marking tactics were naïve in concept. About a dozen He 111s would attempt to mark a target by dropping canisters of 2.2lb, stick-shaped incendiary bombs. These weapons had poor ballistics, however, and when dropped from high altitude they scattered themselves over a wide area. Moreover, the bombers in the main force dropped the same weapons, so that even if the Pathfinders' marking was accurate its effect was quickly diluted. All in all, this was a poor way to mark targets for attack and it failed more often than it succeeded. (For comparison, during a major RAF night attack later in the war up to 80 Pathfinder aircraft might take part and these dropped specially developed marker bombs which produced distinctively coloured spot fires at the target or flares in the sky above it.)

Several sources ascribe the success of the attack on Coventry to the successful marking of the target by pathfinders. However, that attack occurred on a moonlit night with clear skies, and it is likely that the main force of bombers would have found the target without assistance.

From late 1942, the strengthening of the British defences forced the *Luftwaffe* to employed compact 'bomber stream' tactics similar to those used by the RAF. The raiders flew in a single concentrated wave and delivered their attack within the space of about an hour.

As an example of German night raiding tactics in the latter part of the war, let us observe those employed on the night of 18/19 April 1944. A force of about 125 bombers, Ju 88s, Ju 188s, He 177s, Do 217s and Me 410s, set out to attack London. After take-off the aircraft climbed to altitude and headed for the radio beacon at Noordwijk in Holland, where they formed into the 'bomber stream' and headed out over the North Sea. Off the coast of Suffolk, pathfinders dropped clusters of flame floats into the sea to provide a fixing point. The bombers crossed the coast just north of Orfordness, flying at their highest possible cruising altitudes. Twice per minute each bomber released *Düppel* radar reflective foil (the German equivalent of 'Window') in order to confuse defending radars.

East of Newmarket the raiders swung on to a south-westerly heading for London, that turning point being marked with clusters of red parachute flares. As each bomber approached the capital it began a shallow descent to increase speed, and the crew released *Düppel* at high rates to counter radar-laid anti-aircraft fire. For the bombing run the aircraft levelled out for as short a time as necessary to aim their bombs at more clusters of red flares laid by the pathfinders. After bomb release the attackers resumed their descent, heading south-east to cross the coast near Dungeness. During this dash for the safety, some of the bombers reached speeds in excess of 400 mph. Their high speeds, combined with the release of large amounts of *Düppel*, produced a difficult interception problem for RAF night fighter crews. Nevertheless, the *Luftwaffe* lost thirteen aircraft destroyed that night, or just over 10 per cent of the force committed.

Air-Launched Flying Bombs

The final part of the bomber offensive against Great Britain lasted from mid-1944 until early 1945, using Heinkel 111s modified to air-launch V.1 flying bombs. To avoid RAF night fighters, the bombers usually attacked during spells of poor weather and they approached over the North Sea at low altitude and at night. When it neared the previously briefed launch point, the Heinkel would commence a climb to 1,500 feet (the minimum safe altitude to release the missile). At the same time it accelerated to 200 mph (the speed necessary to sustain the running of the missile's pulse jet engine). Once the pulse jet was running it gushed flames that lit up the sky for miles around. As soon as possible after starting the pulse jet, therefore, the missile was launched. Then the bomber entered a steep turn and returned to low altitude, to get as far as possible from the missile before RAF night fighters arrived in the area.

Jet Bomber Attacks

Finally, mention should be made of the attack modes available to the jet-propelled Arado Ar 234, the most advanced bomber type to enter service with the *Luftwaffe*. A single-seater, this aircraft was designed to carry out three types of visual bombing attack: shallow-dive, low-altitude horizontal and high-altitude horizontal.

In action, the shallow-dive attack was the one most used. This began at around 13,000 feet with a descent at an angle of about 30 degrees. Sighting via the periscopic sight mounted in the roof of the cabin, the pilot released the bombs at about 6,500 feet (2,000 metres). During the low-altitude horizontal attack the pilot released his bombs 'by eye' as he flew low over the target.

The most interesting mode of bomb delivery was the high-altitude horizontal attack. The pilot would fly to a distinctive initial point about 20 miles from the target. Then he engaged the Patin autopilot, disconnected the control column and folded it away to his right and leaned forward over the *Lotfe* bomb sight mounted between his legs. The *Lotfe* controlled the automatic pilot via what would now be called an analogue computer. As the pilot adjusted the bomb sight to hold the sighting graticule over the target, he fed appropriate commands to the autopilot to 'fly' the aircraft on the required path. When it reached the release point the mechanism released the bombs automatically. After bomb release the pilot swung the control column back into position, switched out the autopilot and recovered manual control of the jet.

The Ar 234 could also carry out blind attacks using the *Egon* equipment, in which it was controlled throughout its bombing from a pair of *Freya* ground radar stations working together (*Egon* worked along similar lines to the British Oboe system).

The Dive-Bomber and Ground-Attack Forces

Dive-Bomber Tactics

Until the advent of air-to-surface guided weapons late in World War II, the steep diving attack was the most accurate means of delivering bombs on a defended target. For an air attack to be effective, accurate delivery of weapons was (and still is) essential. Obviously, if the bombs impacted too far from the target to cause it damage, the attack was a failure and the aircraft and their crews had been put at risk for nothing.

The blast force from an exploding bomb decreases rapidly as distance from detonation increases. Consider the typical effects the detonation of a 550lb bomb. If it scored a direct hit on a medium-sized building, it would knock down the entire structure. If it went off 20 yards away, the blast might blow down one or more walls. If the detonation was 40 yards from the building the latter would suffer serious but repairable damage. If the detonation was 80 yards from the building the latter might suffer only minor damage. The difference between those extremes was only 80 yards, less than the distance covered in one second by a bomber flying straight and level at 180 mph.

Despite valiant efforts to improve matters, during World War II the accuracy of bombing from horizontal bombers flying at high altitude by day was poor. Usually an attacking force had to drop a large number of bombs in order to get a small proportion of militarily useful hits. To carry the necessary bombs, the aircraft needed to be large and therefore relatively expensive.

The steep-diving attack offered a better solution. In a dive-bomber a well-trained pilot could place half his bombs inside a circle with a radius of 25 yards centred on the aiming point. (For a horizontal bomber, the circular error from a single bomb was two or three times greater.) The dive-bomber had to be strong enough to cope with the severe 'G' forces incurred during the pull-out, which limited its size and also its bomb load. Yet against pinpoint targets—and the majority of military targets were in that category—a relatively cheap dive-bomber releasing a small weight of bombs could inflict greater destruction on a target than a horizontal bomber dropping a far greater weight of bombs. That was the rationale for the dive-bomber.

In the *Luftwaffe*, the prime exponent of this method of attack was the Junkers Ju 87. This aircraft is often referred to as the 'Stuka', though the abbreviation of the German word *Sturzkampfflugzeug*, or dive-bomber, referred to all such aircraft and not any one particular type.

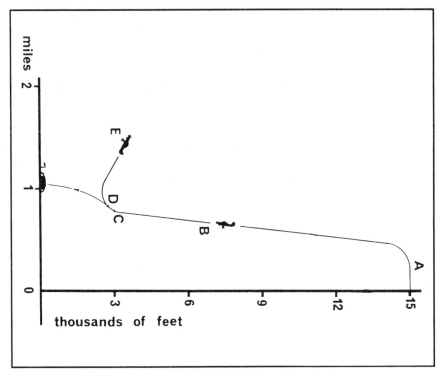

Fig. 11. A typical dive-bombing attack by a Junkers Ju 87.
(A) Aircraft enters dive in a bunt, in this example from 15,000 feet.
(B) Dive angle 80° and maximum speed reached in the dive about 350 mph.
(C) When the aircraft reaches the previously briefed pull-out altitude, about 30 seconds
  after commencing the dive, the pilot presses a button on his control column which initiates
  the automatic pull-out system.
(D) As the aircraft's nose begins to rise, the bomb is released automatically.
(E) After the pull-out the pilot regains control of the aircraft, retracts the dive brakes, opens
  the throttle and climbs away.

To show the nature of the tactics used, let us observe a typical diving attack by Ju 87s. Depending on the size and importance of the target, the attacking force might comprise a *Staffel* or a *Gruppe*. The aircraft flew in three-plane *Ketten* (V-formation), the *Ketten* being in line astern with about 300 yards between each. The dive-bombers usually cruised at speeds around 160 mph and at altitudes between 5,000 and 11,000 feet.

For accuracy it was important that during their attack dives the aircraft headed into wind. Their route was chosen so that the final approach to the target was made flying into the forecast wind. As he neared the target, the formation leader would look for rising smoke or other clues to confirm that the briefed wind direction was correct. If necessary, he would realign the attack to correct for a change in wind direction.

Just in front of his seat, set into the cockpit floor of the Ju 87, the pilot had a window through which he could observe the target sliding beneath his aircraft. When he judged he was over the target, he pulled a lever to rotate the underwing dive brakes to the maximum-drag position. This would cause a severe nose-up trim change, so to compensate for it and hold the aircraft level an extra trim tab lowered automatically beneath the elevator.

The formation leader commenced his attack dive and the rest of the aircraft followed. For attacks on small targets, for example bridges or individual buildings, Ju 87s usually approached in line astern. Against larger targets, for example harbours or marshalling yards, the dive-bombers usually bunted into the dive as a three-aircraft *Kette*, which delivered their attacks in unison.

The Ju 87 had been designed without compromise as a dive-bomber, and once established in its 80-degree dive it was extremely stable. It was a simple matter for the pilot to centre his reflector sight on the target and hold it there. Restrained by the drag from the fixed undercarriage and the dive brakes, the aircraft built up speed slowly: it took a dive through about 8,000 feet before it reached its terminal velocity of 350 mph.

When the aircraft passed a pre-set point, typically 4,300 feet (about 1,300 metres) above the ground, the altimeter sounded a warning horn in the cockpit. When the aircraft reached the previously set bomb-release altitude, typically 2,300 feet (700 m), the horn ceased. That was the signal for the pilot to release the bombs.

It will be remembered that when the pilot moved the dive brakes to the high-drag position before the start of the dive, an elevator trim tab had lowered to compensate for the nose-up pitching moment. When the pilot pressed the bomb release, a powerful spring snapped the tab back into the neutral position. The nose-up trim change now took effect to pull the aircraft firmly, smoothly and automatically out of its dive. As the nose of the dive-bomber rose above the horizontal, the pilot returned the dive brakes to the low-drag position and turned on to his escape heading.

Dive-bombing was the most efficient method of attacking bridges, small military objectives and rail targets. It was also effective against soft-skinned vehicles which were vulnerable to blast and splinter damage. Dive-bombing was not accurate enough to be effective against well-armoured tanks, however, which required a direct hit or a very near miss in order to put them out of action.

Published accounts often speak of 'close air support' missions flown by Ju 87s during the *Blitzkrieg* campaigns early in the war. Most of these authors are ignorant of the true nature of this type of operation, however. Close air support operations are those mounted against targets in the battle area and in close proximity to friendly forces. To make an accurate dive-bombing attack it was necessary to be able to discern the target from an altitude of at least 5,000 feet (nearly a mile high) before commencing the dive. Unless the enemy positions were clearly defined (for example on one side of a river line), or accurately marked with coloured smoke (a technique employed later in the war), identification was often difficult. There was always a risk that bombs might fall on the very troops they were supposed to assist. In truth, for most of the time the dive-bomber's objectives were well behind the battle area—what would now be termed 'battlefield air interdiction targets'.

There was one other type of target against which dive-bombing was particularly effective—shipping. It offered a greater chance of scoring hits than any other method. When engaging a warship manoeuvring in open water, a Ju 87 pilot could often hold his sight over a ship making a hard evasive turn. After release, the bomb's short flight of about five seconds left no time for any subsequent helm change to take effect.

Nemesis for the *'Stuka'*

Germany's enemies quickly came to appreciate the danger posed by the Ju 87s that were able to operate freely. The weapon primarily responsible for ending the dive-bombers' run of successes was the fast-firing medium-calibre AA gun, typified by the 40mm Bofors used by British forces. This weapon fired 2lb shells at a rate of 120 per minute. Viewed from a gun position close to the target, a steep-diving Ju 87 appeared to hang stationary in space. That gave the gunners an easy zero-deflection shot. The Bofors gun was accurate up to 10,000 feet, and a hit from just one of its impact-fused high-explosive shells anywhere on the structure of the Ju 87 was usually sufficient to knock the plane out of control.

From the mid-war period there were few high-value targets within Ju 87 range that lacked effective gun protection. The steep-diving attack became expensive in terms of aircraft and crews, and the Ju 87s were forced to resort to shallow-dive or low-altitude attacks. The latter were less risky, but they were also far less effective.

In the autumn of 1943 the *Sturzkampfgeschwader* (dive-bomber *Geschwader*) were renamed *Schlachtgeschwader* (ground-attack units) and a programme began to re-equip them with fighter-bomber versions of the Fw 190. By the summer of 1944 the Ju 87 was rarely used in its original dive-bombing role.

Ground-Attack Tactics

In the context of this section, the term 'ground attack' embraces low-level and shallow-dive attacks on tactical ground targets close to the battlefield and in enemy rear areas.

Early in the war the *Luftwaffe* possessed only one specialised ground attack type, the Henschel Hs 123. The rugged biplane had a built-in armament of two 7.9mm machine guns and it could carry two 20mm cannon pods, or

440lb of bombs, on racks under the wings. The Hs 123 was used to make low-altitude strafing and bombing attacks in or behind the battle area.

During 1940 the *Luftwaffe* experimented with the use of Bf 109s and Bf 110s in the fighter-bomber role. During low-altitude horizontal attacks it was found that these aircraft could plant bombs on the ground with considerable accuracy. However, if the bombs exploded on impact there was a high risk that the aircraft would incur blast and splinter damage. To give the aircraft time to get clear it was necessary to fit delay fuses to detonate the bombs up to 10 seconds after impact. That raised a further problem, however. Unless the target were sufficiently bulky to stop the bombs hurled into it, and tall enough to catch any that landed short and bounded high on the first impact, the bombs were likely to travel considerable distances across the ground. During an instrumented trial carried out by the RAF, a series of inert 250-pounders were released from fighter-bombers flying at 60 feet altitude at 300 mph. In some cases, following their initial impact with the ground, bombs bounced twice has high as the releasing aircraft; and, tumbling end over end as they bounded across the ground, some bombs came to rest more than half a mile from the initial impact point. Undoubtedly *Luftwaffe* fighter-bomber pilots would have had similar experiences when dropping normal types of bombs.

To overcome these problems the *Luftwaffe* developed a special new bomb for use in low-altitude attacks—the SD 2 (nicknamed the 'Butterfly Bomb' by the Allies), weighing 4.4lb. A cylindrical weapon about the size of a half-pint beer tin, it was carried in large numbers in special containers fixed to the attacking planes. A Bf 109 or a Ju 87 could carried 96; a Ju 88 or a Do 17 could carry 360. After release the SD 2 casing opened to form a pair of 'wings' which killed its forward speed. Then the weapon spun to the ground, falling almost vertically like a sycamore seed. The 7oz explosive charge detonated on impact, hurling out high-velocity fragments. Because the 'wings' slowed the bombs so rapidly, and the explosive charge was so small, there was no risk of the aircraft incurring blast or splinter damage.

SD 2s were first used in large numbers during the initial stages of the attack on the Soviet Union, and proved highly effective. Later, instead of being released individually, the small bombs were dropped in special containers which opened when clear of the aircraft. Thus these bombs could be released from a higher altitude during a dive or a shallow-dive attack, making aircraft less vulnerable to ground fire. The SD 2s would hit the ground in a near-circular pattern, producing a significant area effect. This was the first cluster-type weapon to be used on a large scale.

Heavy Cannon versus Tanks

During the mid-war period the *Luftwaffe* introduced special anti-tank aircraft fitted with heavy cannon. In this role the Ju 87 carried two 3.7cm Flak

18 cannon, modified anti-aircraft guns. The twin-engined Henschel Hs 129 carried one 3cm cannon, later a 3.7cm and finally a 7.5cm weapon. In each case these guns fired solid-shot, armour-piercing rounds. In the case of the 3cm and 3.7cm weapons, pilots had to aim at the thinner armour on the sides and rear of the tank to achieve a penetration. The attacks required the aircraft to close to within 200 yards of the target vehicle, flying at low altitude. This proved a hazardous procedure, particularly if the tanks had protection from anti-aircraft guns. A few pilots secured good results against tanks, but many others were killed before they could achieve anything. Moreover, the weight and drag of the gun installations imposed a severe performance penalty which made these aircraft vulnerable to fighter attack.

Late War Fighter-Bombers

From the beginning of 1944, ground-attack versions of the Focke Wulf 190 bore the brunt of the *Luftwaffe* operations in this role. These aircraft strafed targets with their 20mm cannon and 13mm machine guns. They also carried bombs ranging in size between 110 and 3,700lb, as well as several different types of cluster bomb. Finally, during the closing stages of the war, some of these aircraft employed *Panzerschreck* and *Panzerblitz* rocket projectiles in attacks on ground targets.

During the final year of the war *KG 51* operated Messerschmitt 262s in the fighter-bomber role. The jet plane's high speed enabled it to operate over areas where the enemy held air superiority. Nevertheless, initially, in order to reduce the risk of capture, pilots of the secret aircraft had strict orders not to fly below 4,000 metres (about 13,000 feet) over enemy territory. This limitation made it almost impossible to find and hit small military targets. Later the order was rescinded, and Me 262s usually attacked in 30-degree dives starting from about 15,000 feet and releasing the bombs at about 3,000 feet. The aircraft's usual war load was one SC 500 or two SC 250 bombs. The Me 262 also carried two 30mm cannon, but these low-velocity weapons were designed for air-to-air use and they were not very effective for strafing ground targets.

Night Ground-Attack Operations

Following the successful German *Blitzkrieg* campaign in the east in the summer of 1941, the Soviet Air Force was virtually driven from the skies by day. Its only chance of striking back was at night, and it sent modified Polikarpov Po-2 biplane trainers to carry out nocturnal nuisance raids over the German rear areas. The slow, low-flying, relatively quiet Po-2s fanned out singly over enemy territory, bombing or strafing any lights or other signs of activity seen on the ground. The nuisance raids achieved a degree of disruption out of all proportion to the direct damage they inflicted, or the numbers of aircraft involved. The threat of these attacks forced road vehicles to run on dimmed lights or none at all, obliging them to be driven at a snail's pace to avoid colliding with each other, running off the road or hitting troops moving on foot.

In the autumn of 1942 the *Luftwaffe* decided to imitate these tactics. After all, in areas where that service held air superiority, the Soviet Army conducted the majority of troop movements by night. As an operational experiment the four *Luftflotten* on the Eastern Front each formed a *Behelfskampfstaffel* (auxiliary bomber *Staffel*) operating two-seat biplane trainers like the Arado Ar 66 and Gotha Go 145 modified to carry machine guns and racks for small bombs.

The German initial operations were judged successful, and after a few weeks the units were renamed *Störkampfstaffeln* (harassment bomber *Staffeln*). By the beginning of 1943 there were about a dozen such *Staffeln*, operating some 200 aircraft. These units became an integral part of the *Luftwaffe* and in the following October they were renamed *Nachtschlachtgruppen* (night ground attack *Gruppen*). As Ju 87s were replaced in daylight ground-attack units, many of them went to the night attack units which operated with these and other available types until the end of the war.

The Anti-Shipping Forces

Early War Attacks

To an even greater extent than other types of offensive air operation, anti-shipping tactics were dictated by the type of weapon used. During the early war period, dive-bombers attacked ships at sea using tactics similar to those used against land targets. This worked well, so long as military necessity forced Allied shipping to operate in areas within easy reach of German-held airfields. From bitter experience, the Allied navies quickly learnt the need to give such airfields as wide a berth as possible. On the German side, the need to deliver anti-shipping attacks progressively further out to sea dictated the use of longer-ranging, and therefore larger, aircraft types. Such aircraft were too large for steep-diving attacks. Horizontal bombing attacks from medium or high altitude, using conventional types of bomb against ships manoeuvring in open water, had little success.

At the outbreak of World War II the *Luftwaffe* possessed no bomber type able to carry out attacks on ships more than 600 miles from its base. To remedy this deficiency, the four-engined Focke Wulf Fw 200 *Kondor* airliner was hastily modified to serve as a maritime patrol aircraft. Carrying up to five SC 250 bombs, the *Kondor* had an effective radius of action of nearly 1,000 miles. During 1940 and 1941 these aircraft carried out regular armed-reconnaissance missions between Bordeaux/Mérignac in France and Stavanger/Sola in Norway.

The Focke Wulfs flew a wide arc into the Atlantic, keeping well clear of the British Isles, and attacked any ships they encountered on their way. At that time the Royal Navy was desperately short of escort vessels and convoys often sailed with a bare minimum of protection. As a result the marauding planes achieved a degree of success far beyond their limited numbers or the Fw 200's intrinsic quality as a bomber. The converted airliners made deliberate attacks on individual ships, flying at just above mast-level. The pilots released the bombs 'by eye' and, from that altitude, had a good chance of achieving one or two hits with a stick of five bombs. The merchantmen were almost defenceless against such attacks and several were sunk or damaged.

For the Focke Wulf crews it was too good to last, and it did not. Merchantmen began to carry a makeshift collection of short-range weapons, while the numbers of escorting warships rose steadily. Life for the attackers became increasingly hazardous and losses began to rise. In the end the *Kondore* were forced to cease attacking convoys, and restricted their activities to the pure maritime reconnaissance role.

The Torpedo Bomber Force

A further deficiency in the armoury of the *Luftwaffe* at the beginning of the war was the lack of an effective aerial torpedo or a modern aircraft type able to carry it. The torpedo in service was the ineffective LTF 5 and the principal launching aircraft was the obsolescent Heinkel He 59, a twin-engined, float-equipped biplane. Early in the war the more effective Heinkel He 115 floatplane started to replace the He 59 in front-line units, but still the force lacked an effective torpedo.

Only in the spring of 1942 did the *Luftwaffe* start to field a fully effective torpedo attack force. Then *Kampfgeschwader 26* became operational with the H-6 version of the Heinkel He 111 modified to carry the F5B, a torpedo developed from an Italian Whitehead design. The weapon weighed 1,686lb (764kg), of which 440lb (200kg) comprised the warhead.

By far the most successful torpedo attack by the *Luftwaffe* took place on 13 September 1942, when some forty He 111s attacked convoy PQ.18 off the north coast of Norway. The convoy was shadowed by Blohm und Voss Bv 138 flying boats, and at a previously briefed time one of these began to radiate homing signals to guide in the Heinkels. To maintain the element of surprise for as long as possible, the attackers ran it at 150 feet, flying at their most economical cruising speed of 165 mph. The Heinkels flew in loose vics of between six and ten aircraft, with some two miles between succeeding vics.

As they prepared to commence their attack runs, the torpedo bombers opened out into line abreast formation with about 300 yards between aircraft. Each crew selected a ship to attack and increased speed to 170 mph. Released at that speed and altitude, the F5B would hit the water at its optimum entry angle of 12 degrees. If the torpedo were released from a greater altitude or a lower speed, it was liable to 'nose-dive' into the water and it might go too deep to recover; released from a lower altitude or at a much greater speed, it was liable to 'belly flop' and might suffer damage to its internal mechanism. Each He 111 carried two torpedoes, which were usually released in succession and aimed at the same ship. The optimum release range for the F5B was 1,000 yards from the target ship. The torpedo covered about 250 yards during its air flight of 3 seconds, and running at 33 knots it took about 14 seconds to cover the remainder of the distance. The weapon's minimum effective range, allowing it time to complete its air flight, arm itself and settle in its run, was about 650 yards

By the time it had released its second torpedo, the aircraft was usually within about half a mile from the target ship and by then it was too late to turn away. The most common escape manoeuvre was therefore to accelerate going straight ahead, running past the convoy and keeping as low as possible.

Usually an aircraft would not commence evasive jinking until the last ship in the convoy was behind it.

The attack on PQ.18 sank seven Allied merchant vessels. All of the aircraft regained their bases in Norway, though six had suffered major damage. In later actions the torpedo bombers sank three more merchant ships.

Following this convoy action the German torpedo bomber force was able to achieve little. With the introduction of more and more escort carriers, the Allied navies had sufficient vessels to provide effective fighter cover for any convoy that needed to sail through waters where there was risk of air attack.

New Guided Missiles

Soon after the start of the war German engineers had begun working on new types of anti-shipping weapon to replace the air-launched torpedo. By the summer of 1943 two separate types of anti-shipping guided missile were ready

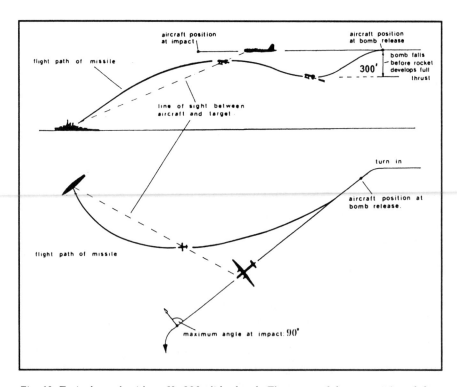

Fig. 12. Typical attack with an Hs 293 glider bomb. The range of the parent aircraft from the target at missile release varied between 4,000 and 20,000 yards, giving a time of flight for the missile of between 30 and 110 seconds. During the final part of its flight the observer in the aircraft guided the flare in the missile so that it remained superimposed over the target. He held it there until the missile impacted.

for action—the Henschel Hs 293 glider bomb and the Ruhrstahl Fritz-X guided bomb.

The Henschel Hs 293 resembled a small aeroplane with a wing span of just over 10 feet and carried a warhead of 1,100lb. After release from the parent aircraft, a liquid-fuel rocket motor mounted under the missile accelerated the weapon to a speed of about 370 mph in 12 seconds. Then the rocket motor cut out and the missile coasted towards the target in a shallow dive, slowly bleeding off its speed. The effective range of the weapon depended on its release altitude. Typically, released from 4,500 feet, the Hs 293 had an effective range of about five miles. In the tail of the missile was a bright flare to enable the observer in the parent aircraft to follow its progress in flight. Using a small joy-stick controller, he transmitted the appropriate left/right, up/down signals to the missile. The Hs 293 was a command-to-line-of-sight missile, and the observer steered the tracking flare until it appeared to be superimposed over the target. He then applied corrections to hold it there throughout the remainder of its flight. The Hs 293 had relatively little penetrative ability and was used principally against merchant ships and unarmoured warships.

The second of the two new weapons, the Fritz-X guided bomb, employed a radio control system similar to that fitted to the Hs 293. However, in all other respects it was a radically different weapon. Intended for use against armoured warships, the 3,100lb Fritz-X resembled an ordinary free-fall bomb with four stub-wings set in cruciform mid-way along its body. The weapon was unpowered. After release from an altitude between 16,000 and 21,000 feet, it accelerated to a speed of around 600 mph to give it sufficient momentum to penetrate a warship's armour. The aircraft's observer aimed the Fritz-X in the same way as a normal bomb, using the standard *Lotfe* bomb sight. Immediately after bomb release the pilot throttled back his engines, climbed the aircraft through 1,000 feet and then levelled off. This manoeuvre reduced the plane's speed rapidly from 290 to 165 mph, and at the end of it the observer was in position to look straight down the final part of the bomb's trajectory as it sped towards the target. As in the case of the Hs 293, the observer steered the tracking flare to hold it over the target until the missile impacted.

When carrying the new guided missiles, aircraft could deliver attacks on shipping with greater accuracy and with less risk to themselves than when using torpedoes. However, the mounting scale of fighter cover meant that even now the German bombers were unable to attack Allied shipping with impunity. The launching aircraft had to approach its target at medium or high altitude. When either type of missile was in flight, the aircraft had to fly a predictable path and that made it vulnerable to fighter attack. If the launching aircraft turned to avoid attack while its missile was in flight, the latter had to be abandoned.

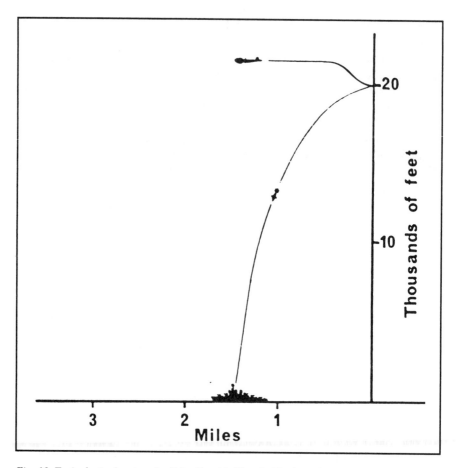

Fig. 13. Typical attack using the Fritz-X guided bomb. The launching aircraft delivered the weapon from an altitude of 20,000 feet or above, to give it sufficient velocity to pierce the armoured deck of a large warship. The observer aimed the weapon in the normal way, using the Lotfe 7 *bomb sight. After release of the guided bomb, the pilot throttled back the engines and climbed the aircraft through 1,000 feet. He thus reduced speed rapidly, which enabled him to hold the aircraft over the bomb's line of trajectory. During the final part of the bomb's fall the observer guided the tracking flare so that it was superimposed on the target, until the weapon impacted.*

The Hs 293 and the Fritz-X both achieved some spectacular successes in the weeks following their introduction. Within a short time, however, the Allied navies had taken the measure of these new threats. The fighter defences were strengthened still further and thereafter the guided missile units went the same way as the rest of the *Luftwaffe* anti-shipping force, and were able to achieve little.

Airborne Assault Operations

General

Airborne assault operations are those where the troops travel by air, and are dropped or landed ready to go into action within a short time of their arrival. Early in World War II the *Luftwaffe* pioneered each of the three methods of delivering an airborne assault—from transport aircraft landing beside the objective, by parachute drop and by landing in gliders. In the German armed services all parachute and glider-borne assault troops belonged to the *Luftwaffe*. Lightly armed army units, for example mountain troops, could be delivered by transport aircraft.

Once the airborne troops reached the ground they functioned as light infantry with no heavy supporting weapons. Although their carrying aircraft gave them a very high degree of strategic mobility, once the men were on the ground the lack of vehicles rendered them almost immobile.

Air Landing Operations

In an air landing operation the troops were carried aboard transport planes which landed in areas that had yet to be cleared of the enemy. This method gave several advantages. The troops taking part did not require any special training, and they and their weapons arrived together and ready for action immediately after leaving their aircraft. Moreover, the transport planes could carry somewhat larger and heavier loads than could be delivered by parachute. The sole, and as it turned out the overriding, disadvantage of this method was the heavy risk incurred by the transport aircraft.

The first and only large-scale opposed air landing assault operation took place on 10 May 1940. That morning, to support the advance of German troops moving into Holland and Belgium, Junkers Ju 52s transported the 22nd Infantry Division to seize positions around The Hague. Simultaneously, other Ju 52s dropped paratroops and towed gliders with troops to seize key points. These landings caused considerable disruption to the defences, but in several cases aircraft landed on airfields that were under artillery fire. For example, at Ypenburg the paratroops came down some distance from the airfield. The Ju 52s carrying the follow-up units arrived before the airfield had been secured, and as they landed they were raked by enemy fire. As a result, 11 of the 13 transport planes were destroyed and the troops on board suffered heavy casualties.

On the first day of the campaign the German air transport units reported the loss of about 160 aircraft, more than one-third of their strength. A few of these were shot down or strafed on the ground by Dutch fighters, but the majority were hit by machine-gun or artillery fire from the ground.

In an interesting variation of the air landing tactic, a dozen obsolete Heinkel He 59 seaplanes alighted on the Nieuwe Maas river at Rotterdam and landed 120 troops to seize two important bridges there. Four of these aircraft were destroyed after their troops had disembarked.

After any battle the victor has the great advantage of possession of the battlefield. Following the victorious conclusion of the campaign in Holland, the *Luftwaffe* found that it was possible to salvage many of the Ju 52s littering the countryside. Of the transports initially recorded as lost, 53 were recovered in a repairable state and another 47 yielded usable components.

Parachute Operations

Compared with an air landing operation, a parachute operation can put down troops in an unsecured area with far less risk to the transporting aircraft. On the other hand, as mentioned above, the weight of supplies or munitions an aircraft could drop by parachute was considerably smaller than that which it could deliver if it landed. Furthermore, there was the ever-present risk that troops delivered by parachute would arrive scattered over a wide area.

The Ju 52 could carry a dozen paratroops, so a *Staffel* of twelve aircraft was necessary to lift a *Kompanie* of 144 men. As they approached the dropping zone the Ju 52s would be flying in three-plane vics about 60 yards apart, at 100 mph and at an altitude of 400 feet. On the signal to jump the troops leapt from the door on the port side at one-second intervals. A static line attached to the aircraft caused the parachute to open fully before the man had fallen 90 feet. From there it took him about 20 seconds to reach the ground.

Up to and including the attack on Crete in the spring of 1941, when a man landed by parachute he was *not* ready to go into action immediately. Normally his only firearm was a 9mm Luger pistol, although he would sometimes be equipped with hand grenades. The paratroops' main weapons—rifles, machine guns, anti-tank rifles and small mortars—were carried in four containers mounted under the aircraft. These containers were released and fell by parachute at the same time as the men, and were brightly coloured for ease of identification on the ground. Only after the men had recovered their weapons were they fully ready to go into action.

During the landings in Crete some units suffered heavy losses trying to recover their weapons. Once the defenders had realised the importance of the brightly coloured containers, they concentrated their fire on any man seen trying to reach them. Later in the war the *Luftwaffe* would develop a technique for dropping the men together with their personal weapons.

Once the dropping zone had been secured, aircraft could drop heavier weapons using clusters of two or more parachutes. The 2.8cm anti-tank rifle, the 2cm anti-tank/anti-aircraft cannon and the 7.5cm light gun could all be delivered in this way.

Glider Operations

Glider operations combined the advantages of air landing and parachute operations. The troops arrived in a concentrated force and were ready for action immediately on leaving their glider. Since the gliders were regarded as expendable, they could land on terrain that was too rugged for a normal aircraft to use. Gliders were particularly useful vehicles for *coup de main* missions, because they could make a long, silent approach to arrive by surprise at their objective. The DFS 230, the only glider type used by the *Luftwaffe* during airborne assault operations, could safely reach a landing zone 15 miles away if released from 5,000 feet.

During *Luftwaffe* glider operations the tugs were nearly always Ju 52s. Such aircraft could also carry small payloads, and were sometimes used to create a diversion after they had released their gliders. During the attack on Belgium, for example, the tugs flew some distance away and dropped dummy paratroops to confuse the defenders.

With a glider in tow on the end of a 400-foot line, a Ju 52 normally cruised at 110 mph. After it was released, the DFS 230 had an optimum gliding speed of 70 mph and it landed at about 40 mph. Typical loads carried by DFS 230, in addition to the pilot (who was a trained infantryman), were as follows:

> 4 riflemen
> 1 machine gun, with crew of three and
>   2,200 rounds of ammunition
> 1 handcart
> 3,000 rounds of rifle ammunition
> 1 box hollow charge anti-tank grenades
> **Total 2,350 lb**

> 9 riflemen
> 1 field radio
> 3,000 rounds of rifle ammunition
> **Total 2,200 lb**

> 1 mortar with crew of 5 and 10 boxes
>   of mortar bombs
> 2 riflemen
> 1 handcart
> **Total 2,100 lb**

Reconnaissance Operations

Tactical Reconnaissance Operations

At the outbreak of World War II the *Luftwaffe* possessed a total of thirty short-range reconnaissance *Staffeln*. One such *Staffel* was assigned to each Army Corps, for tactical reconnaissance and to conduct target spotting for the artillery.

At that time most *Staffeln* were equipped with three Heinkel He 45s and six He 46s, and held a further three He 46s in reserve. Both types had entered service in 1934 and by the start of the war they were obsolescent. These two-seaters lacked armour protection, which made them vulnerable to battle damage, and were not equipped for bad-weather or night operations. In the conditions of air supremacy achieved by the *Luftwaffe* over Poland, however, these outdated machines were perfectly well able to perform their tasks.

The Henschel Hs 126 entered service in 1938 and had started to replace the He 45 and He 46. At the outbreak the war only a few *Staffeln* had converted, however. The performance of the new high-winged monoplane was markedly superior to that of its predecessors and it carried armour protection for the fuel tank and the crew. It was equipped to operate in bad weather or at night, and, in contrast to the earlier fabric-covered types, the all-metal Hs 126 did not require a protective shelter against the weather. By the spring of 1940 almost the whole of the force had re-equipped with the Hs 126 and the type served effectively during the campaigns in the west and in the Balkans.

The next type to enter service, the twin-engined Focke Wulf Fw 189, became available at the end of 1940. Although it was no faster than the Hs 126, it was a considerable improvement over the earlier machine in almost every other respect. It carried a third crew member, a gunner, to cover the all-important rear hemisphere. That freed the observer from this chore and allowed him to concentrate on the main task of the mission. He sat in the nose beside the pilot, rather than behind him as in previous types, allowing for a high degree of cooperation between the two men. The twin-boomed layout of the Fw 189, together with the extensive glazing around the cabin, provided the pilot and the observer with an excellent field of view of the ground below and to the sides of the aircraft.

At the beginning of the attack on the Soviet Union in 1941 there were 36 tactical reconnaissance *Staffeln*, each with seven aircraft. In addition there were twenty *Staffeln*, each with six aircraft, assigned to support major armoured units conducting mobile operations. Although a few Fw 189s were available at that time, most units continued to operate Hs 126s. During the period of intensive fighting following the start of the campaign in the east, tactical reconnaissance units suffered particularly heavy losses. At the end of 1941, when the severe winter halted operations, the force had been reduced to a low ebb.

When large-scale land operations resumed on the Eastern Front, in the spring of 1942, the force had recovered much of its former strength. The Fw 189 was now in large-scale service and for most of that year it fulfilled well the roles assigned to it. From the beginning of 1943, however, the Soviet fighter force gradually became more effective. The Fw 189's lack of speed made it increasingly vulnerable during daytime operations, and except in quiet areas the type was gradually relegated to the night role.

Because it had enjoyed air superiority over most of the battle fronts for so long, the *Luftwaffe* was relatively late in introducing single-seater fighter types converted for the tactical reconnaissance role. Only in the summer of 1943 did Messerschmitt Bf 109Gs and Focke Wulf 190As modified in this way become available in reasonable numbers. Moreover, the modified fighters carried only vertically mounted cameras (in contrast to their Allied counterparts, which carried both vertical and oblique cameras, the latter for taking close-ups and for photography from below a low cloud base).

Usually the single-seaters operated in pairs, with one pilot navigating and conducting the reconnaissance while the other maintained a watch for enemy fighters. If the reconnaissance was to be flown in an area where strong enemy fighter activity could be expected, sometimes a fighter escort would be provided. Most often, however, the reconnaissance aircraft received no such protection and if they were harassed by enemy fighters they had to break off their mission prematurely.

Strategic Reconnaissance Operations

At the start of the war the Dornier Do 17P equipped most long-range reconnaissance *Staffeln*. Over Poland and during the campaign in the west this twin-engined aircraft rendered excellent service. The *Luftwaffe* assigned ten long-range reconnaissance *Staffeln* to the Army, one for each Army Group and one to each field Army. In 1940 the Junkers Ju 88 became available for this role and it quickly became the most-used long-range reconnaissance type.

The *Aufklärungsgruppe der Oberkommando der Luftwaffe*, a unit under the direct control of the *Luftwaffe* High Command, operated a wide range of specialised reconnaissance types. One of the most impressive was the Junkers Ju 86P, an twin-engined, ultra-high-altitude aircraft powered by turbo-supercharged diesel engines. To allow lengthy flights at high altitude, there was a pressurised cabin for the two crewmen. The Ju 86P overflew targets at alti-

tudes above 35,000 feet, where it was almost immune from fighter interception during the early war years. However, this aircraft had was difficult to
keep serviceable and as a result its sortie rates were low.

Night Reconnaissance Operations

Shortly before the invasion of the USSR the *Luftwaffe* formed three night
reconnaissance *Staffeln*, each equipped with nine Dornier Do 17Z aircraft.
One such *Staffel* was assigned to each of the three Army Groups taking part
in the campaign.

During a night mission the aircraft flew over the target area at medium
altitude, the shutters of its cameras set initially in the open position. At measured intervals (typically 10-second) the aircraft released a line of (typically)
five photo-flash bombs set to ignite at about 4,000 feet above the ground.
When the first bomb ignited it produced a flash of 6,000,000 candlepower
lasting one-third of a second. The flash illuminated the ground, and also
triggered photo-electric cells which closed the camera shutters, wound the
film in each to the next frame and reopened the shutters. When the second
flash bomb ignited, this process was repeated until the final flash bomb ignited and the run was complete.

Night photographs gave far less detail than those taken by day. However,
this method was extremely useful for detecting night movements of enemy
troops, equipment and supplies on routes leading to the battle area.

As the war progressed, the gradual loss of air superiority and the growing
interference from enemy fighters made daylight missions hazardous. As a
result the *Luftwaffe* was forced to place progressively greater reliance on night
missions. What had started as a useful but limited tactical expedient became
for a long period the only available method for gaining an insight into troop
dispositions and movements in enemy-held territory.

The Do 17Zs performed this role for several months until they were replaced by higher-performance Dornier Do 217s, Ju 188s and Me 410s.

Jet Reconnaissance Operations

Following the invasion of Normandy in June 1944, the omnipresent Allied
fighter patrols made daytime reconnaissance a dangerous and costly business. Night missions were less vulnerable to fighter attack but, as has been
mentioned, these could give only patchy information. For German army commanders this lack of intelligence on Allied dispositions and movements was a
severe handicap. Often their first inkling that a major Allied thrust was in the
offing was the noise of the preparatory artillery bombardment and reports of
tanks heard or seen approaching the forward positions.

To overcome this deficiency two Arado Ar 234 jet reconnaissance aircraft
from the pre-production batch were sent to operate over France. The first-
ever jet reconnaissance mission took place on 2 August 1944 and lasted 90

minutes. Cruising at 460 mph and at 34,000 feet, and untroubled by Allied fighters, the aircraft systematically photographed the beachhead area. That single mission achieved more than the entire German reconnaissance force in the west had done in the previous eight weeks. The Arado returned with 380 sharp pictures covering almost the entire Allied lodgement area in Normandy. It took a twelve-man team of photo interpreters, working flat-out, more than two days to produce an initial assessment of what was found. By that time the Allies had landed more than 1½ million men and 300,000 vehicles, so there was plenty to see. The more detailed examination of the prints took several weeks.

During the next three weeks the two jet planes flew a total of thirteen further missions. During one of these, an Arado photographed the entire south coast of England, between Bornemouth and Dungeness, from 36,000 feet.

The Ar 234s ranged at will over Allied territory, restoring a capability long denied to the *Luftwaffe* in the west. Ironically, just as the German Army started to receive a detailed picture of the Allied rear areas, it was almost too late to exploit the new-found source of intelligence. Early in August the German Army's defensive line in Normandy collapsed and it began a headlong retreat from France. The jets merely provided a clear picture of a battle that was already lost.

Later that year four Ar 234s carried out a systematic coverage of Allied troop positions in eastern France. The jets often overflew the hilly Ardennes area during their outbound and homeward flights, their cameras running during each such flight. About half a dozen Me 262 jets fitted with cameras also photographed that area. The resultant pictures were used to construct highly detailed photo-mosaics, which proved invaluable in planning of the German Army's all-out offensive which was to open in December. When that offensive began, the rapid initial advances were due in large measure to the accurate intelligence on Allied defences gleaned from these photographs.

Only about forty Ar 234s and Me 262s were delivered to front-line reconnaissance units. However, in this role a relatively small number of capable machines can achieve extremely important results—as was the case in this instance.

Luftwaffe War Diaries

During the final days before the German collapse the *Luftwaffe* High Command ordered the destruction of unit war diaries to prevent their capture. In general the order was obeyed, and of those that escaped destruction by the Germans and fell into Allied hands, many were subsequently destroyed by people who had no regard for their historical value. Only a few sections of unit war diaries have survived, and in this chapter some of these have been translated, to give the reader an idea of the wealth of detail that has been lost. To cover a wide spread of operations, this author has selected excerpts from the war diaries of several different types of unit: a dive-bomber *Gruppe* during the attack on Poland; a fighter *Gruppe* during the Battle of Britain; a twin-engined fighter *Gruppe* which fought against US heavy bombers attacking Germany; a night fighter *Geschwader* which fought against RAF bombers attacking Germany; a ground-attack *Gruppe* which took part in the Battle of Normandy; and a jet bomber *Gruppe* during the latter part of the war.

★ ★ ★

I. Gruppe Sturzkampfgeschwader 1, September 1939

At the beginning of the campaign in Poland in September 1939 this dive-bomber *Gruppe* operated as part of *Luftflotte 1* and was based at Elbing near Danzig in East Prussia (now part of Poland). Commanded by *Hauptmann* Paul-Werner Hozzel, on 26 August 1939 the unit had a strength of 30 Junkers 87Bs plus nine in reserve, three Dornier 17Ps for reconnaissance and to lead attacks, and six Junkers 52 transports; 30 Ju 87s, two Do 17s and all six Ju 52s were serviceable. Given below is the account in the unit's war diary for its operations on 1 September 1939, the first day of what was to become World War II. The target area for the initial operations was the town of Dirschau (now Tczew) on the River Vistula, near the frontier and some 25 miles from the base airfield.

1st Operation, *Stab* and 1st, 2nd and 3rd *Staffeln*
Assignment: The road and railway bridge at Dirschau to be seized in a *coup de main* operation [by ground forces].
The capture to be assisted by *I./StG 1* with supporting units.
Target: Destruction of demolition charges known to be in position on the bridge at Dirschau.

9./KG 3 [with Dornier Do 17s] was assigned to support the operation, under the operational control of *I./StG 1*.

I./StG 1 was to attack at Z hours minus 3 minutes = X-hour for the *Gruppe* = 4.42 hours for the following diversionary targets:

Target I: Low-altitude attack on the power cable beside the railway embankment by two *Ketten* [three-plane flights] of *3./StG 1*.

Target II: High-altitude attack on the electricity generating plant by one *Kette* from 3rd *Staffel* and one *Kette* from 2nd *Staffel*.

Target III: High-altitude attack on the signal box at the station, by two *Ketten* of 2nd Staffel.

Target IV: High-altitude attack on the water and gas works by the *Stabs Kette*.

Target V: High-altitude attack on the embankment immediately to the west of the bridge by three *Ketten* of 1st *Staffel*.

9./KG 3 was to deliver a low-altitude attack on the barracks to the west of Dirschau.

Defences: Small amount of 2cm and 4.5cm *Flak*.

Results: The targets were destroyed as ordered.

Reconnaissance: None was flown before the attack. Afterwards two Do 17Ps took off with two press reporters for a post-strike reconnaissance.

Losses: One Ju 87B of *1./StG 1* was destroyed during the approach to the target when it flew into the ground descending through fog 8km east of Elbing. Crew: *Fw* Giertz and *Uffz* Tessner killed.

After the attack *I./StG 1* transferred to Grieslienen.

Three aircraft of the 2nd *Staffel* were forced by fog to make emergency landings near Heiligenbreit (no damage).

Combat-ready aircraft:

Within 3 hours: 15; within 8 hours: 30.

Munitions expenditure:

Loads carried by attack forces at respective targets:

I.	1 *Kette*	250 kg
	1 *Kette*	500 kg
II.	1 *Kette*	500 kg
	1 *Kette*	250 kg
		50 kg
III.	1 *Kette*	500 kg
	1 *Kette*	50 kg
IV.	2 aircraft	500 kg
	1 aircraft	250 kg
		50 kg
V.	1 *Kette*	500 kg
	1 *Kette*	250 kg
		50 kg

Food supply and health: Very good

Weather: Mist as far as Marienburg up to 50 metres. Over the target: 1/10 at 1,500 metres. Visibility 7–10km.

Action by supporting units: After the attack on the detonation charges and the barracks *9./KG 3* returned to KG 3.

Remarks, lessons learned: It is impossible to bring a dive-bomber unit successfully into action during marginal weather conditions without incurring losses.

[signed] Hozzel
Hauptmann and *Kommandeur*

2nd Operation, *Stab* and 1st, 2nd and 3rd *Staffeln*
Attack time 1715 hours.
Commission: Destruction of the Polish broadcasting transmitters at Babice and
Mokotow near Warsaw.
Operation from Grieslienen forward operating base.
Take off: 1615 hours [by 28 Ju 87s]; landing: 1800 hours.
Results: Target No 4912 (transmitter at Mokotow) and the PZL [aircraft] fac-
tory (targets 743 and 209) destroyed by direct hits.
Defences: Strong Polish fighter and *Flak* (4.5cm and 7.5cm) defences.
1 Polish fighter (PZL 11) shot down in air combat by *Unteroffizier* Ruediger.
Witnesses: *Oblt* Hozzel
          Oblt Mössinger
          Uffz Gentschner
          Ogefr Zupp
Losses: 1 radio operator, *Flg* Mutschisckk, 2nd *Staffel*, wounded.

Due to shortage of fuel eight Ju 87s made forced-landings, of which two were
wrecked, six undamaged.
Combat-ready aircraft: After 3 hours: 18; after 8 hours: 34.
Provisioning and health: very good.
Munition expenditure:
  28 × 250 kg
  112 × 50 kg.
Weather: 6/10 at 4,000m. Visibility 3km in thick haze.
Remarks, lessons learned: An operation by a *Stuka Gruppe* involving a flight
time of more than 1½ hours is not possible, if a dogfight has to be taken into
account. 8 forced landings! Of those one turned over and one stood on its nose.

* * *

I. Gruppe Jagdgeschwader 3, September 1940
In the Battle of Britain this fighter *Gruppe* was part of *Luftflotte 2*, and in
September 1940 was based at Samer, near Boulogne. Commanded by *Hauptmann* Hans von Hahn, on 7 September the unit reported a strength of 23
Messerschmitt Bf 109Es, of which 14 were serviceable after four weeks of
heavy fighting. This part of the diary covers the unit's operations up to and
including the major air battle of 15 September.

12.9.40   1030 Air defence: 3 *Rotte* [pairs] at immediate readiness, stood down
          at 20.30 hours.

13.9.40   Bad weather. No operations. The *Staffeln* [personnel] and pilots went to Boulogne and Lille.

14.9.40   During the day at various states of readiness, released at 14.30.

15.9.40   1200 Escort (by 12 aircraft) of Do 17s against London. *Oblt* Keller shot down a Spitfire, *Leutnant* Rohwer a Hurricane. *Fw* Wollmer dived into the Channel; the impact was seen by *Lt* Springer. This crash appears not to have been caused by enemy action. After a long dive Wollmer's machine rolled a quarter turn into a vertical dive and he did not succeed in bailing out. A motor boat detached from a German convoy near Cap Gris Nez and went to the scene of the crash.

1510 Operation by nine aircraft to escort He 111s against London. At 1,500m there was almost total cloud cover. Over the Thames estuary and to the north of London there were gaps in the cloud. During the flight in there was contact with Spitfires. The bombers flew in loose formation to the north of London. Strong and accurate *Flak*. The Spitfires came from above, fired, and dived away. *Hauptmann* von Hahn shot down a Spitfire, *Lt* Rohwer probably destroyed a Hurricane. During an attack by Spitfires *Oberleutnant* Reumschuessel became separated from his wing-man, *Obfw* Olejnik, and has not returned [this aircraft crashed near Charing, Kent; the pilot bailed out and was taken prisoner]. After he was separated from the formation *Obfw* Hessel was heard on the radio, but he failed to return [this aircraft crashed near Tenterden; the pilot bailed out and was taken prisoner]. *Obfw* Buchholz's aircraft was hit in the cooling system and forced down in the Channel. *Oblt* Keller made contact with a rescue aircraft nearby, which picked up B. He had injuries and was taken to the military hospital at Boulogne. The body of *Lt* Kloiber has been washed ashore near St Cecile, and buried. *Lt* Meckel and two *Feldwebeln* attended the funeral. During the last few days news has been received from the Red Cross in Geneva that *Oblt* Tiedmann, *Oblt* Rau, *Oblt* Loidolt, *Lt* Landry (these last two wounded) and *Obfw* Lamskemper have been captured by the British.

★ ★ ★

III. Gruppe Zerstörergeschwader 26 Horst Wessel, February and March 1944

Early in 1944 *III./ZG 26* was based at Wunstorf near Hanover. The unit's role was to engage US heavy bombers making daylight attacks on targets in Germany, for which its Messerschmitt Bf 110Gs were armed with two 30mm cannon, four 20mm cannon and four 21cm rocket launchers firing forwards, and two 7.9mm machine guns for rear defence. During the first five days of the period described below the US Eighth and Fifteenth Air Forces mounted their so-called 'Big Week' of operations against German aircraft production centres. In the course of its operations *III./ZG 26* frequently encountered American P-38, P-47 and P-51 escort fighters, and suffered accordingly.

16.2.44 *Generalmajor* Ibel [commander of 2. *Jagddivision*] visited the unit and spoke to crews.

17.2.44 Due to re-equipment [arrival of new aircraft to replace previous losses] no operations.

18.2.44 Crews flew training missions in instrument flight, bombing and high-altitude flight.

19.2.44 The *Gruppe* put up 26 Bf 110s to exercise measures for supporting the Army in the land battle.

20.2.44 At 12.03 hours the *Gruppe* received orders from 2. *Jagddivision* to take off and engage reported incoming enemy bomber formation. At 12.13 hours 13 Bf 110s were airborne and assembled at radio beacon *Marie*, after new orders re-assembled overhead base. The *Kommandeur, Major* Kogler, took off late with three more Bf 110s at 12.19 hours but failed to meet up with the aircraft which had taken off at 12.13. At 4,000m the first formation was surprised by enemy fighters attacking out of the sun and as a result 11 Bf 110s were shot down.

Formation Leader: *Hauptmann* Freyschmidt.
Losses:

Pilots	Radio Operators
Hptm Rosenkranz	
Flg Tacke	*Obefr.* Loehr
Ofw Schmeller	*Uffz* Schmidt, H.
Feldw Scherkenbeck	*Uffz* Schmidt, W.
Uffz Nolting	*Uffz* Kucirek
Ofw Brendle	*Feldw* Längle

Wounded:

Feldw Herlitzius	*Feldw* Röder
Feldw v Kovarbasic	*Uffz* Schmalz
	Feldw Tetzalf
	Uffz Messmer

During the incursion two enemy fighters carried out a low-level attack on the airfield. As a result nine aircraft were hit and suffered up to 30 per cent damage.

Armourer	*Ogefr* Hanning killed
Radio Operator	*Uffz* Huber wounded
Mechanic	*Uffz* Dörenkamp wounded

21.2.44 At 12.41 hours the Group received orders to engage incoming enemy formations.
At 12.45 10 Bf 110s were airborne; assembly over Radio Beacon *Marie*. At 13.15 hours these aircraft joined up with the escort of friendly fighters in the Rottenburg area. Our formation made contact with the enemy force, but due to poor direction failed to reach a favourable position from which to attack.

Combat Report D1

1. Order: Scramble to engage enemy formation.
2. Take-off: 10 Bf 110s from Wunstorf, 12.45 hours.
3. Weather at take-off: Light drizzle, 1km visibility, cloud base 500m, tops 1,200, 8–9/10 cover. Wind 030 at 10km/h.
4. Fighter escort: Joined up with own fighter escort over Rottenburg at 13.15 hours.
5. Fighter control instructions received immediately after take-off.
6. Enemy sighted: Approx. 13.40 and 13.45 hours at map reference HS [near Bielefeld].
7. Attack: The attack was not carried out. The relative position of the enemy formation shifted from the south-east to the south, to the south-west, to the west and to the north-west. Our formation was on the outside of the turn and it was not possible to close on the enemy. Three enemy formations were seen with about 1km between each, each with considerable vertical extent. The bombers were flying in arrow formation.
8. Weather in operational area: Between 1500 and 1800 hours, continuous cloud cover with some gaps. Persistent condensation trails and cirrus at 7,000m. Visibility more than 50km.
9. Lessons.
   Tactical: If possible the assembly of the formation should be 1,000 to 2,000m higher than the enemy formation, to give a sufficient reserve of speed to get into position for a successful attack.
   Signals: No contact on Y-Direction, Channel 26 [fighter direction channel] was unusable. There was so much traffic on the [Ist Fighter] Corps radio channel that proper control was not possible.
10. Landing: Eight Bf 110 between 1455 and 1530 hours at Wunstorf [the other two landed at Hildesheim].
11. Successes: Nil.

22.2.44. The *Gruppe* was ordered to take off at 12.22 hours to engage incoming enemy formations.
The *Gruppe* scrambled 8 Bf 110s at 12.28 hours.
Weather at take-off: Fair weather, 50km visibility, cloud base 1,000m, 2–3/10 cover.
At 12.55 to 13.00 hours joined own fighter escort at 7,000m above Lake Steinhude. The *Gruppe* joined up behind *I./ZG 26* [also flying Bf 110s] which was operating under the control of the *2. Jagddivision*. At 13.35 hours three formations of Fortress IIs were sighted.
The leader of our formation (*I./ZG 26*) closed on the enemy formation to attack from head-on. *III./ZG 26*, following, was too close behind for a head-on attack, and had to turn and attack from the rear. While closing in to attack, fire was opened from about 400m. The enemy machine flying on the left outer side of the formation burst into flames along its right side. It began to curve away to the left and a second attack was carried out from above and to the left, from behind. This Fortress dropped away from the formation well ablaze.

There was strong defensive fire from the enemy rear gun positions. Each enemy formation numbered about 60 aircraft, flying in arrow. Weather in operational area: About 3/10 cloud cover, cloud base 500m, tops 2,000m. Visibility above cloud more than 50km.

During the head-on attack, the formation leader turned in too soon, so that the aircraft coming behind were unable to get into an attacking position.

Landing: Two Bf 110s landed at Wunstorf, at 13.58 and at 14.10 hours. Four Bf 110s made belly-landings. No landing reports received so far from two Bf 110s [later found to have been shot down, their crews were killed].

Successes: One Fortress II shot down by *Oblt* Bley.

23.2.44   No operations. The *Gruppe* carried out instrument flying training missions as planned. The 7th *Staffel* is in the process of receiving replacement aircraft.

24.2.44   Operational Report
Take-off: Four Bf 110s from Wunstorf at 12.01 hours.
Order: Scramble take-off to engage incoming enemy formations.
The *Gruppe* assembled at 7,000m over Brunswick with 10 Bf 110s of *I./ZG 26*. *II./JG 11* joined up to provide the escort at 12.15 hours. Instructions received from *JaFue* [fighter controller] during the assembly. At 13.15 hours eight formations each of about 15 Liberators were seen in the area of Nordhausen, stepped up from 4,000m to 7,000m and flying on a south-easterly heading. It was noticeable that the enemy aircraft were wavering about. On the approach of our *Gruppe* the enemy force turned south and later south-west. Attack was carried out at 13.30 hours in the area of Holzminden, from the left and above. *III./ZG 26* scored one victory (*Oblt* Meltz) and one *Herausschuss* [bomber damaged and seen to leave formation] (*Major* Kogler). Several Liberators were observed to be on fire; others were seen to crash. [*Lt* Gern, who was shot down during the action but bailed out of his aircraft, lodged a claim for one Fortress shot down when he returned to his unit.]
The claims of *I./ZG 26* are not to hand.
Landing: Two Bf 110s landed at Wunstorf at 14.08 and 14.14 hours.
One Bf 110 suffered damage to the cabin and turned back.
One Bf 110: No landing report received [Gern's aircraft].
Supplement: The enemy bombers were escorted by Thunderbolts, which flew above the formation. It was ascertained that the leading formation, which I tried to attack, always went into a turn to the right when I was in front shortly before I turned in to make my attack. It is possible that this forced the bombers away from their target.

[signed] Kogler
Major and *Gruppe Kommandeur*

★ ★ ★

Nachtjagdgeschwader 6, March 1944

In March 1944 this night fighter unit operated against RAF night bombers as part of *Jagddivision 7* responsible for the defence of southern Germany. The *Geschwader* comprised two *Gruppen*, the Ist based at Mainz-Finthen and the IInd based at Echterdingen. The *Geschwader* was commanded by *Major* Heinrich Wohlers, and on 6 March each *Gruppe* reported 14 Messerschmitt 110s serviceable.

15 March   Target Stuttgart. Own take-off too early. Consequently there was a lack of fuel. 26 Bf 110s and three Ju 88s took off [the Ju 88s belonged to *Luftbeobachtungsstaffel 7*, which flew from Echterdingen to search for the RAF bomber stream]. Three four-engine bombers shot down for certain, and two probables. Five Bf 110s crashed due to their running out of fuel, one made a belly landing and one force-landed at Zürich/Dübendorf [in Switzerland. Surprisingly there was no mention that the *Geschwader* commander, *Major* Wohlers, had been killed when his aircraft crashed in fog near Echterdingen. RAF losses: 36 out of 863.]

18 March   British penetration in the area Frankfurt–Mannheim–Darmstadt [the target was Frankfurt]. 24 Bf 110s and two Ju 88s took off. One bomber shot down for certain, and three probably destroyed. One Bf 110 was shot down and one was rammed by an enemy night fighter and crashed. [RAF losses: 22 out of 846.]

22 March   Target Frankfurt. 21 Bf 110s and two Ju 88s took off. *Oberleutnant* Becker scored 6 victories. The air situation was not at all clear. The enemy turned when to the north of Terschelling, towards the southeast in the direction of Osnabrück, but this was not recognised. From Osnabrück on no contact was made. The enemy main force was not recognised until it was to the north of Frankfurt. [RAF losses: 33 out of 816.]

23 March   Received false reports of an enemy force moving in an easterly direction. The target was Paris [in fact it was Laon]. 20 Bf 110s and one Ju 88 took off, but in vain. [RAF losses: 2 out of 143.]

24 March   The enemy approached over the North Sea and Jutland, to Berlin. The return flight touched the northern tip of our own divisional area. Radio Beacon 12 was subjected to music-type interference. Crews encountered severe icing when breaking through the overcast. Vain attempts were made to make contact with the bomber stream during its return flight. Our own flares over Berlin were too high (6,000m). Very disciplined firing by the *Flak* over Berlin [i.e., the gunners engaged targets up to a certain altitude, and the night fighters engaged targets above that altitude]. *Korps* communications channels could be heard well, in spite of the enemy interference. In action were 11 Bf 110s to Berlin, five Bf 110s against the returning stream, three Bf 110s engaged in *Himmelbett* [ground-controlled interception] operations, and one Ju 88 reconnaissance aircraft. One victory to *Oberleutnant* Bekker. [RAF losses: 72 out of 811—obviously other German night fighter units did better.]

26 March About 500 bombers approached over the Zuider Zee on an easterly course towards the Rhine. They then turned south towards Essen–Oberhausen–Duisburg [the target was Essen]. Our radar and ground observers recognised the turn too late. Our own reconnaissance aircraft, a Ju 88 flown by *Hauptmann* Wallner, reported enemy activity only over the Ruhr area as a whole. The direction of the [enemy's] approach and return flights could not be recognised from the running commentary. Therefore, it was not possible to get into the bomber stream. Due to the devious approach and the strong headwind, *II./NJG 6* did not arrive at the target before the end of the attack. Severe icing was reported. 21 Bf 110s on *Zähme Sau* [freelance night fighter] operations, three Bf 110s on *Himmelbett*, one Ju 88 on reconnaissance. Three Bf 110s ran out of fuel and crashed, and one made a belly landing. [RAF losses: 9 out of 705.]

* * *

III. Gruppe Schlachtgeschwader 4, June 1944

At the time of the Allied landings in Normandy on 6 June 1944 this ground-attack unit was commanded by *Major* Gerhard Weyert and operated from Clastres near St Quentin in eastern France and Le Luc and Frières in the south. On 4 June the unit possessed 50 Focke Wulf 190F fighter-bombers, of which 38 were serviceable. Following the invasion the unit was redeployed to bases in the north of France, where it attempted operations in the face of overwhelming Allied air superiority. Considering this was an official document, the account contains remarkably forthright language concerning some of the orders the unit received from the High Command.

6.6.44 At 03.00 hours the *Kommandeur* was informed by Derfflinger Ia [operations officer at headquarters], *Major* Fahrenberg, that there had been landings by enemy airborne forces to the north of Caen and landings of seaborne forces near the mouth of the Seine. At 06.45 hours, on his own discretion, the commander ordered the *Gruppe* to come to Readiness State I. At 07.45 hours Derfflinger Ia gave orders for the *Gruppe* to prepare to move to [forward airfields in] the Le Mans area. On the question of whether to begin moving immediately, the reply came that teleprinter confirmation should be awaited. A codeword for use in the event of an enemy landing had not been given. The order to prepare for the move was given to unit commanders by the [*Gruppe*] *Kommandeur*. All airworthy combat aircraft are to prepare to leave, with their pilots and 1st mechanics [it was standard practice to carry a mechanic in the rear fuselage of each single-seat fighter, during operational deployments of this type]. Key personnel and the doctor will follow in two Ju 52s. After the teleprinter order to move to Laval was received at 09.35 hours, individual *Staffeln* took off as follows:

12.15 hours, *Stab* and 9th *Staffel* from Clastres, to land at Laval at 13.35 hours.

13.45 hours, 8th *Staffel* from Frières, to land at Tours at 14.45 hours.

12.00 hours, 7th *Staffel* from Le Luc, to land at Laval at 19.00 hours.

For safety [to reduce the risk of encounters with enemy fighters], the aircraft which took off from St Quentin were ordered to fly round the south of Paris at low level. In spite of this, all units were intercepted by the enemy and there were dogfights with American Mustangs and Thunderbolts.

The losses of the *Gruppe* on 6.6.44 were:

Pilots: *Oblt* Pühringer killed
        Obfw Kollberg killed
        Fw Brauneis killed
        Uffz Speer killed
        Lt Limberg wounded

Mechanics: *Fw* Eidam killed
        Uffz Krüsmann killed
        Uffz Ebert killed
        Obgef Ohlwein killed
        Obgef Kleinker wounded

From 1700 hours the 9th *Staffel* mounted *Schwarm*-strength attacks [four-aircraft units] against enemy landings and vehicle concentrations near the mouth of the Orne, with a total of three operations with 13 aircraft. In one case it was not possible to reach the target area, due to the presence of strong enemy fighter defence.

Lessons learned from the move:

1. The *Gruppe* could have deployed earlier, if the order to begin the move had been issued earlier by *Korps*.

2. In view of the superiority of the RAF and the USAAF over France, it is unwise to carry mechanics in combat aircraft.

3. The airfield at Laval was quite unprepared for the arrival of the ground-attack unit. There were no refuelling vehicles, no bomb-loading trolleys, no personnel to assist and, above all, no airfield defence. The airfield commander had been told to expect the unit to arrive in the evening, and that missions would be flown only from the following morning. There was little room to disperse [the aircraft] and accommodation had been prepared too close to the airfield.

7.6.44   At 0430 hours the two Ju 52s took off from Clastres carrying key personnel for Tours. They should have taken off at 1300 hours the previous day and arrived eight hours late. When they arrived it was impossible to go further by road, in spite of strenuous efforts. Further flights by Ju 52 [to take the personnel closer to the combat area] were out of the question. Only two days later, on 9 June, did the servicing team arrive at Laval.

From 0600 hours four operations were mounted, in which 24 aircraft were sent against landings and tank concentrations in the area of the mouth of the Orne river [where British troops had established a bridgehead]. Due to the strong fighter defences, three of the operations had to be broken off before reaching the target and the bombs jettisoned. At about 10.00 hours ten Mustangs carried out a strafing attack on the airfield. *Lt* Essau was shot down and severely wounded; four Fw 190s were destroyed on the ground.

At about 21.00 hours there was an attack on aircraft of the 8th *Staffel* as they were coming in from Tours, by three Mustangs. *Oblt* Dahle was shot down and severely wounded; *Obfw* Schneider was shot down and wounded.

Despite favourable weather we achieved little, because successful operations are impossible without effective fighter protection. The day's losses in pilots and aircraft can be blamed on the absence of any flak defence at the airfield.

8.6.44   At 12.40 hours three operations with 17 aircraft were flown against the enemy troops landing near Riva Bella and the Orne Bridge near Benouville. Due to the strength of the fighter defences one operation had to be broken off prematurely. *Fw* George is missing. For the first time there was a fighter escort, provided by *I./JG 11* [with Bf 109s]. The operations achieved little, because it was impossible to keep to the planned rendezvous points and routes ordered by *Fliegerführer West*. Due to continuous enemy air activity over the airfields, individual units could not meet their assigned take-off times. And due to dogfights on the approach routes it was not possible to keep rendezvous times. About 22.00 hours the vehicle column arrived from Clastres. Losses due to air attack: One car, one lorry, one mobile workshop with trailer.

That evening the *Kommandeur* attended a conference to discuss operational policy, held at [headquarters] *Fliegerführer West*. The operations planned by *II. Fliegerkorps* the previous day could not be carried out at the times given. Operational matters such as the strength of attacks, timing, routing and defensive tactics in the light of the prevailing weather situation should be left to *Fliegerführer West* [commanding the fighter and fighter-bomber units] or, better still, to *Gruppe* commanders. The last order, for an attack on Arromanches with an approach from Trouville along the whole length of the invasion coast, was nonsensical and disregarded the fact that the flight distance [to the target] was more than 200km [125 miles]. It could have been ordered only by people who had no idea of the situation or the strength of the enemy defences. *II Fliegerkorps* would not be argued out of its previous inflexible way of giving orders.

9.6.44   0610 hours. Early operation in poor weather at the lowest possible altitude. The target was not reached. A late attack, at 20.10 hours, was made against the landings at Riva Bella. The *Kommandeur* made an emergency landing at Falaise. Altogether 14 aircraft operated. During the night there was a heavy attack by four-engined bombers. The runway was cut in several places by bomb craters.

10.6   Released from operations, airfield still cannot be used. *Hptm* Wedekind and *Lt* Limberg visit *Fliegerführer West*.

11.6   Released from operations, work on runway.

12.6   0635 hours, operation by four aircraft against the landing area at Riva Bella. The target could not be reached and the bombs were jettisoned. *Ofw* Schopper made an emergency landing. Operations should have started to fly supplies to *Luftwaffe* personnel at the strongpoint at Douvres [a radar station near the coast encircled by British troops and still holding out]. But at the take-off point all four Fw 190s were destroyed in a strafing attack by eight Spitfires. Two fighters (Bf 109s) were shot down. After that the unit was stood down.
Ten pilots were sent to Le Bourget to pick up new aircraft.

★ ★ ★

9. Staffel Kampfgeschwader 76, December 1944

In the autumn and winter of 1944 the IIIrd *Gruppe* of *Kampfgeschwader 76* was working up with its new Arado 234 jet bombers at Burg bei Magdeburg. By mid-December the unit possessed sixteen serviceable Ar 234s. On 17 December the 9th *Staffel*, commanded by *Hauptmann* Dieter Luckesch, began moving to Münster-Handorf in western Germany with ten of the jet bombers. By 21 December the move was complete and the *Staffel* prepared to begin operations in support of German troops heavily engaged in the Ardennes salient—'The Battle of the Bulge'.

22.12.44   Operational orders see Appendix C, Teleprinter message 11a,12a/44, Secret, 21.12.44.
Due to bad weather the operation which had been ordered could not be carried out. The *Staffel* continued to improve operational readiness by getting the available aircraft serviceable and improving the ground organisation.

23.12.44   Operational orders see Appendix C, Teleprinter message 15a, 1944, Secret, 22.12.44.
Due to bad weather the operation which had been ordered could not be carried out. *Staffel* personnel were employed to improve the ground organisation and for technical services.

24.12.44   Operational orders see Appendix C, Teleprinter message 17a/44, Secret, 23.12.44.

1st operation: Operation by nine Arado 234s, take-off time 10.14–10.26 hours.
Flight route: Base–Radio Beacon Iburg at low altitude [after take-off pilots remained at low altitude and began their climb only when they were well clear of base, to conceal its location from the enemy]—climb to 4,000 metres heading towards Cologne—flight to the target at Liége

from out of the sun—return flight over Cologne or Bonn, thence to
base.

Landed: 11.22–11.48 hours.

Attack: The cities of Liége and Namur were attacked in shallow dive,
10.50–11.00 hours. Bomb release altitude 2,000 metres. Nine SC 500
bombs (Trialen) [a powerful new explosive] released on railway and
factory facilities which were operating, and large complex of buildings in the centre of the city. Five hits observed.

Defences: Weak ground defences observed, moderate flak. Spitfires
and Thunderbolts observed flying defensive patrols in the target area.
No interceptions, because obviously the Arado 234 was not yet known
to the enemy.

Losses: Undercarriage of aircraft F1+PT collapsed on landing, causing damage to the wing. The pilot, *Uffz* Winguth, was uninjured.

2nd operation: Operation by eight Arado 234s, take-off time 14.52–
15.20.

Flight route: As during first operation. Landed 16.00–16.25 hours.

Attack: Attack carried out on the same target as during the first operation, with shallow-dive attacks at 15.31–16.00 hours from release
altitudes between 2,000 and 2,400 metres. There were eight SC 500
bombs (Trialen) but due to a technical failure one SC 500 could not
be released and had to be brought back. Results of the attack on Liége-
North railway station were not observed by any of the pilots.

Defences: Ground defences were not observed. In the target area [our
aircraft] had to fly through strong formations of [enemy] fighters and
bombers, and this hindered accurate bombing. No fighter attacks observed.

Losses: None.

During both missions the [ground along the] route and the target
could be clearly seen, and the mission was a complete success. The
railway stations at Liége and Namur were seen to be working. The
airfield north of the city was observed to be in use by fighters.

Remarks: Arrival of the remaining six Arado 234s at the operational
base, from Burg.

25.12.44 Operational orders see Appendix C Nr 20a/44, Secret, 24.12.44.

1st operation: Operation by eight Arado 234s, take-off 0825–0848
hours.

Track: As during first operation on 24.12.44, landed 09.17–09.48
hours.

Attack: Shallow-dive attack on the city of Liége from altitudes of 5,000
to 2,000 metres, between 08.46 and 09.24 hours. The target was the
railway station west of the junction of the Maas and Ourthe [rivers]
and the factory area south-west of the station. Five hits were observed
on railway lines and sheds in the station area, one on a block of houses

east of the station which started a large fire, and one hit the factory area to the south-west of the station.

Defences: Strong flak was observed. Thunderbolts operated in 4–6 aircraft patrols in the target area. On one occasion an unsuccessful gun attack was observed. It must now be taken into account that the enemy has identified the Arado 234.

Losses: *Leutnant* Frank in F1+DT crash-landed near Teuge in Holland. Pilot uninjured. [His aircraft was hit by a Tempest of No 80 Squadron RAF.]

Despite the failure of one engine *Oberfeldwebel* Dierks carried out his orders and returned to base in F1+NT. On landing the aircraft was damaged. Pilot uninjured.

The railway installations on the south and north of Liége are still in full use. Reconnaissance reports that as a result of the attacks rail traffic has halted in the northern part of the town.

2nd operation: Attack by eight Arado 234s, take-off 14.00–14.03 hours. Flight route: Base–Datteln (canal junction) at low altitude, then climb to 5,000 metres on course Bonn–Laacher Lake–Bastogne. Approached Liége out of the sun in a shallow dive to 2,000 metres. Returned to base via Bonn and Dortmund. Landed 15.03–15.18 hours.

Attack: On the railway station in the north-western part of Liége, traversing the entire battle area in order to intimidate enemy forces. The attack was carried out in a shallow dive from 5,000 to 1,500 metres, 14.35–14.45 hours. Eight SC 500 bombs (Trialen) were released. Seven hits observed in the station area (three hits on lines in use, one hit on the south-east corner of a large transhipment shed, one hit on a block of houses north-west of the station, one hit on a block of houses north of the station). One hit close to railway lines at the south-west corner of the station. One hit on the factory area to the south of the station started a fierce fire.

Defences: Powerful medium flak defences were observed in the target area. Formations of Spitfires flew barrier patrols in the Liége–Bastogne area. It appears that the enemy is trying to use fighters to seal off the entire area of our breakthrough on the Western Front.

Losses: Aircraft F1+FT, pilot *Oblt* Fendrich, burst a tyre on landing. Damage to the canopy.

Both operations can be stated to have been successful. The results of the shallow-dive attacks could be assessed as average, even though the aircraft reached speeds up to 900 km/h [560 mph]. Pilots must familiarise themselves on details of new targets and the new attack procedures. Our aircraft type is now recognised by the enemy and we are liable to come under fighter attack. Attacks have come mostly from ahead or obliquely from ahead and above, so far without success. Because of the high speed of our aircraft, attacks from behind have not been successful.

Due to the powerful fighter defences, so far horizontal attacks using the *Lotfe* [high-altitude bomb sight] have not been possible.

★ ★ ★

III. Gruppe Kampfgeschwader 76, April and May 1945

Arado 234s from this *Gruppe* continued in action until the final week of the war. On 5 April the unit moved to Kaltenkirchen near Hamburg and continued operations from there. Often under severe pressure from Allied fighters, the *Gruppe* saw action on both the Western and the Eastern Fronts.

6.4   6th *Staffel*: attack on [British] armoured units west of Achmer. Following this attack, the 6th *Staffel* ceased operations until 12.4 in order to re-group.
            III. *Gruppe*: Shallow dive attack, from 1,200m to 800m, on the canal bridge at Vinte sw Achmer.

7.4   *III. Gruppe*: Attack [on Soviet troops] in the area Jüterbog-Zossen south of Berlin.

10.4   *III Gruppe*, evening. Target: Autobahn between Bad Oeynhausen and Hanover.

13.4   *III Gruppe*. Due to the presence of [enemy] low-flyers, four Arados were unable to take off for a mission.

14.4   *6 Staffel*, mid-day. Attack on [British] vehicle concentration in the bridgehead over the Aller [river] at Essel, 30km ENE Nienburg.

15.4   *6 Staffel*, morning. Attack on [British] vehicles at Meine, 11km south of Gifhorn, and armoured columns on autobahn Hanover–Brunswick. Four enemy fighters made vain attempt to chase *Lt* Croissant over Gifhorn. Due to fighters he flew at low altitude to Ratzeburg south of Lübeck.
            During the landing at Kaltenkirchen a fighter, believed to have been a Tempest, shot down *Ofw* Luther of the *6. Staffel*. He made a crash landing and suffered severe injuries [the loss links with a claim by two Tempest pilots of No 56 Squadron].

18.4   Early afternoon. Weather reconnaissance of the area of the bridges over the Aller near Rethem, 17km north-east Nienburg [over which British troops were advancing]. Attack on the bridges from 500m. Defended by fighters and flak of all calibres.

19.4   Midday, operation as on previous day. *Major* Polletien, Ia [Operations Officer] of the *Geschwader*, returned to Lübeck-Blankensee from an operation in the Berlin area, and despite a radio warning from the airfield he was shot down by an English fighter and killed.

20.4   *III. Gruppe* at Kaltenkirchen, evening. Shallow-dive attack 2,500/1,000m on [Soviet] tanks and vehicles on the road between Zossen and Baruth, south of Berlin. Negligible defences. The flight to the target began with an easterly flight over the Baltic before heading from there to the area of Berlin.

ANTI-SHIPPING AIRCRAFT

(Above) During 1940 and 1941 the Focke Wulf Fw 200 Condors of Kampfgeschwader 40 *achieved considerable success against Allied merchant shipping in the Atlantic. (Kowalewski)*

(Right, upper) Armourers moving a 250kg bomb into position for loading on an Fw 200. Note the 'world in a ring' emblem of KG 40 *on the fuselage of the aircraft. (Kowalewski)*

(Right, lower) A Heinkel He 111 releasing an F5B torpedo. This weapon carried a 440lb warhead and had an effective running range of about 1,000 yards. (Via Schliephake)

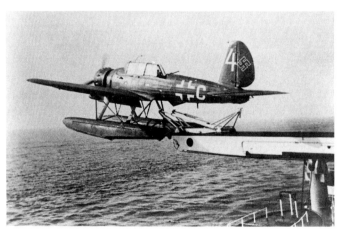

(Above) A Dornier 217 of II. Gruppe KG 100 carrying a Henschel Hs 293 glider bomb under the starboard wing. (Via Girbig)

(Left, upper) The Fritz-X armour-piercing, radio-guided bomb was released from high altitude and attained an impact velocity close to the speed of sound. Control surfaces recessed into the fins at the rear of the missile allowed the observer in the parent aircraft to steer the bomb on to the target during the final part of its trajectory.

(Left, lower) The Arado Ar 196 reconnaissance seaplane saw service throughout the entire war, operating from fixed bases and also from the larger warships.

RECONNAISSANCE AIRCRAFT

(Right, top) The rugged if ungainly fabric-covered Heinkel He 46 was the main tactical reconnaissance type employed during the campaign in Poland in 1939.

(Right, centre) The all-metal Henschel Hs 126 replaced the He 46 early in the war and was a great improvement over its predecessor.

(Right, bottom) In 1942 the Focke Wulf Fw 189 became the main tactical reconnaissance type in use. The twin-boom layout and extensively glazed cabin gave the crew excellent visibility in most directions.

(Above) The Junkers Ju 88 was the most-used long-range reconnaissance type. These examples, pictured on the central sector of the Eastern Front during the early winter of 1943, belonged to Aufklärungsgruppe 22.

(Left, upper) An Arado Ar 234 reconnaissance aircraft of Kommando Sperling about to take off for a mission late in 1944. Flying fast and high, these aircraft photographed Allied-held areas at will during the final nine months of the war. (Götz)

(Left, lower) Technicians removing the film cassettes from an Ar 234 after a sortie. (Götz`

TRANSPORT AIRCRAFT

(Above) During German airborne
assault operations the main transport
aircraft used was the Junkers Ju 52,
which was able to carry up to 12
paratroops. (Via Schliephake)

(Right, top) The six-engined
Messerschmitt Me 323 was the
heaviest transport type employed by
any air force during World War II.
This example is delivering fuel to
German forces in Tunisia in 1943.
(Stehle)

(Right, centre) The remarkable five-
engined Heinkel He 111Z, comprising
two He 111s joined at the wing and
with an additional engine mounted in
the middle. This unusual aircraft was
employed as a tug for the Me 321
gliders used to transport priority
cargoes to the Eastern Front. (Via
Ethell)

(Right, bottom) An He 111Z with an
Me 321 in tow, pictured soon after
take-off. (Via Schliephake)

(Top) Junkers Ju 86s, obsolete aircraft used at bomber training schools, were pressed into use during the desperate operation to carry supplies to the beleaguered German 6th Army cut off at Stalingrad.

TRAINING AIRCRAFT
(Above and below) The Focke Wulf 44 primary trainer. (Via Schliephake)

(Above) The Arado 66 advanced trainer. (Via Schliephake)

(Below) Arado 96 trainers of the pilot training school near Paris, February 1942. (Wiegand)

(Bottom) Large numbers of aircraft were written off in accidents at the pilot training schools. This spectacular collision occurred at Cracow in Poland. A Bf 109 of the resident training unit and a Ju 52 from the flying school at Pütnitz tried to land on the same part of the runway at the same time, fortunately without injury to any of those on board.

FLAK

(Left) The 12.8 cm Flak 40 was the heaviest anti-aircraft gun used by the Luftwaffe. Some of these weapons were employed in paired installations, as depicted here, with two barrels on a common traversing and elevating mounting. The use of these paired weapons was confined to the giant Flak towers erected in the larger German cities.

(Right, upper) A 10.5 cm Flak 38 in action from a flak tower. (Via Schliephake)

(Right, lower) The Friedrichshain Flak tower near the centre of Berlin. As well as providing raised platforms to support anti-aircraft guns, these massive bomb-proof structures housed civil defence headquarters and provided shelter for the civilian population. (Via Schliephake)

(Below) The Kommandogerät 40 was the standard German fire control predictor during the latter half of the war. (Via Schliephake)

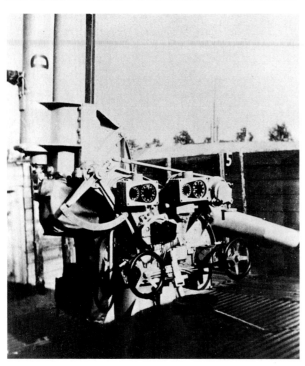

(Left, upper) The 8.8cm Flak, *the most-used German heavy anti-aircraft weapon. (Via Schliephake)*

(Left, lower) A close-up view of the receiver dials of the data-transmission system for an 8.8cm gun. By matching the gun position pointers with the gun aiming pointers, the gun crew aligned the weapon on the aiming point calculated by the predictor. (Via Bergander)

(Right, top) The standard Flak *control radar was the Würzburg D, manufactured by the Telefunken company. Initially this set operated on frequencies in the 553–566MHz band, but when Allied jamming became more serious it was modified to operate on frequencies down to 440MHz. (Via Heise)*

(Above) A mobile 3.7cm Flak *weapon on a half-track mounting, defending a target in Italy.*

(Right) A quadruple-barrelled 2cm Flak *weapon with its crew, in a camouflage firing position in Italy.*

THE V.1 FLYING BOMB

(Left, upper) A V.1 (Fieseler Fi 103) flying bomb being manhandled on to the launching ramp.

(Left, lower) A V.1 launching site at Vignacourt, near Abbeville in France, photographed in June 1944. The only 'give-away' amongst the innocuous-looking cluster of farm buildings is the launching ramp in the top right corner, aligned on London.

(Right, top) A V.1 in flight, pictured shortly after launch.

(Right, centre and bottom) From the autumn of 1944 the only effective strategic bomber force available to the Luftwaffe *was* Kampfgeschwader 53, *whose He 111s had been modified to air-launch V.1 flying bombs. This method of bombardment was extremely inaccurate, however, and few of the missiles reached their targets. (Via Heise)*

SENIOR COMMANDERS

(Left) Reichsmarschall *Hermann Göring pictured in 1943, during an inspection visit to a* Wilde Sau *night fighter unit. Standing behind and to his side is* Oberstleutnant *Hajo Herrmann, the originator of this tactical concept. Göring was Commander-in-Chief of the* Luftwaffe *from its formation until April 1945 when, following a disagreement with Hitler, he was stripped of all offices. (Herrmann)*

(Above) Generalfeldmarschal *Robert* Ritter *von* Greim became the last Commander-in-Chief of the Luftwaffe *in April 1945, replacing Göring in that post.*

(Above) Generalfeldmarschall *Albert Kesselring, centre, pictured during the Battle of Britain when he commanded* Luftflotte 2. *(Von Lossberg)*

(Left) Generalfeld-
marschall *Wolfram
Freiherr von Richt-
hofen, second from
left, pictured at his
forward command
post overlooking the
Allied landings at
Anzio in 1944 when
he commanded*
Luftflotte 2. *(Via
Riggelsworth)*

(Above) Generalfeldmarschall *Hugo Sperrle
commanded* Luftflotte 3 *during the Battle of
Britain, and was still in that post when Allied
forces landed in France in 1944. Hitler blamed
him for the failure of the* Luftwaffe *to support
the Army during the latter campaign, and had
him transferred to the reserve in August 1944.*

(Above) Generaloberst *Hans-Jürgen Stumpff
commanded* Luftflotte 5 *during the Battle of
Britain and headed* Luftflotte Reich *during the
'Battle of Britain in reverse' actions of 1944.*

(Above left) Generalfeldmarschall *Erhard Milch held the post of Director General of Equipment in the* Luftwaffe *from November 1941 until May 1944.*

(Above right) Generaloberst *Günther Korten was Chief of the General Staff of the* Luftwaffe *from September 1943 until July 1944, when he suffered fatal injuries during the bomb attack on Hitler's life.*

(Left) After a brilliant career as a front-line fighter pilot, Adolf Galland became Inspector of Fighters in November 1941. While in that post he rose to the rank of Generalleutnant, *but he remained outspoken in his criticism of decisions made by Göring and others in the High Command. Relieved of his position early in 1945, Galland commanded an Me 262 fighter unit during the final weeks of the war. (Sachs)*

26.4   *Stab*, morning. Target: Russian tanks at the Hallenschen Tor in Berlin. *Ofw* Breme reported: The area from Tempelhof–Neu Köln–Hermann-platz is already occupied by Russian troops; no firing seen. North of the Hermannplatz was ablaze with flames reaching to 300m. By the Hallenschen Tor was a sea of fire. Did not wish to drop bombs there so jettisoned them into a lake ESE of Schwerin.

29.4   *Stab*, morning. Target Berlin.
Evening. Shallow dive attack on [Soviet] armoured column east of Berlin. *Ofw* Breme praised the way in which *Fw* Wördemann in the control tower at Blankensee airfield kept watch on the air situation [for patrolling enemy fighters] and guided him in safely by means of radio calls and light signals.

30.4   *Stab*, afternoon. Target: Government district of Berlin. Due to attacks by five enemy fighters *Fw* Woerdemann was forced to jettison his bombs.

3.5   *III. Gruppe*: *Fw* Drews, *8 Staffel*, flew from Leck during the afternoon on the last recorded operation by *KG 76*: shallow-dive attack from 1,500m to 800m on vehicles south of Bremerförde; strong flak defences.

Pilot Training

During the course of World War II the period of training given to new pilots in the *Luftwaffe* underwent a steady reduction. The description given below covers the situation to the autumn of 1941, before the shortages of fuel and other operational pressures had taken effect.

For recruits entering the *Luftwaffe* from civilian life, the first step was six months with a *Fliegerersatzabteilung* or recruit training depot. This was the equivalent to the 'square-bashing' or 'boot camps' in other air forces. The main emphasis was on drill and physical training, with elementary lectures on the principles of flight, radio communications and map-reading.

Having passed through his initial training, the prospective student pilot moved to a *Fluganwänterkompanie*, where he spent two months studying general aeronautical subjects. Thus prepared, he moved to an *A/B Schule* (elementary flying school), where he flew light aircraft such as the Klemm Kl 35, the Focke Wulf Fw 44 and the Bücker Bü 131. For the A_2 licence the pupil received instruction in aerodynamics, aeronautical engineering, elementary navigation, meteorology, flying procedures and training in the use of the Morse code. For his B licence the trainee flew higher-performance aircraft like the Arado Ar 66 and the Gotha Go 145. He also flew heavier types like the Junkers W 33 and W 44, and obsolescent combat planes like the He 51, the Ar 65 and the Hs 123. On successful completion of his B_2 training the student pilot had amassed between 100 and 150 hours' flying time and received his pilot's licence and wings.

Pilots selected for single-engined fighters or dive-bombers now went straight to the specialist training schools for these roles. Significantly, they would receive no formal training in instrument flying before they reached their operational units.

Pilots selected for multi-engined aircraft went to the C Flying Schools, where they received a further 50 or so hours' additional flying. This included instruction in instrument flying and, for bomber pilots, in the handling of obsolescent combat types such as the Ju 86, the Do 17 and early versions of the He 111. Graduates from the C Flying School received the advanced pilot's licence. By the end of the course they could fly high-performance aircraft by day or night on instruments with reasonable proficiency, and they could make simple cross-country navigational flights under fair weather conditions.

At the various specialist training schools, pilots flying multi-seat aircraft joined up with their crews. Combined crew training then began, flying in modern combat aircraft. The flying exercises at specialist schools were similar to those flown at the C Schools, but with longer night and cross-country flights, some of which were made in less favourable weather. On completion of this training, the crews went on to their assigned operational *Geschwader*.

Early in the war the observer (*Beobachter*) in multi-seat aircraft performed a task different from that of a navigator in the RAF or the USAAF. A German observer was trained as an aircraft captain. He received pilot training up to C standard, before moving to the observers' school for a nine-month course for further training in blind-flying and navigation.

Following the outbreak of war, the role of aircraft captain was more often taken over by the pilot. The length of observer training was progressively shortened, until by 1944 it was down to five months and there was little pilot training content.

After leaving their respective specialist training schools, crews went to the *Ergänzungs* (replenishment) units attached to the various operational *Geschwader* or *Gruppen*. These units served as holding centres to replace losses in front-line units. While awaiting their assignments, these crews received operational training that was specific to the units they were about to join.

From the time he joined the *Luftwaffe* until he arrived at his *Ergänzungs* unit, a fighter or dive-bomber pilot would have received about 13 months' training with between 150 and 200 flying hours. Bomber or reconnaissance pilots received about 20 months' training and between 220 and 270 flying hours. It is important to note, however, that these figures referred only to those who had completed their training by the end of 1941. For from then on the *Luftwaffe* training organisation, previously efficient and smooth-running, began to buckle under the strains imposed on it.

Up to mid-1941 the *Luftwaffe* replaced its aircrew losses by drawing on its reserves of trained crews. Following the invasion of the Soviet Union, however, the heavy losses placed impossible demands on the flying training organisation. In the first six months of the campaign *Luftwaffe* losses in aircrew in all categories, in all theatres and from all causes, amounted to about 2,200. This rate of loss continued during the second six months.

Quite apart from these personnel losses, the campaign on the Eastern Front imposed more direct forms of pressure on the training schools. During the Soviet winter offensive early in 1942, substantial bodies of German troops were cut off in the pockets at Demjansk and Cholm. Large numbers of Junkers Ju 52s and instructor pilots from the C and blind-flying schools were diverted to the Eastern Front to assist with the airlift to supply these troops. Due to the losses suffered and the needs of front-line units, many instructors and Ju 52s were never returned to the training organisation. Later that year, the pace of air operations led to shortages of aviation fuel throughout the

Luftwaffe. Again the flying schools, which had the lowest priority, were the first to suffer.

The shortages of aviation fuel, instructors and aircraft threw out of gear the programmes for training bomber and reconnaissance crews. In the short term there was a surplus of partially trained pilots from the A/B Schools. However, at the other end of the pipeline, there was a lack of trained crews arriving at the *Ergänzungs* units. In July 1942 *General* Kühl, the Director of Training, wrote to Göring setting out the impossible position that had arisen at the C Schools. As was often his way, the *Reichsmarschall* came up with a glib solution: he ordered that the C Schools be disbanded and their functions be taken over by the *Ergänzungs* units. This was beyond the latter's capacity, however, for they had insufficient aircraft or instructors to cope with so large an influx of trainees. So the *Ergänzungs* units in their turn passed many of the trainees to the operational *Gruppen* for training there. The result was a confused situation in which the standard of training of new crews fell dramatically. As an inevitable result, the efficiency of operational bomber and reconnaissance units also fell.

The winter of 1942/43 saw the largest airlift operation of all, the all-out attempt to carry supplies to the German 6th Army cut off at Stalingrad. Once again the training organisation was stripped of aircraft and instructors to bolster the airlift, and yet again many planes and crews were never returned.

During 1943 *Generalleutnant* Kreipe took over as Director of Training and found the organisation in a very poor state. He slowed the rate of its deterioration, but could not halt it altogether. He introduced some useful expedients, like short courses on gliders to provide initial flying experience for trainee pilots. But he failed to overcome the perennial shortages of flying instructors, modern aircraft and, above all, aviation fuel.

By the beginning of 1944 new German fighter pilots were arriving at their operational units with about 160 hours' flying time in total. By comparison, their counterparts in the RAF and the USAAF had more than twice as many flying hours. During the first half of the year the *Luftwaffe* day fighter units suffered debilitating losses at the hands of better-trained American pilots flying higher-performance fighters. In this period the German home-defence units lost some 2,000 pilots killed, missing or wounded. When the training organisation tried to make good these casualties, it entered a vicious circle. The ill-trained replacement fighter pilots were no match for their opponents and suffered heavy losses. In their place came newer pilots with even less training and who were even less well able to survive.

A further factor disrupting the training programmes was the frequent incursions by American raiding forces. Each time that happened, there would be frantic radio broadcasts to trainee pilots and crews to land as soon as possible. Anyone who failed to hear or to heed these calls was liable to learn the finer points of air combat in the hardest school of all—from a band of marauding Mustangs or Thunderbolts.

That spring the training standards fell even further, when the B flying schools were disbanded. From then on fighter pilots were sent into action with about 112 hours' flying made up as follows: A School two hours' glider flying, followed by 50 hours' powered flying in elementary trainers; Fighter School 40 hours; and *Ergänzungs* Fighter *Gruppe* 20 hours.

At the same time the *Luftwaffe* instituted the so-called *Windhund* programme, under which ex-bomber pilots whose units had been disbanded received 20 hours' fighter training before going to an operational unit. With their greater previous flying experience these pilots were more effective than the straight-through trainees. Yet in fighter-versus-fighter combat even these were a poor match for their opponents.

In the summer of 1944 the Allied strategic bomber forces mounted a systematic programme of attacks aimed at wrecking the German synthetic fuel industry. The production of aviation fuel fell far below requirements. Operational flying had to be curtailed in several areas, and most of the remaining bomber units were disbanded. In such a climate the training schools, who were always regarded as the poor relations, suffered hardest of all. First the elementary and many of the specialist flying schools were closed. Then, as the last of their trainees passed out, the specialist fighter schools were also disbanded and their instructors went to front-line units. By February 1945 the *Luftwaffe* aircrew training organisation had, to all intents and purposes, ceased to exist.

The *Flak* Arm

Compared with other nations involved in World War II, the Germans had devoted the greatest resources to the development and deployment of anti-aircraft artillery before the conflict started. Moreover, alone amongst the major air forces, the *Luftwaffe* was responsible for the gun defence of cities and industrial targets (in other nations that was an army prerogative).

At the outbreak of war nearly a million men, almost two-thirds of the total *Luftwaffe* manpower, served in the *Flak* arm (*Flak* was an abbreviation for *Fliegerabwehrkanonen*, or anti-aircraft guns). The size of this arm gradually increased until at its peak in the autumn of 1944 there were 1,250,000 men and women—about half the personnel strength of the *Luftwaffe*—so employed. Because of its size and its importance within the *Luftwaffe*, and not least because most published accounts have ignored it, the *Flak* arm deserves a detailed coverage in this book.

The German Army and Navy also possessed *Flak* units of their own. However, those two services were relatively weak in this respect: taken together, they possessed less than a quarter of the weapons available to the *Luftwaffe*.

Flak Organisation

The *Flak* arm of the *Luftwaffe* had a twofold responsibility. First, it was to protect potential targets in metropolitan Germany and *Luftwaffe* installations wherever they might be. Secondly, it was to provide mobile air defence for the field armies and, on occasions, fire support against ground targets. This dual role was reflected in the layout of higher formations. The highest headquarters formation was the *Korps*, which was fully motorised and operated with the field armies. A *Korps* controlled between two and four *Divisionen*. The staff of a *Flak Division* could be either motorised or static. In the former case it might serve under a *Korps* near the front; in the latter case (usually for home defence) it came under control of the local *Luftgau* headquarters. In static defence a *Division* controlled two or more *Brigaden* (brigades), each of between two and four *Regimenter* (regiments). A motorised *Division* controlled between two and four *Regimenter*. A *Regiment* normally controlled between four and six *Abteilungen* (battalions) in static defence, or four *Abteilungen* if it was motorised. By the beginning of 1945 the *Luftwaffe* possessed seven *Flak Korps*, 29 *Divisionen*, 13 *Brigaden*, and 160 *Regimenter* with their subordinated *Flak Abteilungen*.

The basic *Flak* unit, the *Abteilung*, came in four main types: *Schwere* (heavy), *Leichte* (light), *Gemischte* (mixed, with both heavy and light AA weapons) and *Scheinwerfer* (searchlight). The *Abteilung* were further sub-divided according to their state of motorisation into fully motorised, semi-motorised and static units.

As the war progressed there was a steady drain of able-bodied men away from the static home defence *Flak* units and into the field units. In their place came a hotch-potch collection of men and women from various sources. There were *Flak Wehrmänner*, workers serving in the 'Home Guard' role with *Flak* units in their locality. There were *Luftwaffenhelfer*, 15- and 16-year-old school-boys who were called away from their lessons by day, or from their beds at night, to man the guns. There were youths of the *Reichs Arbeit Dienst*, the labour service, into which all young men were inducted on leaving school unless they went directly into a fighting service. There were *Flak Kampf-helferinnen*, women auxiliaries employed on non-combat duties at gun sites. There were Italian and Hungarian volunteers. And, finally, for the various labouring tasks there were turncoat Russian prisoners.

In October 1944 the *14. Flak Division*, responsible for the defence of the important Leuna synthetic oil refinery and other industrial installations in southern Germany, had a strength of 62,550 personnel of all ranks. These were divided as follows:

Regular *Luftwaffe* personnel	28,000
Reichs Arbeit Dienst	18,000
Luftwaffenhelfer	6,000
Flak Helferinnen	3,050
Hungarian and Italian volunteers	900
Russian prisoners	3,600
Others	3,000

Heavy *Flak*, Weapons and Ammunition

For the purpose of this section the term 'heavy *Flak*' includes all weapons of 7.5cm calibre and larger. These weapons employed predictor control when engaging aircraft, in contrast to the lighter and faster-firing weapons which were fired over open sights.

The smallest-calibre heavy *Flak* weapon produced in quantity in Germany was the 8.8cm. The first version to enter service was the *8.8 cm Flak 18*, introduced in 1933. Fitted with a semi-automatic breech mechanism, this weapon had a practical rate of fire of 15 rounds per minute. The firing crew numbered ten, later reduced to seven. The *8.8 cm Flak 37* had an improved mounting and an electrical data transmission system which carried fire control information directly from the predictor. The *8.8 cm Flak 41* was the first

Main Types of Heavy Flak Weapon used by the *Luftwaffe*

Weapon	Practical max rate of fire	Weight of shell	Max engagement altitude
8.8cm Flak 18	15rds/min	19.8lb	26,250ft
8.8cm Flak 37	15rds/min	19.8lb	26,250ft
8.8cm Flak 41	20rds/min	19.8 lb	35,000ft
10.5cm Flak 38	15rds/min	32.2lb	31,000ft
12.8 cm Flak 40	10rds/min	57lb	35,000ft

major redesign of the gun itself, with a longer and stronger barrel and a powered ramming system. This version entered service in 1943.

The *10.5 cm Flak 37* entered service just before the outbreak of war. It had a powered ramming system and power-assisted laying and a normal crew of nine men. The *38* was similar, but it incorporated an electrical data transmission system and other detailed improvements. The *12.8 cm Flak 40* was the heaviest *Flak* weapon employed by the *Luftwaffe*. It had powered ramming, elevation and traverse. The *12.8 cm Flakzwilling 40* comprised two barrels on a common traversing and elevating mounting. The use of these paired weapons was confined to the giant *Flak* towers erected in the principal German cities.

As the war progressed, the *Flak* arm made increasing use of captured foreign weapons. These included the British Vickers 3in and 3.7in guns, the French 7.5cm, the Italian 9cm and 10.2cm, the Czech 7.65mm and the Russian 7.62cm and 8.5cm weapons. Normally these weapons fired captured ammunition, though in some cases guns were re-bored to fire the standard German 8.8cm shell.

When engaging aircraft, for most of the war heavy *Flak* weapons fired time-fused high-explosive shells (the Germans failed to develop a workable proximity-fused shell). In 1943 controlled-fragmentation rounds were introduced for 8.8cm and 10.5cm weapons. These had grooves cut on the inside face of the casings, so that when the charge detonated the case broke up into a smaller number of larger fragments. The new rounds were considerably more effective against heavy bombers than their predecessors.

Towards the end of the war a new type of shell, the *Brandschrapnel*, (incendiary shrapnel) entered service. This was a thin-walled projectile containing, in the case of an 8.8cm round, 51 small incendiary pellets. When the shell detonated, the pellets were blown forwards and outwards rather like pellets in a shotgun blast. The pellets were designed to pierce the skin of the aircraft, enter fuel tanks and start fires there. The *Brandschrapnel* rounds were considerably more effective than the controlled-fragmentation rounds, which in turn had been a major improvement over the earlier non-grooved projectiles.

In addition to these normal forms of ammunition, heavy *Flak* units sometimes fired star shells. These could be used to provide navigational assistance
for German fighters, or they might be fired in attempts to confuse enemy
bomber crews guided by flares dropped over the target. A typical round of
this type was the 8.8cm *Leuchtgeschoss*. Activated by a time fuse, it ejected a
parachute carrying a white or coloured flare that burnt for about 15 seconds.

'Scarecrows'

During the war there were frequent reports from Allied bomber crews concerning sightings of so-called 'Scarecrow' shells at night. One Allied document described these as 'an explosion releasing a quantity of smoke, coloured stars and flaming debris, resembling an aircraft which had been destroyed. Distinguishable from the real thing, and apparently not lethal at
close range.' The purpose of these explosions was said to be the sapping of
bomber crews' morale, rather than to inflict injury on them or on their aircraft.

During 1940 the *Luftwaffe* experimented with an 8.8cm shell that exploded
with an especially bright flash. As well as the shell's destructive effect, it was
hoped that bomber crews flying at night would find its brighter flash discon-
certing. On analysis following operational trials it was found that the shell
had a negligible effect on bombing accuracy or the evasive action taken by
bombers. After a short period of use, these rounds were withdrawn from
service.

German sources mention no other type of weapon that might fit the 'Scarecrow' category. Certainly the military value of any weapon that was 'apparently not lethal at close range' was highly questionable. Moreover, there would
have been great difficulty in fitting the pyrotechnics necessary to produce a
convincing likeness of a falling bomber into the space available inside even a
large-calibre *Flak* shell. Having investigated the available evidence on the
phenomenon, this author has concluded that the German armed forces *never*
employed types of ammunition designed to affect the morale of enemy aircrew without causing physical damage.

Nevertheless, there is powerful, if one-sided, evidence that some odd effects were seen in the night skies over Germany. If the effects were not deliberate, one may speculate on how they might have occurred accidentally. There
are several possibilities. The 12.8cm shells burst with a very bright flash which
sometimes produced a 'catherine wheel' appearance. This effect resulted from
the large explosive charge, however, and was not deliberate. The pellets from
incendiary shrapnel shells produced a 'swarm of bees' effect at night. Other
unusual phenomena might have resulted from the slow detonation of defec-
tive rounds. And, there can be little doubt, many of the sightings that were
confidently reported as 'Scarecrows' were, in fact, real aircraft exploding and
falling in flames.

Fire Control Equipment for Heavy Flak

The standard German predictor for use with heavy *Flak* at the beginning of the war was the *Kommandogerät 36*. This instrument incorporated a range-finder with a 4-metre baseline. The predictor produced a flow of information on the plane's future flight path, in the form of bearing and elevation settings for the guns and time-fuse settings for the shells. The instrument could not cope with manoeuvring targets, however. Moreover, the maximum aircraft speed it could accept was 400 mph (a figure easily exceeded by a slower aircraft with a good tail wind).

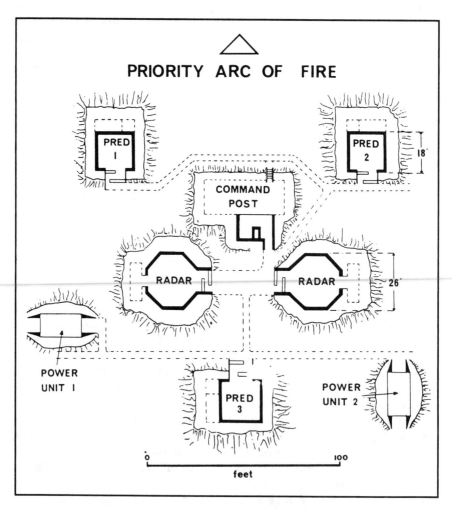

Fig. 14. Layout of the fire control equipment for a typical Grossbatterie. *The third predictor and the second power unit were held in reserve, in case of a failure of one of the main units.*

The *Kommandogerät 40*, which superseded the *-36* in production, was able to track a target in a steady turn. This predictor could calculate fire control information on targets flying at speeds of up to 670 mph.

Layout of a Heavy *Flakbatterie*

During the course of the war several different layouts for *Flakbatterien* were employed. The description given below must be regarded only as representative. In 1939 the standard arrangement comprised four guns at the corners of a square with 35-yard sides, and with the command post in the centre. Early in the conflict the command post with the predictor were moved outside the square, to a position about 100 yards from the nearest gun. That placed the delicate instrument and its operators outside the area affected by the flash and muzzle blast from the guns. If a site was equipped with a radar set, this was placed close to the command post.

At the end of 1941 there was a change in policy, and to concentrate firepower heavy guns were deployed in six-gun batteries. At existing sites this was achieved by placing a extra gun at either end of the square. At new sites the six guns were set out in a circle, or in a circle of five weapons with the sixth in the centre. Later still eight-gun batteries became common, typically laid out in a circle of seven with the eighth in the centre.

By 1942 there was a need to bring concentrated fire to bear on formations of bombers by day, or in compact streams by night. This led to the formation of *Grossbatterien*, with two or three normal batteries situated close together and engaging the same target using firing data from a common command post. During the latter part of the war, a rising proportion of the heavy *Flak* units were grouped into *Grossbatterien*.

In very large cities, such as Berlin, Hamburg and Vienna, massive concrete *Flak* towers were constructed in pairs. The larger structure served as a platform for four heavy guns—10.5cm, 12.8cm or even double 12.8cm. The smaller tower, some distance away, carried the fire control radar and the command post. As well as providing space for ammunition, the lower storeys of the towers served as air raid shelters and civil defence headquarters.

Another important aspect of the *Flak* defences was the so-called *Eisenbahnflak* (railway *Flak*) units. These comprised self-contained units with both light and heavy *Batterien*, the guns and fire-control instruments being mounted on railway flats. These units served as a mobile reserve, to provide for rapid reinforcement to targets considered likely to come under attack. The weapons fired from their flats, which were drawn up in sidings close to the point to be defended.

Searchlights Operating with Heavy *Flak*

At the beginning of the war the most-used type of searchlight in the *Luftwaffe* was the *150 cm Flakscheinwerefer 37*. The unit for the deployment of search-

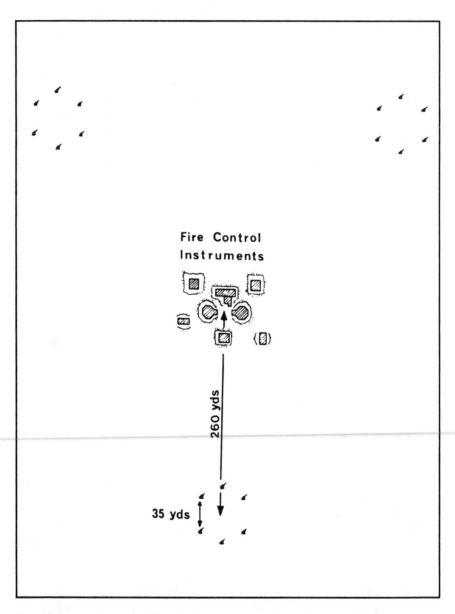

Fig. 15. Layout of a typical Grossbatterie, *showing the positioning of the three six-gun* Batterien *at the corners of a triangle centred on their fire-control instruments. The individual gun emplacements were about 37 yards apart. When the* Grossbatterie *went into action, all eighteen guns fired simultaneous salvos at the single target aircraft being tracked by the predictor.*

lights was the *Abteilung* with three (later four) *Batterien* each with nine (later between 12 and 16) lights. During the early war period the searchlights were laid out in a chessboard pattern, with intervals of about three miles between individual lights. The searchlight zone lay outside the *Flak* engagement area, in the 'zone of preparation' (see below). Sound locators, and later fire-control radars, assisted the lights to find their targets.

In 1942 the more powerful *200 cm Flakscheinwerfer 40* entered service. These were usually positioned close to the radar at a heavy *Flakbatterie*, which helped it to find targets. When used in this way the 200cm light served as the Master Light. When it found a target, the three 150cm satellite lights working with it came on to 'cone' the aircraft. Typically, a searchlight battery was laid out in a triangle. The Master Light was in the centre, and the satellite lights were positioned about 1½ miles away from it at the corners.

It should be noted that a searchlight battery constituted an effective means of target defence in its own right. If one or more lights held a night bomber in their beams, the glare blinded its crew and prevented any sort of accurate bombing run.

Principles of Siting Heavy Flak

So far as the gunners were concerned, enemy bombers had to be expected to approach a vulnerable point from any direction. Therefore the guns had to be positioned to provide all-round defence. During the early war period the defences were laid out on the assumption that the bombers would fly no faster than 265 mph and no higher than 20,000 feet. A bomb released from such an aircraft would have a forward throw of about 4,400 yards. A circle or near circle of radius 4,400 yards from the outer edge of the vulnerable area, joining the points of bomb release, was the Line of Bomb Release (LBR). *Flak* sites were positioned so that enemy planes would be under fire throughout most or all of their bombing run, for a period of about 50 seconds. In that time an aircraft flying at 265 mph covered 6,600 yards. So the *Flak* engagement zone was a concentric circle running from points 6,600 yards outside the LBR, to the LBR itself. Beyond the *Flak* engagement zone lay the so-called 'zone of preparation'. There the predictors tracked targets and computed fire-control data, so that the guns could open fire accurately the moment the aircraft came in their range.

Any aircraft flying slower than the assumed figure had to cross the LBR to release its bombs at the target, so engaging these raised no new problems. Later in the war, with the newer Allied bombers attacking at somewhat higher speeds, the LBR at each target had to be recalculated to take this into account.

The siting of individual *Batterien* depended on the number of those available to defend the target. If there were three *Batterien*, these were laid out in an approximately equilateral triangle each about 3,000 yards from the near-

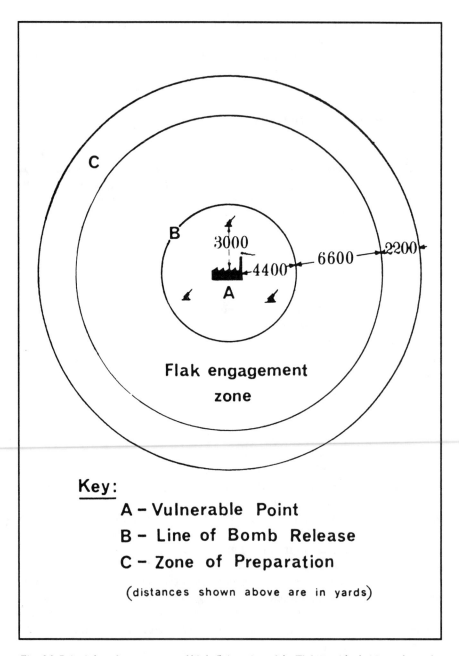

C

B

3000

4400

6600

2200

A

Flak engagement
zone

Key:
A – Vulnerable Point
B – Line of Bomb Release
C – Zone of Preparation

(distances shown above are in yards)

Fig. 16. Principles of engagement of high-flying aircraft by Flak: *an ideal siting scheme for* three *Flak* Batterien *to cover a vulnerable point. Each* Batterie *is indicated by a single gun symbol.*

est point to be defended. If there were five *Batterien*, four would be at the corners of a square about 4,400 yards from the vulnerable point, with the fifth as near the vulnerable point as practicable. Where guns were deployed to protect a large target, for example a city, the latter was divided into a number of vulnerable areas around which the guns were positioned.

Principles of Engagement of High-Flying Aircraft by *Flak*

If they had accurate fire-control data from their predictors, the guns would open fire at the aircraft at their maximum effective range. In the case of the *8.8 cm Flak 18/37*, that was about 10,000 yards. If the guns engaged a formation of bombers, the priority target was the aircraft at the head of the formation. All guns in the battery engaged the same target aircraft, firing by salvos as rapidly as possible.

The Tactical Control Officer, usually the battery commander, decided when to shift fire to another target. Usually this happened when the aircraft being engaged had passed the Line of Bomb Release.

To ensure a smooth switching between a succession of targets, each *Grossbatterie* was equipped with at least two radars and two predictors. The first radar/predictor combination to produce good data on a designated target aircraft controlled the guns during the initial engagement. Meanwhile the other radar/predictor combination tracked another target in the zone of preparation. When fire was shifted to the second target, the Tactical Control Officer switched to the data from the second radar/predictor combination and the engagement continued with a minimum of delay. As soon as it relinquished control of the guns, the first radar/predictor combination swung back to the zone of preparation and searched for a third target.

Light and Medium *Flak* Weapons

The principal automatic weapon used by *Luftwaffe* light *Flak* units was the 2cm gun. There were two models, the *2 cm Flak 30* and the *-38*, which entered service early in the war. Ballistically the two weapons were identical, though the latter had a somewhat greater rate of fire. Ammunition was fed in using 20-round box magazines.

The 2cm gun could be mounted on its own two-wheeled trailer, or it could be fitted to railway wagons, lorries or tracked vehicles. The *2 cm Flakvierling 38* comprised four 2cm weapons on a quadruple mounting that might be either mobile or static.

The standard medium AA guns used by the *Luftwaffe* were the *3.7 cm Flak 18* and the similar *-36* and *-43* models that followed it into service. Ammunition was fed in by six-round clips. When engaging aircraft, these weapons fired high-explosive rounds with percussion fuses. A self-destruction mechanism detonated the shells when they reached their maximum effective range, to prevent their causing damage when they hit the ground. Usually the clips

Type of weapon	Practical max rate of fire	Weight of shell
2 cm Flak 30	120rds/min	4oz
2 cm Flak 38	180rds/min	4oz
3.7 cm Flak 18	80rds/min	1lb 5oz

Main Types of Light and Medium Flak Weapon used by the *Luftwaffe*

were loaded with a mixture of tracer and non-tracer rounds. Both the 2cm and 3.7cm weapons were fired over open sights, and corrected on to the target by observing the flight of tracer rounds.

The standard fire unit was the *Zug* (section) with three guns. A 2cm gun *Batterie* comprised four of five sections, while a 3.7cm *Batterie* was made up of three or four. Early in the war a *Zug* was usually laid out in a triangle with sides of about 250 yards, with the apex towards the vulnerable point. From 1944 the policy changed, and, to provide more concentrated fire-power, the spacing between guns was reduced to about 60 yards. In the centre of the triangle there was usually a small dug-out from which the *Zug* commander directed the fire from his guns.

Principles of Siting Light and Medium *Flak* Weapons

Normally the light and medium *Flak* weapons were sited in the same way as heavy guns, to cover a zone of engagement leading up to the Line of Bomb Release. For the lighter weapons the LBR was calculated for aircraft flying at 500 feet and at 330 mph, which placed the line about 1,000 yards from the vulnerable point. Thus when both heavy and light weapons were deployed for the protection of the same vulnerable point, the heavy weapons were positioned well outside the lighter guns.

Principles for the Engagement of Low-Flying Aircraft by Light or Medium *Flak*

Against a closing target, the effective range of the 2cm gun was about 1,100 yards and that of the 3.7cm gun was about 1,600 yards. Since an aircraft flying at 330 mph covered 150 yards in a second, such a target was in firing range for only a short time. It was therefore important to bring guns to bear quickly on low flying aircraft, and open fire as soon as the target was in range. Because they lacked accurate prediction equipment, these weapons were effective only against aircraft flying almost directly towards, or away from, their site.

Light and medium *Flak* weapons mounted on lorries or half-tracks were much used during the latter part of the war, to protect road convoys from fighter-bomber attack. When engaged in this task the guns had to be ready to go into action at any time, and the gun crews remained in their seats. When enemy fighter-bombers were seen approaching, the gun crew making the initial sighting raised the alarm by opening fire in the general direction of the threat. The entire convoy then came to a halt and all personnel except those manning the *Flak* weapons took cover. The individual *Flak* vehicles pulled off the road on either side (if there was room) and went into action.

Vergeltungswaffe 1: The Flying Bomb

The Weapon

The *Vergeltungswaffe 1* (Revenge Weapon No 1) flying bomb was known in the *Luftwaffe* by its manufacturer's designation, the Fieseler Fi 103, and also by the code-names *Kirschkern* (Cherry Stone) and *Flakzielgerät* (*Flak* target device). To the Allies it was the V.1 or 'Doodle-Bug'. Following the demise of much of the conventional bomber arm in the summer of 1944, the flying bomb was that service's only means available for mounting attacks on strategic targets (the rival V.2 bombardment rocket belonged to the German Army and so falls outside the compass of this volume).

The V.1 was a small pilotless aircraft with a wing span of 17ft 6in and an overall length of 25ft 4in. Its launch weight was 4,858lb and, with a wing area of 55 sq ft, it had a wing loading of 88lb/sq ft. The warhead, mounted in the nose, contained 1,870lb of high explosive.

The V.1 was unlike any other flying machine that appeared in World War II. It was designed to be produced as cheaply as possible, and to make a single flight lasting a maximum of 40 minutes. Most of the structure was fabricated cheaply from mild steel, and there was a minimum of sophistication. The tailplane, for example, was formed out of a single piece of sheet steel, 0.034in thick, with stiffening strips. After the sheet was cut to size, it was bent into shape in a jig and spot-welded along the trailing edge. There were no ribs. The tailplane tips were unfinished steel pressings spot-welded in place.

The Argus pulse-jet engine fitted to the flying bomb ran on low grade (75 octane) petrol. There was no fuel pump. The petrol was pushed through to the burners by compressed air held in containers in the rear fuselage. Compressed air also drove the gyros for the autopilot, and the servo systems for the rudder and elevators (the missile had no ailerons).

During its flight a magnetic compass held the flying bomb on its pre-set heading, while a barometric capsule held it at the pre-set cruising altitude. A small propeller on the nose of the missile, turning in the airflow, drove a simple mechanical counter which measured the distance travelled. At pre-set distances along the track this air-log mechanism armed the warhead, switched on the radio beacon (if fitted) and, finally, initiated the missile's terminal dive.

The Ground Launching Organisation

The unit responsible for launching the V.1s was code-named *Flak Regiment 155 (W)* and later *Flak Gruppe Creil*. The unit was organised along the same general lines as a normal *Flak Regiment*, being sub-divided into *Abteilungen*, *Batterien* and *Züge*. *Abteilungen I, II, III* and *IV* controlled the firing units. *Abteilung V* was responsible for communications. Each firing *Abteilung* comprised four firing and two supply *Batterien*. Each firing *Batterie* controlled two *Züge*, which in turn comprised two firing sites and their crews. Thus a *Zug* controlled two launchers, a *Batterie* four, a firing *Abteilung* 16 and the *Regiment* 64 launchers. At each launching site the crew comprised 50 men under a senior NCO.

The Firing Sequence

Flying bombs arrived at their firing site by lorry, in a partially dismantled condition. The missile was then reassembled and checks were carried out on the operation of the autopilot and control servo units. The flying bomb was then moved to a special non-magnetic building, where the compass system was carefully aligned.

Meanwhile the launching ramp was being prepared. This was 156ft long and elevated at one end to a height of 16ft. It was constructed from eight pre-fabricated sections, each supported at the higher end by an A-frame set in a concrete base. Running up the length of the ramp was a firing tube with a diameter of 11½in, along the top of which was a slot about ½in wide. A cast iron firing piston, shaped like a dumb-bell, fitted into the firing tube and carried a lug which projected out of the slot running along the top of the ramp. The lug engaged the U-shaped launching shoe attached to the underside of the flying bomb.

When the flying bomb was ready for launching, it was moved by trolley to the base of the ramp. There it was lowered on the launching cradle, which was already in position over the lug projecting from the firing piston. The flat wooden underside of the cradle rested between guide rails on the ramp, whose slideway had been covered with a liberal layer of grease. Meanwhile a squad was preparing the launching ramp. Two separate tanks were filled with the rocket-type chemical fuels, hydrogen peroxide (*T Stoff*) and calcium permanganate (*Z Stoff*). At the same time the compressed air bottles fitted to the ramp were fully charged.

When the pre-launching checks were complete, all non-essential personnel withdrew to positions of safety clear of the ramp. The site commander in the concrete firing bunker alongside the ramp controlled the rest of the operation. When all was ready, the site commander pushed the switches to initiate the launch. Compressed air forced petrol from the missile's fuel tank into the burners, where it was mixed with air and ignited by high-energy spark plugs. The pulse-jet engine roared into life and began to build up power.

Simultaneously, compressed air forced the *T Stoff* and *Z Stoff* rocket fuels into the combustion chamber mounted at the base of the launch ramp. On coming into contact the two chemicals reacted violently, producing super-heated steam and oxygen at rapidly increasing pressure. The thrust from the pulse-jet, coupled with the pressure on the firing piston, pushed hard against the steel bolt holding the launching cradle in place. When that pressure exceeded a certain level, the bolt sheared, allowing the cradle with the flying bomb to shoot forward. The two then slid up the ramp, gaining speed rapidly.

If the launch went according to plan, by the time the V.1 reached the end of the ramp it was moving at a speed of about 250 mph, comfortably in excess of its minimum flying speed of 190 mph. As the V.1 left the ramp, the launching cradle and firing piston fell to the ground. Later they would be recovered for re-use.

Flight of the V.1

The V.1 left its launching ramp in a shallow 500ft/min climb, which continued until it reached its pre-set cruising altitude around 1,000 metres (about

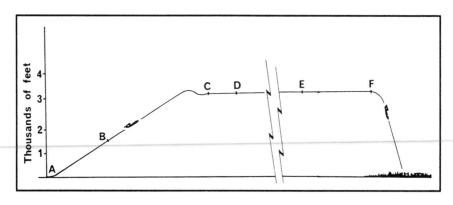

Fig. 17. Flight of the V.1.
(A) After launch, the V.1 made its climb away at about 500 ft/min.
(B) Three minutes after launch the missile began turning on to the previously set heading for the target.
(C) At the previously set cruising altitude, the auto-pilot levelled off the missile.
(D) When the flying bomb was safely clear of friendly territory, the air-log made the warhead 'live'.
(E) About 35 miles from the target the air-log switched on the missile's radio transmitter (if one was carried).
(F) When the missile reached the previously set range of the target, the air-log fired detonators which locked the elevator and rudder. At the same time, spoilers came down under the tailplane to force the missile into a sharp bunt. At that point the rush of fuel to the top of the nearly empty tank caused the motor to cut out. The missile held its steep dive until it struck the ground.

3,200 feet). Three minutes after launch, when the missile was about half-way through its climb, the auto-pilot initiated a slow turn on to its pre-set cruising heading. Soon after the missile crossed the French coast, the air-log counter closed a pair of electrical contacts to make the warhead 'live'.

The V.1s were not manufactured to normal aircraft tolerances, so there were wide variations in the performance of individual missiles. Flying bombs crossed the English coast at any altitude between tree-top height (which usually led to their rapid demise) and 8,000 feet, with most flying at between 3,000 and 4,000 feet. Their speeds also varied greatly. The slowest missiles flew at about 300 mph and the fastest was recorded at 420 mph. Their usual speed was around 350 mph.

Some flying bombs carried a simple radio beacon, which was switched on about five minutes before reaching the target. Ground direction-finding stations tracked the missile during the final part of the flight, and when the transmission ceased that indicated that the bomb had impacted. The intention was that appropriate corrections could be passed to the launching sites, so that subsequent missiles could be adjusted to allow for wind drift.

When the flying bomb reached the pre-set target range, the air-log fired electrical detonators which locked the elevator and rudder in the neutral position and lowered spoilers beneath the tailplane. These spoilers forced the tail to rise and the machine went into a sharp bunt, followed by a steep dive. The bunt and the sudden negative 'G' hurled the remaining fuel to the top of the almost empty tank. That uncovered the feed pipe, causing the pulse-jet to flame out. Thus, shortly before the weapon impacted, the loud rumble of its motor suddenly ceased. Many Londoners owed their lives to the few seconds' warning they received of the missile's imminent arrival.

The V.1 carried two separate impact fusing systems to detonate the warhead, backed up by a clockwork time fuse. In combination these were highly effective: of the first 2,700 flying bombs to fall on the British Isles, only four failed to explode.

The V.1 Summed Up

Although the flying bomb had many clever features, its accuracy fell far short of bombing by conventional aircraft. A major source of error was the wind. If no allowance was made, during a 40-minute flight a 30 mph side wind would blow a missile twenty miles away from its intended track. In 1944 the Greater London built-up area had a diameter of about 12 miles. Nor were the V.1 transmissions of much value in correcting the fall of missiles. The RAF jamming organisation 'meaconed' the transmissions to ensure they gave erroneous information on the missiles' impact points.

Overall, ground-launched flying bombs fired from a range of about 120 miles gave a 50 per cent impact zone of about *eight miles* (the air-launched V.1s, described in Chapter 12, were even less accurate). And those figures discounted the one bomb in ten that failed to reach sustained flight and crashed after launch. So even if there were no losses from fighters, guns or balloon defences, less than half of the bombs that launched successfully were likely reach the London area. Although the V.1s caused considerable damage and large numbers of civilian casualties in London, the weapon was virtually ineffective against a target much smaller in area.

The *Luftwaffe* Fighter Aces' Victory Scores

Over the years there has been controversy, much of it ill-informed, concerning the validity of the German fighter aces' victory claims. *Major* Erich Hartmann, the top scorer in the *Luftwaffe*, is credited with 352 victories; 35 German pilots are credited with victory totals exceeding 150. On the other hand, Group Captain 'Johnny' Johnson, the RAF top-scorer in the late-war period, is credited with 'only' 38 victories; Major Richard Bong, the top-scoring US Army Air Forces pilot, is credited with 40; and Guards Colonel Ivan Kozhedub, the top-scoring Soviet Air Force pilot, is credited with 62. If the German pilots' victory claims are accurate, why was there such a great disparity in the claims of the different nations' pilots? Were the top German fighter aces eight or nine times as good as those of the Allied Air Forces?

This author has no evidence that the top German fighter pilots were any better than their Allied counterparts. The main difference between them was that German pilots had greater opportunities to amass large scores than Allied pilots—if they survived long enough. During the early part of the war the *Luftwaffe* often went into action against opponents with inferior training and equipment, and these opponents suffered accordingly. The days of the easy victories soon passed, however, and from the beginning of 1943 the *Luftwaffe* faced a hard fight on all fronts. To survive for any length of time against numerically superior enemy forces, a German pilot needed to be good and he needed to be lucky. For those who knew their business, however, there were usually plenty of enemy aircraft to pick off.

Another important factor that assisted German fighter pilots to amass large scores was that they did not fly limited tours of combat duty like those in the RAF or the USAAF. Take the top scorer, Erich Hartmann, who joined *JG 52* on the Eastern Front in October 1942. He flew on operations almost continually from then until the end of the war, with only short breaks for leave. By the end of October 1943 his score had reached 148 and in March 1944 it passed the 200 mark. He flew more than 800 operational missions, an average of nearly one per day over the 2½-year period, and on average gained one victory per 2½ sorties. No British or American pilot was allowed fly combat missions for such a long period without a break. At the peak of their scoring careers there were several Allied fighter pilots who achieved victories at the same rate as Hartmann. However, none did so for more than a few months before being sent on a rest tour.

Some writers have suggested that *Dr* Goebbels' propaganda service inflated the victory scores of individual German pilots. This author has studied these claims in detail and can assert with confidence that this was not the case. The Germans are nothing if not good bureaucrats. Before a victory claim was confirmed it underwent rigorous checking by the *Abschusskommission* (the Commission for the Adjudication of Victory Claims). No claim was even considered unless there was an independent witness of the action, or a wrecked enemy aircraft that appeared to link with the claim. If the action took place over German-held territory and no wreck was found, a pilot would have considerable difficulty getting the victory confirmed. No credit was given for shared or probable victories. If more than one fighter had engaged the enemy aircraft shot down, the pilot judged to have played the major part in its destruction received the credit.

This is not to say that every German pilot's victory score was 100 per cent accurate. The *Abschusskommission* was not perfect. Sometimes mistakes were made, and in all air forces there were some pilots who claimed dishonestly in action. But the German organisation was as effective as could be expected in time of war, and it was more thorough than any counterpart run by the Allies.

To sum up, the German fighter pilots' victories were recorded as accurately as could be expected in time of war—and certainly more accurately than those of their British or American counterparts. The German pilot's scores were higher than those in other air forces because they had greater opportunities to achieve victories, and they spent longer periods on front-line operations.

Luftwaffe Pilots Credited With More Than 100 Victories

Hauptmann Erich Hartmann	352	*Hauptmann* Helmut Lipfert	203
Major Gerhard Barkhorn,	301	*Major* Walter Krupinski	197
Major Günther Rall	275	*Major* Anton Hackl	192
Oberleutnant Otto Kittel	267	*Hauptmann* Joachim Brendel	189
Major Walter Nowotny	258	*Hauptmann* Max Stotz	189
Major Wilhelm Batz	237	*Hauptmann* Joachim Kirschner	188
Major Erich Rudorffer	222	*Major* Kurt Brändle	180
Oberstleutnant Heinrich Bär	220	*Oberstleutnant* Günther Josten	178
Oberst Hermann Graf	212	*Oberst* Johannes Steinhoff	176
Major Theodor Weissenberger	208	*Oberleutnant* Ernst-Wilhelm	
Oberstleutnant Hans Philipp	206	Reinert	174
Oberleutnant Walter Schuck	206	*Hauptmann* Günther Schack	174
Major Heinrich Ehrler	204	*Hauptmann* Emil Lang	173
Oberleutnant Anton Hafner	204	*Hauptmann* Heinz Schmidt	173

Major Horst Ademeit	166	*Fj. Oberfeldwebel* Heinz	
Oberst Wolf-Dietrich Wilcke	162	Marquardt	121
Hauptmann Hans-Joachim		*Major* Heinz-Wolfgang	
Marseille	158	Schnaufer	121
Hauptmann Heinrich Sturm	158	*Hauptmann* Robert Weiss	121
Oberleutnant Gerhard Thyben	157	*Oberstleutnant* Friedrich Obleser	120
Oberleutnant Hans Beisswenger	152	*Oberstleutnant* Erich Leie	118
Leutnant Peter Düttmann	152	*Leutnant* Franz-Josef	
Oberst Gordon Gollob	150	Beerenbrock	117
Leutnant Fritz Tegtmeier	146	*Leutnant* Hans-Joachim Birkner	117
Oberleutnant Albin Wolf	144	*Leutnant* Jakob Norz	117
Leutnant Kurt Tanzer	143	*Leutnant* Heinz Wernicke	117
Oberstleutnant Friedrich-Karl		*Oberleutnant* August Lambert	116
Müller	140	*Oberst* Werner Mölders	115
Leutnant Karl Gratz	138	*Leutnant* Wilhelm Crinius	114
Major Heinrich Setz	138	*Major* Werner Schroer	114
Hauptmann Franz Schall	137	*Leutnant* Hans Dammers	113
Oberleutnant Walter Wolfrum	137	*Leutnant* Berthold Korts	113
Hauptmann Rudolf Trenkel	138	*Oberstleutnant* Kurt Bühligen	112
Oberst Adolf Dickfeld	136	*Oberst* Helmut Lent	110
Hauptmann Horst-Günther von		*Oberleutnant* Franz Woidich	110
Fassong	136	*Major* Kurt Ubben	110
Oberleutnant Otto Fönnekold	136	*Major* Reinhard Seiler	109
Hauptmann Karl-Heinz Weber	136	*Hauptmann* Emil Bitsch	108
Major Joachim Müncheberg	135	*Major* Hans Hahn	108
Oberleutnant Hans Waldmann	134	*Oberst* Günther Lützow	108
Major Johannes Wiese	133	*Oberleutnant* Bernhard Vechtel	108
Alfred Grislawski	133	*Oberst* Victor Bauer	106
Major Adolf Borchers	132	*Hauptmann* Werner Lucas	106
Major Erwin Clausen	132	*Generalleutnant* Adolf Galland	104
Hauptmann Wilhelm Lemke	131	*Leutnant* Heinz Sachsenberg	104
Oberst Herbert Ihlefeld	130	*Major* Hartmann Grasser	103
Oberleutnant Heinrich Sterr	130	*Major* Siegfried Freytag	102
Major Franz Eisenach	129	*Hauptmann* Friedrich	
Oberst Walther Dahl	128	Geisshardt	102
Hauptmann Franz Dörr	128	*Oberstleutnant* Egon Mayer	102
Leutnant Rudi Rademacher	126	*Oberleutnant* Max-Hellmuth	
Oberleutnant Josef Zwernemann	126	Ostermann	102
Leutnant Gerhard Hoffmann	125	*Oberleutnant* Herbert Rollwage	102
Oberst Dietrich Hrabak	125	*Major* Josef Wurmheller	102
Oberst Walter Oesau	125	*Hauptmann* Rudolf Miethig	101
Oberleutnant Wolf Ettel	124	*Oberst* Josef Priller	101
Hauptmann Wolfgang Tonne	122	Ulrich Wernitz	101

Biographies of Senior Commanders

Reichsmarschall **Hermann Göring**

Born in 1893, Hermann Göring was commissioned in the Imperial Army in 1912. He first saw action as an infantry officer during the early stages of World War I. In October 1914 he transferred to the Imperial Flying Service and flew initially as an artillery observer. He then trained as a pilot and was posted to a fighter unit. In May 1918, following his 18th aerial victory while flying with *Jasta 27*, he received the *Pour le Mérite* (the so-called 'Blue Max', the nation's highest decoration for bravery in action). Two months later he took command of the famous *Jagdgeschwader Richthofen* and held that post until the Armistice, when his victory score stood at 22.

Demobilised after the war, he engaged in a series of aviation ventures in Germany and in Sweden. He also joined the newly formed National Socialist Party and played a leading part in its rise to power. In 1923 he played an active role when the Party attempted to seize power in Munich, and when the *Putsch* failed he fled to Sweden. Following a government amnesty in 1927 he returned to Germany, and again became active in politics. In May 1928 he was elected as a National Socialist deputy to Parliament.

In 1933, after the National Socialist government took power, he held several important posts, including that of State Minister for Air. Now Göring wielded considerable political power and, when the occasion demanded, he showed that he could be both astute and ruthless. His position in the Party was now second only to that of Hitler himself. Under his leadership the build-up of the secret *Luftwaffe* received high priority for money, resources and personnel. From the time of the public unveiling of the new *Luftwaffe*, in 1935, he was its Commander-in-Chief.

Following the impressive part played by the *Luftwaffe* during the campaigns in Poland, in Flanders and in the Soviet Union, in the autumn of 1941 Göring was at the height of his popularity and power. Hitler had proclaimed him as his successor. Although Allied propaganda characterised him as a rotund buffoon with a vanity for dressing up, few Germans held that view of Göring at this time.

The spell of popularity did not last long, however. By the end of 1942 the *Luftwaffe* was under severe pressure on each of the battle fronts. As the air attacks on the German homeland became more damaging, Göring's personal position declined steadily. At the same time the *Reichsmarschall*'s many assumed duties in government, and frequent periods of leave, left him relatively little time to run the *Luftwaffe*. Finally in April 1945, after an unsuccessful attempt to take power from Hitler, he was dismissed from all posts. After the war he went on trial at Nuremberg on charges of conspiracy, crimes against peace, general war crimes and crimes against humanity. Convicted on all four counts, he was sentenced to death by hanging. Before that sentence could be carried out, however, he committed suicide by taking poison on 15 October 1946.

Generalfeldmarschall Robert, *Ritter* von Greim

Robert von Greim was born in 1892 and entered the Royal Bavarian Army as a cadet in 1906. During the early part of World War I he served in the artillery before transferring to the Flying Service in 1916. He became a successful fighter pilot and rose to command *Jagdstaffel 34*. Later he led *Jagdgruppe 10*, then *Jagdgruppe 9*. At the end of the war he was credited with 28 aerial victories and held the *Pour le Mérite*.

Following the Armistice he was in China from 1924 to 1927, where he helped organise an air force for General Chiang Kai-shek. He then returned to Germany and started a flying school for commercial pilots. During the secret rebuilding of the *Luftwaffe*, he commanded the re-formed *Richthofen Geschwader*. In 1935 he was appointed Inspector of Fighters and Dive Bombers, and in the following year became Inspector of Equipment and Flight Safety. In 1937 he became head of the Personnel Section at the Air Ministry. In 1939 he took command of *Fliegerdivision 5* (later renamed *Fliegerkorps V*). He held the post during the campaign in Flanders, in the Battle of Britain and during the invasion of the Soviet Union. In April 1942 the formation was renamed yet again, as *Luftwaffe* Command East; then, in July 1943, it became *Luftflotte 6*.

Hitler held von Greim in high esteem as a fighting commander. Following the dismissal of Göring in April 1945, he was promoted to *Generalfeldmarschall* and appointed Commander-in-Chief of the *Luftwaffe*. In May 1945, shortly after he was taken prisoner, he committed suicide.

Generalfeldmarschall Albert Kesselring

Born in 1895, Albert Kesselring entered the Imperial Army in 1914 and served as a Brigade Adjutant and General Staff officer during World War I. After the Armistice he remained in the Army and gained a reputation as an extremely capable administrator.

In October 1933 he transferred to the new *Luftwaffe* and became the head of that service's Administrative Office. In the years that followed he held a succession of progressively more important posts. In 1938 he took command of *Luftwaffengruppe 1* (later renamed *Luftflotte 1*) and led the formation during the campaign in Poland. Early in 1940 he took command of *Luftflotte 2*, then the largest of the *Luftflotten*, as it prepared for the planned all-out offensive in the West. During that offensive he commanded his force with distinction, and he went on to command that formation during the Battle of Britain.

In December 1941 *Luftflotte 2* moved to the Mediterranean, still with Kesselring in command. In addition, he was appointed to command all German forces in that theatre. In 1943 he gave up command of *Luftflotte 2*, but he remained as C-in-C South in command of German forces in Italy. In March 1945 he was appointed C-in-C West. He died in 1960.

Generalfeldmarschall Erhard Milch

Born in 1892, Erhard Milch was commissioned into an artillery regiment in the Imperial Army in 1909. Following active service on the Eastern Front, he transferred to the Flying Service in 1915. For much of the war he flew with reconnaissance units, but in 1918 he took command of the fighter unit *Jagdgruppe 6*.

After the war he entered business and in 1926 became the Director of the airline Deutsche Lufthansa. In 1933 he became State Secretary for Aviation, and played a major part in the building up of the German aircraft industry. Three years later he was promoted to *General der Flieger*, and in 1938 to *Generaloberst*. In 1940 he became a *Generalfeldmarschall*. Following the suicide of Ernst Udet in November 1941, Milch became Director General of Equipment in addition to his other duties.

In the years that followed relations between Milch and Göring became increasingly strained. Finally, following a stormy meeting with Hitler in May 1944 on the failure to produce the Me 262 as a fighter-bomber, Milch was stripped of his powers. After the war he was tried and convicted for the forced transportation of foreign workers to Germany. He was sentenced to life imprisonment, but later the term was reduced to 15 years. Released on parole in 1955, he died in January 1972.

Generalfeldmarschall Dr Ing. Wolfram *Freiherr* von Richthofen

Wolfram von Richthofen, born in 1895, was commissioned into a Hussar regiment of the Imperial Army in 1913. He transferred to the Flying Service in 1917 and served as a pilot in *Jasta 11* of *Jagdgeschwader Richthofen* (named after his cousin Manfred). When the war ended he had been credited with eight aerial victories.

After the Armistice he left the service to study engineering and received his doctorate before re-joining the *Reichswehr* in 1923. In 1933 he transferred to the secret *Luftwaffe* and moved to the Air Ministry. In November 1936, for a brief period, he commanded the small German expeditionary air force sent fight in the civil war in Spain. Two years later he returned to Spain and took command of the much expanded *Legion Kondor*.

During the campaigns of the early war period he commanded the hard-hitting *Fliegerkorps VIII* with the bulk of the Ju 87 dive-bomber units. While in that post he established a reputation as a leading exponent of air operations to support of the Army. In July 1942 he took command of *Luftflotte 4*. The following year he was promoted to *Generalfeldmarschall* and moved to command *Luftflotte 2* in the Mediterranean theatre. In November 1944 he contracted a brain tumour and was transferred to the reserve. When the war ended he was taken prisoner, and in June 1945, while in captivity, he died of a brain haemorrhage.

Generalfeldmarschall Hugo Sperrle

Born in 1885, Hugo Sperrle joined an infantry regiment in the Imperial Army in 1903. During World War I he served in the Imperial Flying Service, and rose to command the flying units attached to the 7th Army. After the war he transferred to the Army, but when the new *Luftwaffe* came out into the open he transferred to that service. In 1936 he commanded the the the *Luftwaffe* contingent sent to fight in the Spanish Civil War, the *Legion Kondor*.

On his return from Spain in 1938 he commanded *Luftwaffengruppe 3*, and remained in the post when it was renamed *Luftflotte 3* shortly before the outbreak of war. In 1940 Sperrle commanded the *Luftflotte* during the campaign in the West and provided the air support for the powerful armoured thrust through southern Belgium and northern France. The thrust reached the coast west of Calais, splitting the Allied armies into two and leading to the evacuation at Dunkirk. Sperrle remained in command during the Battle of Britain and the night attacks that followed.

In the spring of 1941 bulk of his flying units were transferred to the East in preparation for the attack on the Soviet Union and the fighting strength of *Luftflotte 3* waned. Nevertheless Sperrle maintained a steady pressure on the British Isles with his small bomber force, tying down many RAF fighter squadrons and a large anti-aircraft organisation that might otherwise have been used to effect in other theatres.

Following the invasion of Normandy in 1944, Sperrle's forces were overwhelmed by the Allied air forces and could do little to influence events. Hitler placed personal blame on Sperrle for this failure, though given the disparity in forces it is doubtful whether anyone else could have done better. In August 1944 he was transferred to the reserve. After the war he was placed on trial at Nuremberg for war crimes but was acquitted.

Generaloberst Hans Jeschonnek

Hans Jeschonnek was born in 1899. He entered the Imperial Army in 1914 as a cadet infantry officer. In 1917 he transferred to the Flying Service and fought with *Jagdstaffel 40*. After the Armistice he remained in the *Reichswehr* as a cavalry officer. In 1933 he transferred to the *Luftwaffe* as a staff officer with the rank of *Hauptmann*. Thus he began a meteoric career which, in six years, took him to the position of Chief of the General Staff of the *Luftwaffe* with the rank of *Generalmajor*.

In 1940 he was promoted direct to *General der Flieger*, without serving in the intermediate rank of *Generalleutnant*. During the years of victory he was held in high esteem and in March 1942 he reached the rank of *Generaloberst*. By the middle of 1943, however, the *Luftwaffe* no longer had control over events. Hitler and Göring placed personal blame on Jeschonnek for this deterioration in the service's fighting power. On 19 August 1943, during a spell of depression, he shot himself.

Generaloberst Günther Korten

Born in 1898, Günther Korten joined an artillery regiment of the Imperial Army as an officer cadet in 1914. During World War I he served in the Army, and he remained with the *Reichswehr* afterwards. In 1934 he transferred to the *Luftwaffe* and by 1939 he was Chief of Staff of *Luftlotte 4* during the Polish campaign. During the Flanders campaign he served as Chief of Staff of *Luftflotte 3*. The following year he returned to *Luftflotte 4* and served there during the Balkans campaign and the invasion of the Soviet Union.

In August 1942 he became head of *Luftwaffe* Command Don with the rank of *Generalleutnant*. In the following January he was promoted to *General der Flieger* and in June 1943 he assumed command of *Luftflotte 1*. He was in this post for only a short time, however. Following the suicide of *General* Jeschonnek (see above), Korten became Chief of the General Staff of the *Luftwaffe*. He suffered severe injuries during the bomb attempt on Hitler's life on 20 July 1944 and died a few days later.

Generaloberst Hans-Jurgen Stumpff

Born in 1890, Hans-Jurgen Stumpff entered the Imperial Army in 1907. He served as an infantry officer in World War I, and later joined the Army General Staff. After 1918 he remained in the Army, and in 1933 he transferred to the new *Luftwaffe*.

From June 1937 until January 1939 he was Chief of General Staff of the *Luftwaffe*, with the rank of *Generalleutnant*. Early in 1940 he commanded *Luftflotte 1* based in north-east Germany and Poland. Following promotion to *Generaloberst* in May 1940, he took command of the newly formed *Luftflotte 5* in Norway and Denmark. After the disastrous action on 15 August, when his aircraft attempted to attack targets in the north of England and suffered heavy losses, Stumpff's force played little further part in the Battle of Britain.

Early in 1944 he was appointed commander of *Luftflotte Reich*, responsible for the air defence of the German homeland. Thus he had the task of fighting a 'Battle of Britain in reverse'. Stumpff had to face the increasingly strong American attacking forces with a collection of units that were inferior in numbers, in the quality of their equipment and in the quality of pilot training. Perhaps surprisingly, in view of his lack of success, Stumpff held that post until the end of the war.

Generaloberst Ernst Udet

Born in 1896, Ernst Udet joined the Imperial Army shortly after the outbreak of World War I. In 1915 he entered the Flying Service and trained as a pilot. In April 1918, following his 20th aerial victory, he received the *Pour le Mérite*. At the end of the war his victory total stood at 62, and he was the highest-scoring German pilot to survive the conflict.

After the war he achieved international fame as a test, sports and aerobatic pilot. In 1935 he entered the new *Luftwaffe* and the following year became Inspector of Fighters and Dive Bombers. In June 1936 he became Director of the Technical Department at the Air Ministry, and in February 1939 he became Director General of Equipment with the rank of *Generalleutnant*. In July 1940 he was promoted to *Generaloberst*.

However, Udet's skill as a pilot in no way fitted him for the exacting task of overseeing the production of aircraft for the *Luftwaffe*. One by one the programmes he instituted for the production of new aircraft types ran into difficulties. At the same time, following the invasion of the Soviet Union, the *Luftwaffe* suffered extremely heavy losses in aircraft. When the German aircraft industry failed to produce the sufficient replacements, the strength of front-line units fell well below establishment. Udet suffered increasingly severe bouts of depression, and on 17 November 1941 he shot himself.

General der Flieger Josef Kammhuber

Born in 1896, Josef Kammhuber entered the Imperial Army in 1914. During World War I he served first with a Pioneer battalion, then with the infantry. After the Armistice he served with the *Reichswehr*. In 1933 he transferred to the *Luftwaffe* and served initially as a staff officer at the Air Ministry. During the Flanders campaign he commanded *Kampfgeschwader 51*. Shot down over France and taken prisoner, he was freed after the Armistice.

In the summer of 1940, with the rank of *Oberst*, he set up a night fighter force to counter the RAF attacks on Germany. By the middle of 1941 the force had grown into *Fliegerkorps XII* and at the end of the year Kammhuber received promotion to *Generalleutnant*. The night fighter force expanded steadily to keep pace with the strengthening RAF attacks, and by the beginning of 1943 it was among the most important *Luftwaffe* commands. In January 1943 Kammhuber was promoted to *General der Flieger*. In the following July, however, the RAF countered his system of radar close-controlled interceptions by the use of 'Window' radar reflective foil.

With the failure of his defensive system, and a series of devastating attacks on the port of Hamburg, Kammhuber fell from favour. In November 1943

he took command the less important *Luftflotte 5* in Norway and Finland. He
returned to favour in February 1945, when he became Special Plenipotenti-
ary for Jet and Rocket Aircraft. By then it was too late for him to influence
events, however. After the war, in 1956, Kammhuber joined the *Bundeswehr*
and became Inspector of the re-formed *Luftwaffe*. He held that post until
1962 when he retired.

General der Flieger Karl Koller

Karl Koller, who was born in 1898, entered the Imperial Army in 1914. In
1917 he transferred to the Flying Service and trained as a pilot. After the war
he served with the Bavarian Police Force until 1935, when he joined the
Luftwaffe. In 1938 he became Chief of the Operations Staff of *Luftwaffengruppe
3* (renamed *Luftflotte 3* soon afterwards) and in January 1941 its Chief of
Staff. He became head of the *Luftwaffe* Operations Staff in September 1943.
In November 1944 he replaced Werner Kreipe (see below) as Chief of the
General Staff of the *Luftwaffe*, a post he held for the remainder of the war.

General der Flieger Werner Kreipe

Born in 1904, Werner Kreipe entered the *Reichswehr* in 1922. The following
November, while attending the Military Academy, he took part in the abor-
tive National Socialist *Putsch* in Munich. In 1930 he underwent flying training and in 1934 he transferred from the Army to the *Luftwaffe* with the rank
of *Hauptmann*. He served as a liaison officer with the Italian Air Force in
1936, and in a similar capacity with the Belgian Air Force in 1937.

In 1940 he commanded *Kampfgeschwader 2* during the campaign in the
West. The following year he became Chief of Staff of *Fliegerkorps I*. In July
1943 he was appointed *General* in charge of training. In August 1944 he
became Chief of General Staff of the *Luftwaffe*, following the death of *Generaloberst* Korten (see above).

Following the failure of the *Luftwaffe* to influence events on each of the
battle fronts, he was in the unfortunate position of having to face of Hitler's
wrath. When Korten tried to defend his service by answering the criticisms in
detail, the *Führer* banished him from his headquarters. In November Korten
was relieved of his post, and he spent the rest of the war in command of the
Air Warfare College in Berlin. After the war he served with the Federal Ministry of Traffic in Bonn.

Generalleutnant Adolf Galland

Born in 1912, Adolf Galland began his flying training in 1932 at a school for
airline pilots. In 1934 he entered the *Luftwaffe* and commissioned as a *Leutnant*.
Between May 1937 and June 1938 he commanded the 3rd *Staffel* of *Jagdgruppe
88* in Spain, flying the Heinkel He 51.

During the Polish campaign he flew Henschel Hs 123s in the ground-attack role with *II. (Schlacht)/LG 2*. In June 1940, with the rank of *Hauptmann*, he took command of the fighter unit *III./JG 26* and led it during the campaign in the Flanders. In August 1940, following promotion to *Major*, he assumed command of *Jagdgeschwader 26* and led the unit during the Battle of Britain. Also that month, following his 17th aerial victory, he was awarded the *Ritterkreuz*. His success as a fighter pilot brought him a steady stream of decorations. In September 1940, following his 40th victory, he received the Oakleaves; nine months later, following his 69th victory, he received the Swords; and in January 1942, after his 94th victory, he received the *Ritterkreuz* with Oakleaves, Swords and Diamonds.

Following the death of *Oberst* Werner Mölders in November 1941, Galland was appointed Inspector of Fighters and promoted to *Oberst*. In November 1942, at the age of 30, he became a *Generalmajor*, the youngest-ever recipient of the rank. By then the *Luftwaffe* was on the defensive, however, and the days of easy victories were over. Galland was outspoken in his criticism of the ineffectiveness of the *Luftwaffe*'s re-equipment and training programmes, and this brought him into open conflict with Göring. In January 1945, following a particularly stormy meeting, Galland was relieved of his staff duties. Göring made no objection when Galland then appointed himself commander of the élite Messerschmitt Me 262 jet fighter unit *Jagdverband 44*, which he led until the end of the war. Galland's final victory total stood at 104. After being active for many years as a consultant on World War II aviation matters, he died in February1996.

Generalmajor Dietrich Peltz

Born in 1914, Dietrich Peltz joined the *Luftwaffe* in 1935. During the campaigns in Poland and in the West in 1940 he commanded a *Staffel* of Junkers Ju 87 dive-bombers. In the Battle of Britain he flew Junkers Ju 88s with *Kampfgeschwader 77* and in the spring of 1941 he was appointed a *Gruppe* commander.

In September 1942 he took command of the Ist *Gruppe* of *Kampfgeschwader 66*, a Ju 88 unit active over the Mediterranean. In the following December he was appointed Inspector of Bomber Units and in March 1943 he took command of operations against England (*Angriffsführer England*). In September he also became commander of *Fliegerkorps IX*. Between then and May 1944, with limited forces, his attacks on Britain tied down large numbers of fighters and anti-aircraft guns. Despite imaginative tactics, his force suffered heavy losses. Following D-day *Fliegerkorps IX* engaged in nightly attacks against the lodgement area and shipping off the coast. During the German offensive in the Ardennes in December 1944 Peltz commanded *Jagdkorps II*, which attempted to provide air support for that operation. In the face of overwhelming Allied air supremacy, however, he was able to achieve little.

Literature on the *Luftwaffe*: A Critical Bibliography

Since World War II numerous books have been published on the *Luftwaffe*. They range from carefully researched works of considerable historical importance to catchpenny accounts based on the work of others and filled with errors. Limitations of space prevent a critical mention of all the works published on this subject. Those described below are the ones which, in the opinion of this author, are the most reliable works on the *Luftwaffe* and its operations. Unless otherwise stated, the works named are published in the English language.

General Accounts on *Luftwaffe* Operations

Aders, Gebhard, *History of the German Night Fighter Force 1917–1945*, Jane's, 1978. A comprehensive account of the evolution of the night fighter arm of the *Luftwaffe* and its operations.

Air Ministry, London, *The Rise and Fall of the German Air Force 1933 to 1945*. Issued by the Assistant Chief of Air Staff (Intelligence) of the RAF in 1948, this is a very good general account of the *Luftwaffe* and the factors which influenced its operations during the war. A copy may be examined at the Public Record Office, Kew, London; others have found their way into private hands.

Beale, Nick, et al, *AirWar Italy 1944–45*, Airlife Publishing, Shrewsbury, 1996. A well-researched and detailed account of air operations by the *Luftwaffe* and the Italian National Republican Air Force between June 1944 and the end of the war.

Bekker, Cajus, *The LuftwaffeWar Diaries*, Macdonald, London 1966. This book has its faults. The title is quite misleading, for the book contains virtually no material from *Luftwaffe* war diaries. Although it purports to describe the *Luftwaffe* and its operations during World War II, its coverage is very uneven. The author devotes 310 pages to the first 52 months of the conflict, and only 27 pages to the final 17 months. Perhaps worst of all, to achieve dramatic effect the author resorts in several places to using made-up dialogue. These points mar an otherwise useful historical work which provides a good general history on *Luftwaffe* air operations during the first four years of the war.

Ethell, Jeffrey, and Price, Alfred, *WorldWar II Combat Jets*, Airlife, Shrewsbury, 1994. A detailed account of the service careers of the jet aircraft types that went into service during WorldWar II. Includes descriptions of the Messerschmitt 163, the Me 262, the Arado Ar 234, the Heinkel He 162 and the Bachem Ba 349 Natter.

Hinsley, F. H., *British Intelligence in the Second WorldWar: Volumes I, II, III, Parts I and II*, HMSO, London, 1979 to 1988. The Official History on the work of the British Intelligence organisation during WorldWar II, including the information gained from decrypted German signals traffic. Although the series covers material gleaned on all aspects of the German war effort, there is a wealth of useful information on the *Luftwaffe* and its operations.

Irving, David, *The Rise and Fall of the Luftwaffe: The Life of Erhard Milch*, Weidenfeld & Nicolson, London, 1973. An excellent account on the leadership of the *Luftwaffe*, based on the personal diaries and recollections of *Generalfeldmarschall* Erhard Milch, backed by the transcripts of numerous wartime conferences.

Koch, Horst Adalbert, *Flak: die Geschichte der deutschen Flakartillerie und der Einsatz der Luftwaffenhelfer*, Podzun Verlag, Bad Nauheim, 1954. A comprehensive German-language account of operations by *Luftwaffe* anti-aircraft gun units during the conflict.

Price, Alfred, *Battle Over the Reich*, Ian Allan, Shepperton, 1973. A detailed overview of air attacks by the RAF and the USAAF on Germany, and the reaction of the German air defence system.

———, *Blitz on Britain*, Ian Allan, Shepperton, 1976. A detailed overview of *Luftwaffe* operations by manned aircraft against Great Britain during the war and the reaction of the British defences.

———, *The Last Year of the Luftwaffe*, Arms & Armour Press, London, 1991. This book gives a detailed overview of *Luftwaffe* operations during the period May 1944 to May 1945, an area that is omitted in many other histories of that service.

USAF Historical Studies on the German Air Force in World War II, Arno Press Inc, New York, 1968–1970. These lengthy monographs were written after the war by ex-*Luftwaffe* senior officers, and were intended for use by students at the USAF Air University at Maxwell, Alabama. They contain a wealth of information, both general and detailed, on their respective subjects:

Morzik, *Generalmajor* Fritz, *German Air Force Airlift Operations*.

Nielsen, *Generalleutnant* Andreas, *The German Air Force General Staff*.

Plocher, *Generalleutnant* Hermann, *The German Air Force Versus Russia, 1941*.

———, *The German Air Force Versus Russia, 1942*.

———, *The German Air Force Versus Russia, 1943*.

Suchenwirth, Richard, *Command and Leadership in the German Air Force*.

———, *Historical Turning Points in the German Air Force War Effort*.

————, *The Development of the German Air Force, 1919–1939*.

Deichmann, *General der Flieger* Paul, *Spearhead for Blitzkrieg: Luftwaffe Operations in Support of the Army, 1939–1945*. A revised version of the book, part of the above series but re-edited by Alfred Price and published by Greenhill Books, London, in 1996.

Young, Richard, *The Flying Bomb*, Ian Allan, Shepperton, 1978. A detailed and comprehensive account of the development and operational use of the V.1 flying bomb.

Accounts of Actions which Give a
Detailed Insight into *Luftwaffe* Operations

Ethell, Jeffrey, and Price, Alfred, *Target Berlin*, Jane's, London, 1981, reissued by Arms & Armour Press, London, 1989. A in-depth reconstruction of the air battle on 6 March 1944, when the USAAF launched their first full-scale attack on the German capital by day and suffered their heaviest ever loss of aircraft.

Middlebrook, Martin, *The Battle of Hamburg*, Allen Lane, London, 1980. Reconstructions of the series of six attacks on Hamburg by the RAF and the USAAF between 24 July and 3 August 1943 which destroyed large parts of the city.

————, *The Nuremberg Raid*, Allen Lane, London, 1973. A in-depth reconstruction of the action on the night of 30 March 1944 when RAF Bomber Command lost 96 bombers out of 779 which set out to attack Nuremberg.

————, *The Schweinfurt-Regensburg Mission*, Allen Lane, London, 1983. A detailed reconstruction of the air actions on 17 August 1943 when the USAAF launched simultaneous unescorted daylight attacks on Schweinfurt and Regensburg and suffered a severe reverse at the hands of the German fighter force.

Parker, Danny, *To Win the Winter Sky*, Combined Books, Pennsylvania, 1994. A detailed, two-sided account of the air actions during the Battle of the Ardennes in December 1944 and January 1945.

Price, Alfred, *Battle of Britain: The Hardest Day, 18 August 1940*, Macdonald & Jane's, London, 1979, reissued by Arms & Armour Press, London, 1988. An in-depth reconstruction of the air action fought over southern England on that day, which saw the largest number of aircraft destroyed on both sides of any during the Battle of Britain.

————, *Battle of Britain Day, 15 September 1940*, Sidgwick & Jackson, London, 1990. A in-depth reconstruction of the air action fought over southern England on the date celebrated as 'Battle of Britain Day'.

Ramsey, Winston, et al, *The Battle of Britain Then and Now*, After the Battle Publications, London, 1980, Fifth Edition 1989. A large tome containing day-by-day listings of aircraft lost by each side during the Battle. Contains a mass of detailed information on the *Luftwaffe*.

———, *The Blitz, Then and Now, Volumes 1, 2 and 3*, After The Battle Publications, London, 1987. The volumes give a brief day-by-day account of each German air attack on Great Britain during the Second World War, including detailed listings of *Luftwaffe* aircraft. Contain much useful information on *Luftwaffe* tactics, types of bombs and other aspects of equipment.

Sarkar, Dilip, *Angriff Westland*, Ramrod Publications, Malvern, Worcs, 1992. Reconstructions of the air actions which took place over southern England on 25 and 27 September 1940, during the Battle of Britain.

Shores, Christopher; Ring, Hans; and Hess, William, *Fighters over Tunisia*, Neville Spearman, London, 1975. A detailed, two-sided account of fighter operations over Tunisia from November 1942 to May 1943.

Wakefield, Kenneth, *Luftwaffe Encore*, William Kimber, London, 1979. Reconstructions of the air actions which took place over southern England on 30 September and 7 October 1940, during the Battle of Britain.

Histories of *Luftwaffe* Units

Balke, Ulf, *Kampfgeschwader 100 Wiking*, Motorbuch Verlag, Stuttgart, 1981. A comprehensive account, in German, of operations by *Kampfgruppe 100* and *Kampfgeschwader 100*. The former flew He 111s in the pathfinder role during the early part of the war and was expanded into a *Geschwader* in December 1941. In 1943 the unit first used air-to-surface guided missiles in action, the Henschel 293 and Fritz-X.

Boehme, Manfred, *Jagdgeschwader 7*, Motorbuch Verlag, Stuttgart, 1983. A comprehensive account, in German, of the development of the Messerschmitt 262 jet fighter and its operational use by *JG 7* during the final months of the war.

Caldwell, Donald, *JG 26*, Ballantine Books, New York, 1991. A well-researched history of the operations flown by this unit, from its formation until the end of World War II.

Dierich, Wolfgang, *Die Verbände der Luftwaffe*, Motorbuch Verlag, Stuttgart, 1976. A large book (703 pages) giving potted histories, in German, of *Luftwaffe* operational flying units, airborne units, *Flak* and signals units and ground fighting units.

———, *Kampfgeschwader 'Edelweiss'*, Ian Allan, Shepperton, 1975. An account of operations by *KG 51*, which flew Ju 88s during most of the war and, from the summer of 1944, Messerschmitt 262s in the fighter-bomber role.

———, *Kampfgeschwader 55*, Motorbuch Verlag, Stuttgart, 1975. A comprehensive account, in German, of operations by *KG 55*, which flew Heinkel 111s throughout almost the entire conflict.

Gundelach, Karl, *Kampfgeschwader 'General Wever' 4*, Motorbuch Verlag, Stuttgart, 1978. A comprehensive account, in German, of operations by *KG 4*, which flew Heinkel 111s throughout the war.

Kiehl, Heinz, *Kampfgeschwader 'Legion Condor' 53*, Motorbuch Verlag, Stuttgart, 1983. A comprehensive account, in German, of operations by *KG 53*, which flew Heinkel 111s throughout the conflict.

Priller, Josef, *Geschichte Eines Jagdgeschwaders*, Kurt Wowinckel Verlag, Neckargemuend, 1969. A comprehensive account, in German, of operations by *Jagdgeschwader 26*, which flew Messerschmitt Bf 109s and Focke Wulf Fw 190s on the Western Front throughout the war.

Ring, Hans, and Girbig, Werner, *Jagdgeschwader 27*, Motorbuch Verlag, Stuttgart, 1971. A comprehensive account, in German, of operations by *JG 27* on the Western Front, in the Mediterranean theatre and in the defence of the homeland.

Smith, Peter, *Stuka Squadron*, Patrick Stephens, Wellingborough, 1990. A well-researched and well-illustrated history on *I. Gruppe Sturzkampfgeschwader 77* from before the war until 1944, when it gave up its Ju 87s and became a ground-attack unit.

Wakefield, Kenneth, *The First Pathfinders*, William Kimber, London, 1981. A very detailed account of pathfinder operations over Britain by *Kampfgruppe 100* during 1940 and 1941.

Collected Biographies of *Luftwaffe* Personnel

Obermaier, Ernst, *Die Ritterkreuztraeger der Luftwaffe, Jagdflieger 1939–1945*, Verlag Dieter Hoffmann, Mainz, 1966. A reference work containing photographs and biographies of the 566 fighter aircrewmen of the *Luftwaffe* awarded the *Ritterkreuz*. Dual text in both German and English.

Bruetting, Georg, *Das Waren die Deutschen Kampfflieger-Asse 1939–1945*, Motorbuch Verlag, Stuttgart, 1975. A reference work, in German, containing biographies of bomber aircrewmen awarded the *Ritterkreuz*.

———, *Das Waren die Deutschen Stuka-Asse 1939–1945*, Motorbuch Verlag, Stuttgart, 1976. A reference work, in German, containing biographies of dive-bomber and ground-attack aircrewmen of the *Luftwaffe* awarded the *Ritterkreuz*. It also contains an overview of dive-bomber and ground-attack operations during the conflict.

Spick, Mike, *Luftwaffe Fighter Aces*, Greenhill Books, London, 1996. This readable and well-researched account covers the fighting careers of the most successful German fighter aces. It also covers the tactics they employed, setting them in the context of the varied conditions the pilots met on each of the fighting fronts during the conflict.

Details of Aircraft Types Operated by the *Luftwaffe*

Brown, Eric, *Wings of the Luftwaffe*, Macdonald & Jane's, London, 1977. Eric Brown served in the Fleet Air Arm and early in 1944 he became that service's chief test pilot at the Royal Aircraft Establishment at Farnborough. For much of the next two years he concentrated on flying captured German aircraft, and logged time in 55 different types. In this book he gives his detailed impressions of what it was like to fly seventeen of the more noteworthy of them.

Green, William, *Warplanes of the Third Reich*, Macdonald, London, 1970. A huge (672-page, large format), profusely illustrated book which covers the subject comprehensively. An excellent reference work on German military aircraft during World War II, with much information on operations flown by the various aircraft types.

Profile Publications, various authors. A total of 262 of these booklets on individual aircraft types appeared between 1965 and 1974, initially with 12 pages and latterly with 48 pages. Each booklet covered the aircraft's development and operational career. They were profusely illustrated and included artwork showing colour schemes. The quality of individual Profiles varied between good and excellent, and the following can be recommended to those interested in the *Luftwaffe*:

No 3	Focke Wulf Fw 190A	No 164	Dornier Do 17
No 15	Heinkel He 111	No 177	Junkers Ju 52
No 23	Messerschmitt Bf 110	No 184	Messerschmitt Bf
No 29	Junkers Ju 88		109F
No 40	Messerschmitt Bf	No 203	Heinkel He 162
	109E	No 207	Messerschmitt Bf 110
No 69	Henschel Hs 129		Night Fighters
No 76	Junkers Ju 87A and B	No 211	Junkers Ju 87D
No 94	Focke Wulf Fw 190D	No 215	Arado Ar 234
No 99	Focke Wulf Fw 200	No 219	Heinkel He 219
No 113	Messerschmitt Bf	No 222	Bücker Bü 131
	109G	No 225	Messerschmitt Me 163
No 130	Messerschmitt Me 262	No 228	Fieseler Fi 156
No 148	Junkers Ju 88 Night	No 234	Heinkel He 177
	Fighters	No 261	Dornier Do 217
No 161	Messerschmitt Me 210		
	and Me 410		

Smith, J. R., and Creek, E. J., *German Aircraft of the Second World War*, Putnam, London, 1972. Further useful reference, particularly on aircraft and weapons systems under development when the war ended.

Luftwaffe Aircraft Markings

Merrick, K. A.; Smith, J. R.; and Gallaspy, J. D., *Luftwaffe Camouflage and Markings 1935–45*, Volumes 1, 2 and 3, Kookaburra Technical Publications, Melbourne, Australia, 1973. Comprehensive works giving details of the camouflage schemes and markings worn by *Luftwaffe* aircraft.

Ries, Karl, *Luftwaffe Embleme,* Verlag Dieter Hoffmann, 1975. A reference work containing photographs of almost every unit emblem carried by *Luftwaffe* aircraft.

Autobiographies of ex-*Luftwaffe* Personnel

Several autobiographies of ex-*Luftwaffe* personnel have appeared, varying in quality and historical importance. Those listed below are, in the author's opinion, numbered among the classic accounts.

Galland, Adolf, *The First and the Last,* Methuen and Co, London, 1955. A very good account, written by the best-known German fighter pilot. Galland's biography appears in Chapter 22.

Heilmann, Willi, *Alert in the West,* William Kimber, London, 1955. A useful account of air operations on the Western Front in 1944 and 1945, written by a pilot who served with *JG 54*.

Johnen, Wilhelm, *Duel Under the Stars,* William Kimber, London, 1957. A very good account of night fighter operations written by a successful pilot who flew with *NJG 1, NJG 5* and *NJG 6*.

Knoke, Heinz, *I Flew for the Führer,* Evans Bros, London, 1953. A vivid account from a pilot who flew with *JG 1* and *JG 11* in home defence operations over Germany against US bomber formations and their escorts.

Steinhoff, Johannes, *The Straits of Messina,* Andre Deutsch, London, 1971. A very good account of the trials and tribulations facing the author, the commander of *JG 77*, on the Mediterranean Front during the summer of 1943.

Other Recommended Publications

Davis, Brian, *Uniforms and Insignia of the Luftwaffe,* Vols 1 and 2, Arms & Armour Press, London, 1995. These heavily illustrated volumes provide a comprehensive and highly detailed account of the multitude of uniforms and insignia that were worn by *Luftwaffe* personnel.

Schliephake, Hanfried, *Flugzeug Bewaffnung,* Motorbuch Verlag, Stuttgart, 1977. A comprehensive account, in German, on the evolution of German aircraft armament—guns, rockets and missiles but not bombs.

———, *The Birth of the Luftwaffe,* Ian Allan, Shepperton, 1971. A useful reference work on German military aviation after 1918 and the build-up of the *Luftwaffe* between 1933 and 1939.

Trenkle, Fritz, *Die Deutsche Funkmessverfahren bis 1945,* Motorbuch Verlag, Stuttgart, 1979. A comprehensive reference work, in German, on the evolution of German radar up to 1945.

———, *Die deutschen Funk-Navigations und Funk-Fuehrungsverfahren bis 1945,* Motorbuch Verlag, Stuttgart, 1979. A comprehensive reference work, in German, on the evolution of German radio navigation systems before and during World War II.

Unit Identification Markings Carried by Aircraft

Most *Luftwaffe* front-line aircraft types carried a code of three letters and a number on the rear fuselage, sometimes repeated under the wings, to denote their unit. For example, a Messerschmitt Bf 110 carried the fuselage markings 'U8 + AH'. The 'U8' to the left of the cross was the identifying code for *Zerstörergeschwader 26*. The 'H' on the extreme right indicated that the aircraft belonged to the *1. Staffel* (part of *I. Gruppe*), and the 'A' was the identification letter of the individual aircraft within the *Staffel*. In addition to the letters-and-number identification code, operational aircraft often carried their *Geschwader*, *Gruppe* or *Staffel* badge, usually on the nose (some carried all three badges, for good measure).

The code letters of the more important *Geschwader* and independent *Gruppen* and *Staffeln* are given below. In some cases units changed their identification codes during the war, and where this happened all their known codes are given.

A1	*Kampfgeschwader 53*	D7	*Wettererkundungsstaffel 1*
A2	*Zerstörergeschwader 52*	D9	*Nachtjagdgeschwader 7*
A3	*Kampfgeschwader 200*	E2 to	Test Establishment Rechlin
A5	*Sturzkampfgeschwader 1*, later	E7	
	Schlachtgeschwader 1	E8	*Nachtschlachtgeschwader 9*
A6	*Aufklärungsgruppe 120*	F1	*Kampfgeschwader 76*
B3	*Kampfgeschwader 54*	F6	*Aufklärungsgruppe 122*
B4	*Nachtjagdstaffel* Finland/	F8	*Kampfgeschwader 40*
	Norway	G1	*Kampfgeschwader 55*
B7	*Wettererkundungsstaffel 1*	G2	*Aufklärungsgruppe 124*
C1	*Erprobungskommando 16*	G6	*Kampfgruppe zbV 2, 101, 102,*
C2	*Aufklärungsgruppe 41*, later		*104, 105*; later *Transport-*
	Nahaufklärungsgruppe 3		*geschwader 4*
C6	*Kampfgruppe zbV 600*	G9	*Zerstörergeschwader 1*, later
C8	*Transportgeschwader 5*		*Nachtjagdgeschwader 1*, later
C9	*Nachtjagdgeschwader 5*		*Nachtjagdgeschwader 4*
D1	*Seeaufklärungsgruppe 126*	H1	*Aufklärungsgruppe 12*
D3	*Nachtschlachtgruppe 2*	H4	*Luftlandgeschwader 1*
D5	*Nachtjagdgeschwader 3*	H8	*Aufklärungsgruppe 33*

J2	*Nahaufklärungsgruppe 3*	1T	*Kampfgruppe 126*
J6	*Kampfgruppe zbV 500*	1Z	*Kampfgeschwader zbV 1*, later
J9	*Trägergruppe 186*, later		*Transportgeschwader 1*
	Sturzkampfgeschwader 1	2N	*Zerstörergeschwader 1*
K6	*Küstenfliegergruppe 406*	2S	*Zerstörergeschwader 2*
K7	*Aufklärungsgruppe Nacht*	2Z	*Nachtjagdgeschwader 6*
L1	*Lehrgeschwader 1*	3C	*Nachtjagdgeschwader 4*
L2	*Lehrgeschwader 2*	3E	*Kampfgeschwader 6*
L5	*Kampfgruppe zbV 5*	3K	*Minensuchsgruppe*
M2	*Küstenfliegergruppe 106*	3U	*Zerstörergeschwader 26*
M7	*Kampfgruppe 806*	3W	*Nachtschlachtgruppe 11*
M8	*Zerstörergeschwader 76*	3Z	*Kampfgeschwader 77*
P1	*Kampfgeschwader 60*	4D	*Kampfgeschwader 25*, later
P2	*Aufklärungsgruppe 21*		*Kampfgeschwader 30*
P7	*Seenotstaffel 5, Seenotstaffel 51*	4E	*Aufklärungsgruppe 13*, later
Q9	*Schlachtgeschwader 5*		*Nahaufklärungsgruppe 15*
R4	*Nachtjagdgeschwader 2*	4F	*Kampfgruppe zbV 400*
S2	*Sturzkampfgeschwader 2*, later	4N	*Aufklärungsgruppe 22*
	Schlachtgeschwader 2	4R	*Nachtjagdgeschwader 2*
S3	*Transportgruppe 30*	4T	*Wettererkundungsstaffel 51*
S4	*Küstenfliegergruppe 506*, later	4U	*Aufklärungsgruppe 123*
	Kampfgruppe 506	4V	*Kampfgruppe zbV 9, 106, 172*;
S7	*Sturzkampfgeschwader 3*, later		later *Transportgeschwader 3*
	Schlachtgeschwader 3	5D	*Aufklärungsgruppe 31*
S9	*Erprobungsgruppe 210*, later	5F	*Aufklärungsgruppe 14*
	Schnellkampfgeschwader 210	5J	*Kampfgeschwader 4*
T1	*Aufklärungsgruppe 10*	5K	*Kampfgeschwader 3*
T6	*Sturzkampfgeschwader 2*, later	5W	*Seenotstaffel 10*
	Schlachtgeschwader 2	5Z	*Wettererkundungsstaffel 26*, later
U2	*Nahaufklärungsgruppe 5*		*Wettererkundungsstaffel 76*
U5	*Kampfgeschwader 2*	6I	*Küstenfliegergruppe 706*, later
U8	*Zerstörergeschwader 26*		*Seeaufklärungsgruppe 130*
U9	*Nachtschlachtgruppe 3*	6J	*Nachtschlachtgruppe 8*
V4	*Kampfgeschwader 1*	6K	*Aufklärungsgruppe 41*
V7	*Aufklärungsgruppe 32*	6M	*Aufklärungsgruppe 11*
V8	*Nachtschlachtgruppe 1*	6N	*Kampfgruppe 100*, later
W7	*Nachtjagdgeschwader 100*		*Kampfgeschwader 100*
Z6	*Kampfgeschwader 66*	6R	*Seeaufklärungsgruppe 127*
1A	*Wettererkundungsstaffel 5*	6U	*Zerstörergeschwader 1*
1G	*Kampfgeschwader 27*	6W	*Seeaufklärungsgruppe 128*
1H	*Kampfgeschwader 26*	7A	*Aufklärungsgruppe 121*
1K	*Nachtschlachtgruppe 4*	7J	*Nachtjagdgeschwader 102*
1L	*Nachtjagdgruppe 10*	7R	*Seeaufklärungsgruppe 125*

7T	*Kampfgruppe 606*	8V	*Nachtjagdgeschwader 200*
7U	*Kampfgruppe zbV 108*	9K	*Kampfgeschwader 51*
7V	*Kampfgruppe zbV 700*	9P	*Kampfgruppe zbV 9, 40, 50, 60*
8H	*Aufklärungsgruppe 33*	9V	*Fernaufklärungsgruppe 5*
8L	*Küstenfliegergruppe 906*	9W	*Nachtjagdgeschwader 101*
8Q	*Transportgruppe 10*		
8T	*Kampfgruppe zbV 800*, later		
	Transportgeschwader 2		

As mentioned above, the final letter of the identification code denoted the *Staffel* (or *Stab* unit) to which the aircraft belonged. The full list of *Staffel* and *Stab* letters was as follows:

A	*Geschwader Stab*	P	*6. Staffel (II. Gruppe)*
B	*I. Gruppe Stab*	R	*7. Staffel (III. Gruppe)*
C	*II. Gruppe Stab*	S	*8. Staffel (III. Gruppe)*
D	*III. Gruppe Stab*	T	*9. Staffel (III. Gruppe)*
E	*IV. Gruppe Stab*	U	*10. Staffel (IV. Gruppe)*
F	*V. Gruppe Stab* (if appropriate)	V	*11. Staffel (IV. Gruppe)*
H	*1. Staffel (I. Gruppe)*	W	*12. Staffel (IV. Gruppe)*
K	*2. Staffel (I. Gruppe)*	X	*13. Staffel (V. Gruppe)*
L	*3. Staffel (I. Gruppe)*	Y	*14. Staffel (V. Gruppe)*
M	*4. Staffel (II. Gruppe)*	Z	*15. Staffel (V. Gruppe)*
N	*5. Staffel (II. Gruppe)*		

Identification Markings of Single-engined Day Fighter and Ground-Attack Aircraft

The system of unit identification markings applied to single-engined day fighter and ground-attack planes (but *not* dive-bombers) differed markedly from that applied to other aircraft types. There was no letter-and-number code to denote their *Geschwader, Gruppe* or *Staffel*. Instead, until almost the end of the war, the unit was identified by the badge painted on the nose or (less often) the rear fuselage. Sometimes, if a unit was hard-pressed and there was no time to paint it on newly delivered aircraft, the unit badge was omitted. In that case there was no simple way of determining its unit.

Within the *Geschwader*, aircraft from the individual *Gruppen* were identified by the symbol to the rear of the fuselage cross as follows: *I. Gruppe*, no marking; *II. Gruppe*, a horizontal bar; *III. Gruppe*, a wavy line or a horizontal bar; and *IV. Gruppe*, a filled-in circle or a cross. See Fig. 18.

Forward of the fuselage cross, a fighter or ground-attack aircraft usually carried a number between 1 and 16 to identify the individual aircraft within its *Staffel*. In place of this identifying number, aircraft belonging to officers

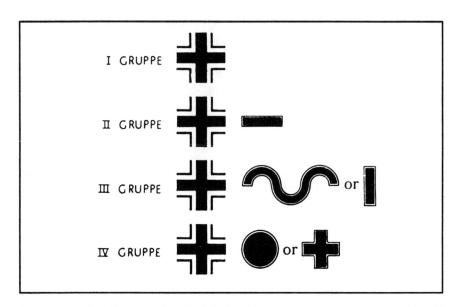

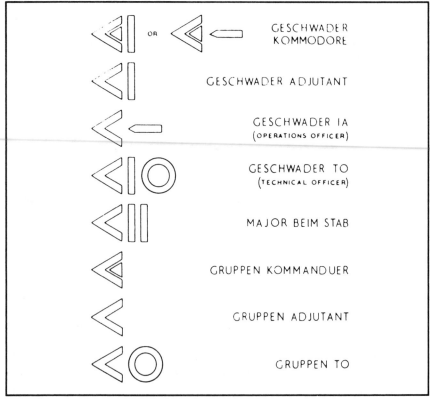

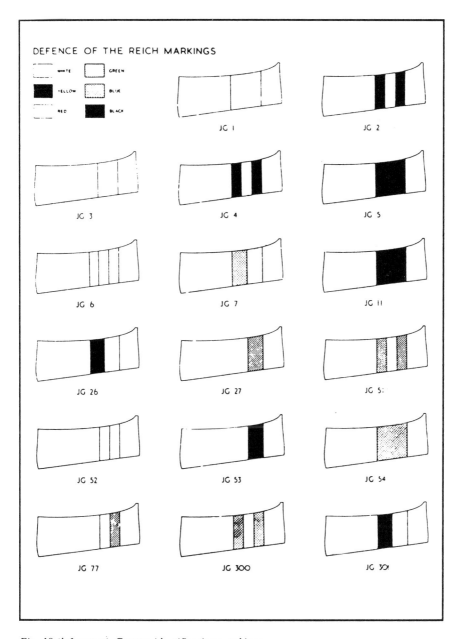

Fig. 18 (left upper). Gruppe *identification markings.*

Fig. 19 (left lower). Fighter Executive Officers' Markings.

Fig. 20 (above) Reich Air Defence Markings.

holding executive positions within the *Geschwader* or *Gruppe* carried identifying chevrons, bars and/or circles. See Fig. 19.

In February 1945 day fighter units engaged in the air defence of the Reich (which meant nearly all day fighter units still operational) began carrying coloured bands around the rear fuselage denoting their *Geschwader*. A complete list of these identifying bands is given in Fig. 20.

From time to time German day fighters units would paint all or part of their engine cowlings in distinctive colours (yellow, white or red) or with distinctive patterns (black and white stripes, checks etc) to assist identification in combat. Such markings were not often used, and if they were they did not constitute a permanent means of identification. Moreover, despite copious and persistent Allied reports to the contrary, they did *not* signify that the aircraft bearing them belonged to 'crack' units. A yellow nose on a Messerschmitt might or might not denote that the pilot was an ace—it depended on who happened to be flying it that day!

APPENDIX B

Main Aircraft Types Accepted by the *Luftwaffe*, January 1939–December 1944

Arado Ar 96*	Trainer	2,279
Arado Ar 196	Reconnaissance floatplane	526
Arado Ar 234*	Jet bomber, reconnaissance	148
Blohm und Voss Bv 138	Reconnaissance flying boat	235
Dornier Do 17	Bomber, reconnaissance	114
Dornier Do 24	Reconnaissance flying boat	233
Dornier Do 217b	Bomber, reconnaissance, night fighter	1,905
Fieseler Fi 156*	Reconnaissance, communications	2,758
Focke Wulf Fw 189	Reconnaissance	797
Focke Wulf Fw 190*	Fighter, fighter-bomber, reconnaissance	16,724
Focke Wulf Fw 200	Reconnaissance-bomber	268
Heinkel He 111	Bomber, transport	6,615
Heinkel He 177	Bomber	1,094
Heinkel He 219*	Night fighter	320
Henschel Hs 129	Ground attack	876

Junkers Ju 52	Transport, trainer	3,229
Junkers Ju 87	Dive-bomber)	5314
Junkers Ju 88*	Bomber, ground attack, night fighter, reconnaissance	14,321
Junkers Ju 188*	Bomber, reconnaissance	1,076
Messerschmitt Bf 109*	Fighter, fighter-bomber, reconnaissance	29,350
Messerschmitt Bf 110*	Fighter, fighter-bomber, night fighter, reconnaissance	5,904
Messerschmitt Me 163*	Rocket powered fighter	237
Messerschmitt Me 210	Fighter, fighter-bomber	382
Messerschmitt Me 262*	Jet fighter, fighter-bomber, night fighter, reconnaissance	564
Messerschmitt Me 323	Heavy transport	198
Messerschmitt Me 410	Fighter, fighter-bomber, bomber	1,160
Siebel Si 204*	Trainer, light transport	1,115

Note: Aircraft types marked * were still in production in December 1944.

APPENDIX C

Equivalent Wartime Ranks

In the case of the *Luftwaffe* ranks, the numbers in the left-hand column refer to the rank badges shown in Fig. 21.

Luftwaffe	**Royal Air Force**	**USAAF**
1. *Generalfeldmarschal*	Marshal of the RAF	(No equivalent)
2. *Generaloberst*	Air Chief Marshal	General (4-star)
3. *General der Flieger*	Air Marshal	General (3-star)
4. *Generalleutnant*	Air Vice-Marshal	General (2-star)
5. *Generalmajor*	Air Commodore	General (1 star)
6. *Oberst*	Group Captain	Colonel
7. *Oberstleutnant*	Wing Commander	Lieutenant-Colonel
8. *Major*	Squadron Leader	Major
9. *Hauptmann*	Flight Lieutenant	Captain
10. *Oberleutnant*	Flying Officer	1st Lieutenant
11. *Leutnant*	Pilot Officer	2nd Lieutenant

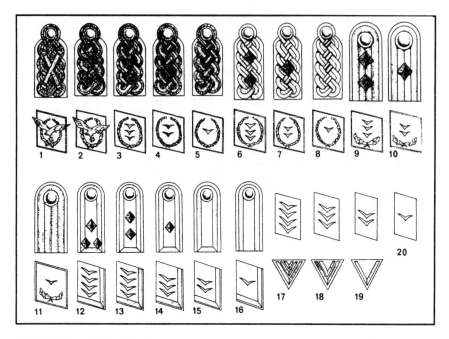

Fig. 21. Luftwaffe *Rank Badges.*

12.	*Stabsfeldwebel*	Warrant Officer	Warrant Officer
13.	*Oberfeldwebel*	Flight Sergeant	Master Sergeant
14.	*Feldwebel*	Sergeant	Technical Sergeant
15.	*Unterfeldwebel*	(No equivalent)	No equivalent)
16.	*Unteroffizier*	Corporal	Staff Sergeant
17.	*Hauptgefreiter*	(No equivalent)	Sergeant
18.	*Obergefreiter*	Leading Aircraftman	Corporal
19.	*Gefreiter*	Aircraftman First Class	Private First Class
20.	*Flieger*	Aircraftman Second Class	Private Second Class